MASTERING HARVARD GRAPHICS

MASTERING HARVARD™ GRAPHICS

Glenn H. Larsen

San Francisco • Paris • Düsseldorf • London

Cover design by Thomas Ingalls + Associates
Cover photography by Michael Lamotte
Series design by Julie Bilski
Screen reproductions produced by XenoFont
Chapter art and layout by Suzanne Albertson

To my father-in-law, Robert B. Pettengill, Ph.D., Professor Emeritus of Economics at SUNY Albany, who inspired this book.

ACKNOWLEDGMENTS

Mastering Harvard Graphics was a book I enjoyed writing, probably because of the many people who contributed to it. Their support, guidance, and professionalism helped mold this book into the finished product you're now holding.

Several people offered guidance during the early stages of this book regarding its content, scope, size, and style. I'd like to thank Dianne King and Barbara Gordon from SYBEX for their comments and suggestions. Paul J. Herer and Michael Champ from the National Science Foundation, as well as John Duff from the UNISYS Corporation, offered many suggestions and recommendations.

I'm especially grateful to George Brosseau of the National Science Foundation and Robert B. Pettengill, Professor Emeritus at the State University of New York. They provided expert guidance throughout this book while making suggestions that only a scientist or economist could offer.

My editor, Nancy O'Donnell, helped organize, clarify, and streamline the presentation of this book. I was fortunate to have such a professional editor; this book is shorter and more precise because of her. My editor's positive, fresh outlook added substantially to the usefulness of this book.

Other people at SYBEX also helped make this book. Joanne Cuthbertson, the supervising editor, made sure things flowed smoothly, while Bob Campbell, my technical editor, provided guidance and assisted greatly in the production of screens. Thanks also go to Chris Mockel, Robert Myren, and Scott Campbell, word processors; Winnie Kelly, typesetter; Suzanne Albertson, design and layout artist; Chris Calder, proofreader; Sonja Schenk, screen producer; and Anne Leach, indexer.

Software Publishing Corporation's Technical Support department helped answer many questions about Harvard Graphics. I'd like to thank Don Brenner, George Patterson, and Chris Thompson for the help they provided. Additionally, I'd like to thank Dick O'Donnell of Software Publishing's Public Relations department for providing general information and insights into Harvard.

I produced most of the charts used in this book from data provided by the U.S. Department of Commerce's Bureau of the Census.

On a more domestic note, I'd like to thank my wife, Evelyn, for her time and patience. I'm also grateful to my four children who tried very hard to be quiet when I was writing.

CONTENTS AT A GLANCE

TABLE OF CONTENTS

INTRODUCTION

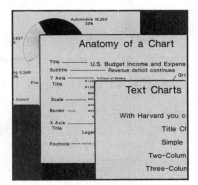

1

INTRODUCING HARVARD

2

GETTING STARTED

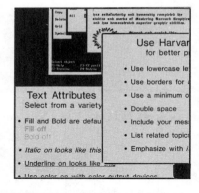

3

CREATING TEXT CHARTS

4

CREATING PIE CHARTS

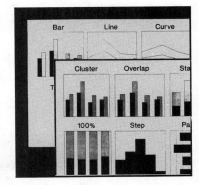

5

CREATING BAR AND LINE CHARTS

6

FINE-TUNING YOUR BAR AND LINE CHARTS

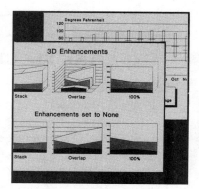

7

CREATING AREA, HIGH/LOW/CLOSE, AND MULTIPLE CHARTS

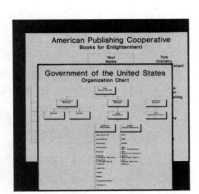

8

CREATING ORGANIZATION CHARTS

9

SAVING TIME WITH HARVARD'S TEMPLATES AND MACROS

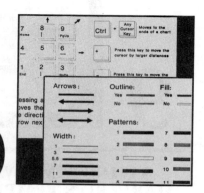

10

DESIGNING CUSTOM CHARTS

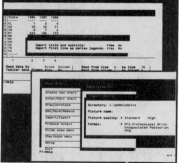

11

TRANSFERRING INFORMATION BETWEEN HARVARD AND OTHER PROGRAMS

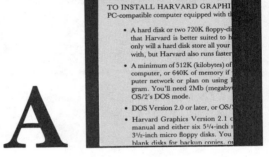

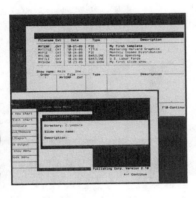

12

CREATING SLIDE SHOWS

A

INSTALLING HARVARD   275

B

SUPPORTED DEVICES   281

INTRODUCTION

COMPUTER GRAPHICS HAVE BECOME INCREASINGLY important for persuasive presentations, as they become more accessible to engineers, students, executives, secretaries, educators, salespeople, accountants, and government officials—in short, to anyone who needs to convey information effectively.

This book will help you produce the powerful and effective graphic communication tools you need to reach your audience quickly. Use graphs to get important points across, manage resources, analyze growth, chart sales statistics, and display other data.

IS THIS BOOK FOR YOU?

This book is written for anyone who wants to master Harvard Graphics. It can be used by people at all levels, from the individual with no prior experience of graphics programs to the experienced professional.

You'll find that this book complements the Harvard Graphics manual by taking you from making charts to constructing an effective presentation. In this book I also discuss chart styles, special effects, and how charts influence your audience. You'll even learn about Harvard's quirks and discover tips to increase your productivity. Often, these tidbits will be in margin notes, which occur throughout the book.

THE MARGIN NOTES

These are three types of margin notes, and each is identified by its symbol, as follows.

This symbol in the margin denotes any related information about the subject at hand. In particular, I use it to remind you about something you previously learned or to tell where to look for more information.

I use this symbol to display tips and shortcuts for using Harvard—anything that will improve Harvard's performance or your understanding of the program's features.

 This symbol tells you to be alert for a potential trouble spot in Harvard. Its accompanying message identifies the problem and explains what can be done to prevent or circumvent it.

VERSION USED

My discussions and instructions are geared for all Version 2.1 users (2.10 through 2.12). In the book I simply refer to Version 2.1, by which I mean all releases. Note, however, that there are slight changes between the different 2.1 releases. For example, Version 2.12 contains some additions and changes to Harvard's configuration setup for film recorders. I also produced the graphs in this book with Harvard Graphics Version 2.11. Nonetheless, the differences between releases will not affect the techniques you learn here.

HOW TO USE THIS BOOK

You can begin producing quality graphics without reading *Mastering Harvard Graphics* cover to cover. The first two chapters give you a quick overview of how to use the program. By the end of the second chapter, you'll have created several simple graphs.

By the end of chapter 8, you will be able to create impressive graphics, rivaling those created by graphic artists. You'll understand the details of chart construction for any type of chart. Chapters 9 through 11 meet more specialized needs—you'll learn how to automate the chart construction process, design your own charts, and transfer data between Harvard and other programs. In Chapter 12, I show you how to give a professional presentation using Harvard's slide show feature. The appendices supply you with additional references for using Harvard; you can consult them as the need arises.

In addition, the inside front and back covers provide you with more references. Refer to the inside front cover when you need to refresh your memory about a particular menu option; its listing will tell you the page number on which the option is discussed. When you want to see Harvard Graphics' menu structure quickly, just check the inside back cover. It gives you an overview of the menus, complete with the available function keys and numbers of the menu options.

Once you have become familiar with Harvard, you will probably want to keep this book near your computer for reference. That way, you can consult it when you are working with commands and features that you use infrequently.

IDENTIFYING YOUR NEEDS

Although I don't assume that you're familiar with Harvard, I do assume that you're somewhat familiar with a computer. For example, I won't tell you how to turn on your computer, printer, or monitor. Nor will I show you how to format your hard disk or install a color graphics board. You'll find these subjects fully explained in DOS and OS/2 books.

I target my instructions to readers with a hard-disk system. If you have a floppy-disk system, you will need to adjust my instructions occasionally, primarily when you set up and run Harvard Graphics initially. Otherwise, you should have no trouble using the techniques discussed here.

As reflected in this book's title, I'll show you how to master Harvard Graphics. However, to master anything, you need practice. You'll gain little by reading this book cover to cover without ever using Harvard. Instead, work through each chapter's "Hands-on" practice session. With a little imagination you can adapt these examples to your own data. You can then experiment with different options on your own.

A PREVIEW OF THE CONTENTS

Following is a summary of the contents of each chapter and appendix. Use this listing as a guide for where you should start. If you're a beginner, you'll want to start at Chapter 1. Experienced users can choose their own appropriate starting point.

Chapter 1: Introducing Harvard This chapter presents Harvard's features. Here you'll learn how to analyze a graph's anatomy and how to select the right graph for your type of data. You'll begin to work with Harvard by configuring your system's output devices, such as your monitor and printer.

Chapter 2: Getting Started This chapter takes you through an accelerated tutorial so you can begin creating simple text, pie, bar, and line charts. In this chapter you'll also learn the essential steps of saving and printing your work. In addition, I discuss when to present printed paper copies, plotted transparencies, and recorded slides to your audience.

Chapter 3: Creating Text Charts In this chapter you'll examine text charts in-depth by creating three different types of text charts and using special text-drawing techniques. These techniques let you arrange text in ways that the standard text charts won't. You'll also learn how to modify your text and check your chart's spelling.

Chapter 4: Creating Pie Charts In this chapter you'll learn how to create an effective pie chart. I also discuss methods of presenting your data, including cutting and linking pie slices. To exploit Harvard's features fully, you'll also learn how to fit more than one pie on your chart.

Chapter 5: Creating Bar and Line Charts In this chapter I cover how and when to use bar and line charts. You'll practice what you've learned and master these charts in "Hands-on" sessions. You'll work with several bar and line chart variations and learn how to use special effects such as 3D and shadowing for emphasis.

Chapter 6: Fine-Tuning Your Bar and Line Charts This chapter builds on the previous chapter, showing you how to refine your charts. For example, you'll learn how to change the bars' widths and the frames and legends' characteristics. In addition, you'll explore the use of labels, grids, ticks, and chart scales.

Chapter 7: Creating Area, High/Low/Close, and Multiple Charts
Borrowing heavily from the previous chapters' chart-building techniques, this chapter shows you how to create area charts, high/low/close charts, and multiple charts. An area chart is simply a variation of a bar chart that emphasizes changes in volume, while a multiple chart can contain up to six graphs, which is useful for data comparisons. On the other hand, stock market enthusiasts and project planners will find the high/low/close chart invaluable for presenting their data.

Chapter 8: Creating Organization Charts   Internal relationships from a family household to billion-dollar corporations can be graphed using an organization chart. This chapter quickly shows you how to design and create organization charts to illustrate a company's hierarchy (a favorite of corporate offices and the government).

Chapter 9: Saving Time with Harvard's Templates and Macros   In this chapter I discuss Harvard's template, chartbook, and macro features, which you can use to create charts automatically. Templates provide blueprints for consistently styled charts and can be grouped in chartbooks for easy retrieval. Macros, on the other hand, automate repetitious tasks for all your charts, streamlining the production process.

Chapter 10: Designing Custom Charts   Here you'll learn how to design lively presentation graphics using an assortment of drawing tools and symbols. For example, you'll practice making a sign that is composed of circles, polygons, and lines. You will also explore Harvard's Symbol menu, using it to save your drawings as symbols and retrieve one of Harvard's symbols. You will then learn how to turn the retrieved symbol into a template chart.

Chapter 11: Transferring Information Between Harvard and Other Programs   In this chapter I present all the importing and exporting methods Harvard provides. In particular, you'll learn how to import data from Lotus 1-2-3 and export Harvard graphs. Since you may work with outside data frequently, you'll also practice setting up a template for importing data.

Chapter 12: Creating Slide Shows   Once you have acquired all the chart-building techniques, you'll need to learn how to tie everything together; Chapter 12 fills that need. In it I'll show you how to sort your graphs, run a computerized slide show, and develop presentation cards.

Appendix A: Installing Harvard   This appendix covers the basics of installing Harvard Graphics. If Harvard has not yet been installed on your system, read this appendix before you tackle Chapter 1, where you will tailor the program more closely to your system.

Appendix B: Supported Devices   This appendix lists the printers, plotters, film recorders, and video screen controllers that Harvard supports. If you have any questions about your system's components, check here before you configure Harvard to them.

Appendix C: Statistics and Calculations   This appendix first examines the rudiments of statistics so that you can take full advantage of Harvard's calculate feature, which is then discussed. This feature helps you sort and analyze your data.

Appendix D: Symbols, Symbols, and More Symbols   This appendix lists all the symbols that Harvard provides for you. Refer to this appendix when you are looking for a particular symbol to incorporate into a chart or when you seek inspiration for your own drawings.

1

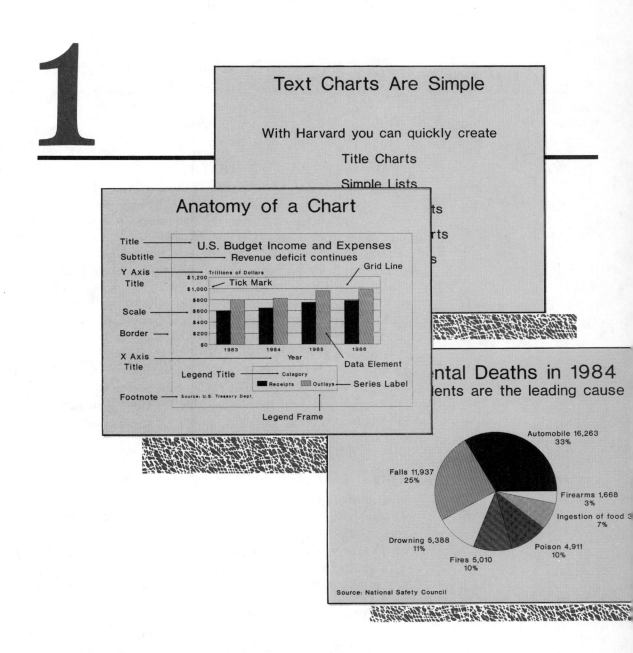

Text Charts Are Simple

With Harvard you can quickly create

Title Charts

Simple Lists

Anatomy of a Chart

Title ——— U.S. Budget Income and Expenses
Subtitle ——— Revenue deficit continues
Y Axis — Grid Line
Title
Trillions of Dollars
$1,200 — Tick Mark
$1,000
$800
Scale — $600
$400
$200
Border — $0
1983 1984 1985 1986
X Axis — Year
Title
Data Element
Legend Title —— Catagory
Receipts Outlays — Series Label

Footnote —— Source: U.S. Treasury Dept.

Legend Frame

ntal Deaths in 1984
ents are the leading cause

Automobile 16,263
33%

Falls 11,937
25%

Firearms 1,668
3%

Ingestion of food 3
7%

Drowning 5,388
11%

Poison 4,911
10%

Fires 5,010
10%

Source: National Safety Council

INTRODUCING HARVARD

CHAPTER *1*

COMPUTERS HAVE REVOLUTIONIZED PRESENTA-
tion graphics. Armed with your computer and Harvard, you can
create masterful, aesthetically pleasing graphs in minutes. Before
computers, graphs were made by gathering stacks of graph paper, a
protractor, and a host of other supplies, taking hours to produce.
Alternatively, you hired a graphic artist if you lacked the time or skill
to produce your own charts. You would then see your charts a week
later, along with a $200 illustration bill.

The computer graphics revolution puts sophisticated, powerful
tools at your disposal for creating charts easily. Unfortunately, many
people lack training in the fundamentals of chart design. They create
meaningless graphs that say nothing or spaghetti graphs that say too
much—often because they choose the wrong type of chart for their
data. To win in the graphics revolution, you need knowledge; this
book helps you gain that knowledge, teaching you how to deliver
your messages with charts.

WHY USE GRAPHICS?

Graphics, particularly charts, can quickly communicate your
ideas. A visual chart will drive a point home decidedly faster than if
you just tried to describe your point verbally. When you present your
ideas rapidly, you conserve both your audience's and your own time.
This greater productivity leads to shorter presentations, meetings,
and conferences. By stressing and highlighting important ideas, you
prevent the audience from misinterpreting your message. Additionally, effective charts project an aura of professionalism. This professional appearance lends credibility to you, your data, and your
message. Even if you just use charts for your own analysis, the
different perspectives on your data can be invaluable.

Here's a summary of the reasons for using graphics:

- To disseminate information for organizational action or approval
- To increase your audience's retention of information and impress upon them the value of your presentation
- To streamline your presentations and meetings
- To establish relationships between the data and your ideas that would otherwise be difficult to explain
- To emphasize important ideas
- To prevent misinterpretation of your data or message
- To project a professional image of yourself and your organization
- To add credibility to your presentation

WHY USE HARVARD?

Now that you understand how graphics can be beneficial, I'll tell you why you should use Harvard: it is easy to use; its files are compatible with other programs; and its many features give you flexible options.

EASE OF USE

Harvard is easy. As you'll learn in Chapter 2, you can create quality graphs in a short period of time. Because Harvard is also intuitive, you can make a selection from a menu and expect to see the functions associated with your choice. If you're stuck, you can reasonably figure out what your options are. If you can't, just use Harvard's built-in help menus. Harvard is simple enough that beginners can easily construct charts within 20 minutes of installing it.

Creating charts is even simpler when you use an electronic pointing device, such as a mouse. A mouse lets you change a graph rapidly using a point-and-click technique. For example, if you want to change the title of a graph, you point to it on the screen, click a mouse button, and type the new title.

COMPATIBILITY

Harvard can save files as a *Computer Graphics Metafile,* or CGM file for short. This means that Harvard can put your graphs into a special format so you can use them with other programs. Because CGM files are quickly becoming an industry standard, you'll be able to exchange data and graphic files between Harvard and dozens of other programs, such as Ventura Publisher and WordPerfect 5.

FEATURES

Harvard Graphics is an extremely flexible program, providing dozens of charting options. For example, when creating text charts, you can choose between title, simple list, bullet, two-column, three-column, or free-form charts. Once you select your chart type, you can change the text's size, color, placement, style, and attributes. You can even add pictures, other graphs, and drawings to your chart.

In addition to producing quality graphs, Harvard can create slide shows and computer presentations. It's an excellent sign-making program that will print professional bulletins and notices. You can also use Harvard as a simple project-management tool by producing scheduling charts. It even comes equipped with a simple drawing package for the artist in you.

WORKING WITH GRAPHS

I will use the terms graph and chart interchangeably throughout this book.

Not all graphs communicate a message. Good charts establish the point you're trying to make quickly, while poor charts fall flat. Just because you used a computer to make a chart doesn't mean it is any good. Figure 1.1 contains a sample pie chart. Would you consider this a useful chart?

If you said no, you're right. This pie chart has too many data elements (pie slices). Even though the numbers are there, it is difficult to

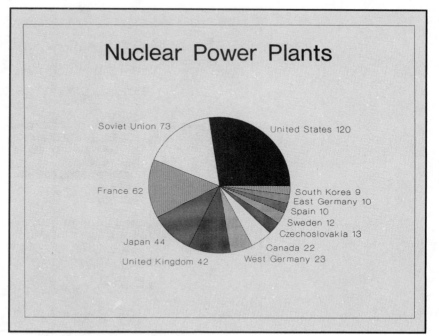

Figure 1.1: One example of a pie chart

see that Canada and West Germany use almost twice as many power plants as Spain and East Germany do; the relationship is lost. If you can't see relationships between your chart's data, you're probably better off not using the chart. This graph doesn't help the presentation; in this case, the presentation has to help the graph.

Compare the crowded pie chart with the chart shown in Figure 1.2. Using the same data, the revised chart now tells a clear story. Unlike the cluttered pie chart, the proportional bars in the numbered scale help you see how the number of nuclear plants varies from country to country. There is also a clear message beneath the chart's title that summarizes the central idea.

The difference between these two sample charts illustrates how the type of chart you choose for your data affects their presentation. Like a master artist, you need to blend graphic tools and your ideas carefully. Understanding this is the first step in mastering Harvard Graphics. Let's continue by exploring a graph's structure.

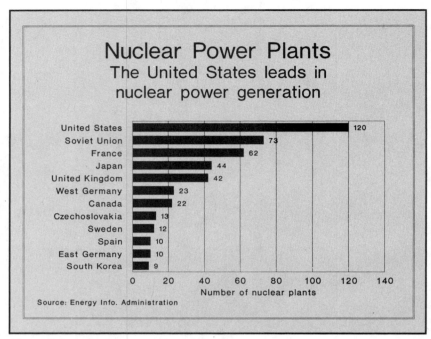

Figure 1.2: A good presentation chart

EXPLORING
THE ANATOMY OF A GRAPH

When artists learn to draw the human figure, they begin by studying human anatomy. Only then are they able to understand their subjects and portray them realistically. Making a professional chart isn't any different. Not until you understand a chart's anatomy can you create an accurate chart.

KNOWING WHAT
ALL CHARTS SHOULD CONTAIN

Although chart types appear strikingly different, they all have some essential elements. For example, include a title, footnote, and border in every chart you create. Figure 1.3 shows the anatomy of a

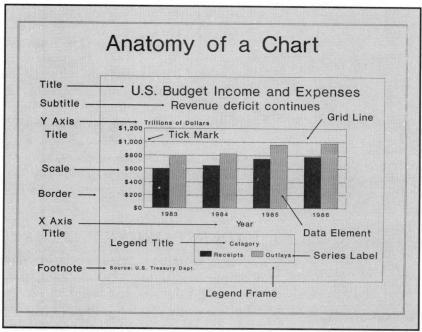

Figure 1.3: Anatomy of a chart

chart depicting the U.S. national economy from 1983 to 1986. The scale along the left side of the chart represents billions of dollars.

Your charts should always contain a *title,* and I recommend using a subtitle as well. Without a title or message, your audience must try to guess what the graph is saying. For example, the graph in Figure 1.3 uses this title and message:

U.S. Budget Income and Expense
Revenue deficit continues

The title uniquely identifies the graph. By adding a message with the subtitle, your central idea is emphasized, saving you presentation time. You have up to three lines for your title and message; I recommend using one title and one subtitle line. This should be sufficient.

You should always consider using a *footnote,* which is also called a *key* or *reference,* to let your audiences know your data source. For example, our U.S. Budget Income and Expense chart includes the following footnote:

Source: U.S. Treasury Department

An audience is more likely to accept the validity of your chart's data if they know where the data come from. However, depending on the composition of your audience, you won't need to include a footnote if you or your organization is the source.

Charts should also include an aesthetic *border*. This border acts like a frame on a painting, since it keeps the the viewer's attention focused on the material inside it. Just like a painting, you shouldn't consider your chart complete until it's framed.

Keep a folder of impressive charts. You can use these as models for your own charts.

UNDERSTANDING THE PARTS OF A CHART

There are other parts to a chart's anatomy besides its title, subtitle, footnote, and border. For example, pie charts also include slices. These pie slices are data elements representing the numerical data within your pie. Other graphs, like line, bar, and area charts, have other parts in addition to their own data elements. As you learn more about graphs, you'll see many similarities. Use the chart displayed in Figure 1.3 to familiarize yourself with the following parts.

- Title: A descriptive heading for the chart.
- Subtitle: A distinctive message or brief description of the chart's data.
- Footnote: Your source for the data or other explanatory text.
- Border: A frame for the chart.
- X axis: The horizontal axis of the graph.
- X axis title: A title describing the data that are displayed along the X axis.
- Y axis: The vertical axis of the graph.
- Scale: The range of numbers or values along the Y axis.
- Y axis title: A title identifying the Y axis's scale.
- Data element: A number or value used in the chart.

- Series: A set of numerical data.
- Series label: A label identifying a single series.
- Legend title: A label identifying the group of series.
- Legend frame: A box around the series labels and legend title.
- Grid line: A graphic line showing the intersection of a data element with a value on the scale.
- Tick mark: A short, thick line that marks a value on the Y axis's scale.

IDENTIFYING THE AXES, SERIES, AND DATA ELEMENTS

Before you can interpret a graph, you need to understand the differences between the X and Y axes, and a series and a data element. Let's assume that you want to graph Table 1.1.

To start, you need to identify your data for the X axis. When you are making a chart, place your groups along the horizontal X axis. For example, use the X axis for groups such as dates, time, items, places, or names. In our table, you would place the years from 1986 to 1989 on the X axis.

Next define the Y axis's data. The Y axis almost always contains numbers, such as dollars or units. Table 1.1 shows widgets ranging from 2,235 to 4,920. When you graph the Y axis's data, Harvard will

Table 1.1: Sample data—the number of widget sales

YEAR	SALES OFFICE		
	NEW YORK	CHICAGO	MIAMI
1986	4,567	2,391	1,429
1987	4,987	3,456	2,986
1988	4,852	4,349	2,235
1989	4,920	5,245	2,429

automatically adjust the scale to the range of 0 to 6,000. You'll find that Harvard does many things for you automatically to make graphing easier.

The sales figures are data elements, occasionally called data points, points, or just plain elements. For example, the numbers 4,567 and 4,987 are elements showing the number of widgets that the New York office sold.

Look carefully at Table 1.1 and see if you can identify the series. A series is a group or set of elements. It can be a single column, a single pie, a single line, or a group of bars. In Table 1.1, a series is one column. For example, all the numbers in the column under New York belong to the New York series. Those under Chicago belong to the Chicago series, and so on.

Now that you know what data go on the X and Y axes and what Table 1.1's series are, sketch a rough graph of Table 1.1. Then compare your sketch to the graph shown in Figure 1.4.

If you're new to charts, use an organizational form similar to the one shown in Figure 1.5. It helps you recognize the important parts of your graph and streamlines data entry.

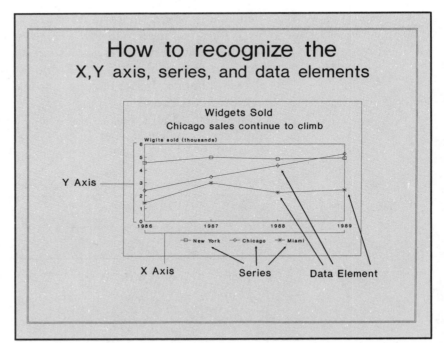

Figure 1.4: Locations of axes, series, and elements

I created the form in Figure 1.5 by using Harvard's Draw/ Annotate option. You'll learn more about this limitless option in Chapters 3 and 10.

Harvard's data-entry screen is similar to the form shown in Figure 1.5. You'll find this form handy if you prepare graphs for other people to present. It can double as a combination order-and-data-entry form.

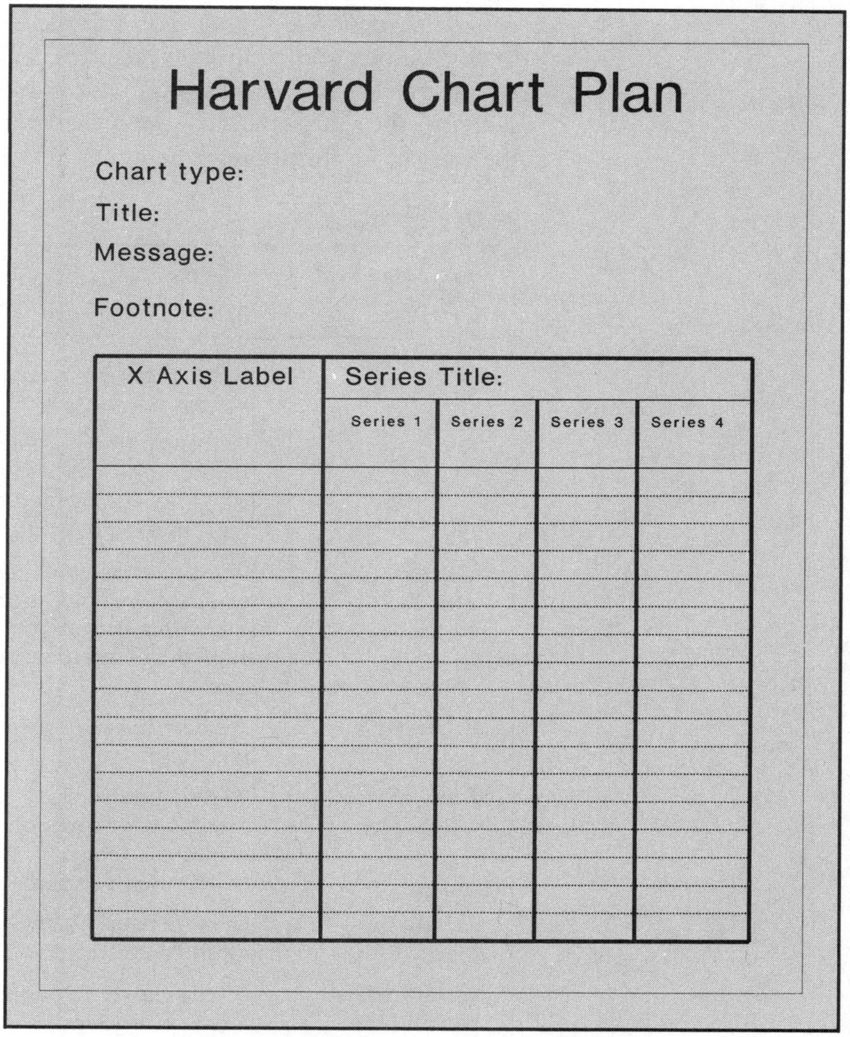

Harvard Chart Plan

Chart type:

Title:

Message:

Footnote:

X Axis Label	Series Title:			
	Series 1	Series 2	Series 3	Series 4

Figure 1.5: Defining and organizing the parts of your graph

SELECTING THE RIGHT CHART

To present your data well, you need to use the type of graph that suits them. As you saw when you compared Figures 1.1 and 1.2, selecting the wrong graph leads to a poor presentation. You will become more confident about selecting the correct type of graph as you work with all of the various graphs in later chapters. For now, refer to Table 1.2, which lists dozens of charts you might want to use. The second column describes the chart's most common use, and the third column gives you the chapter for further information on that chart.

Table 1.2: Choosing the right chart

TYPE OF CHART	USE	CHAPTER
Text	To highlight your main ideas or present nonnumerical data	3
Pie	To show parts of a total including ratios, percentages, shares, or quotas at a given point in time	4
Cut pie	To emphasize an element that is part of a whole; it can also be linked to a column chart to show the components of the slice	4
Line (curve)	To show fluctuations in data over time	5
Line (zigzag)	To illustrate sharp trends and changes over time for frequency, range, and distribution comparisons	5
3D line	To emphasize changes in volume over time	5
Combination bar and line	To emphasize relationships between series as they vary over time	5
Bar	To illustrate changes or growth over time	5

Table 1.2: Choosing the right chart (continued)

TYPE OF CHART	USE	CHAPTER
3D bar	To emphasize magnitude of change or growth over time	5
Cumulative bar	To show increases between consecutive periods	5
Horizontal bar	To rank many similar items or show trends over many time periods	5
Overlap bar	To demonstrate relationships between groups of series	5
Stack bar	To illustrate parts of a total over time, such as sales for several departments	5
Percent bar	To show parts of a whole in percentages at different time periods	5
Dual Y axis (bar or line)	To compare series that have two units or lines of measure, such as dollar amounts and units sold	5
Paired bar	To show correlations between different series using the same X axis, such as the market share between two competitors	5
Deviation bar	To show positive and negative values, such as temperature changes	5
Step bar	To illustrate frequency distributions, ranges, and cumulative totals	5
Dot (scatter)	To compare time periods or individual items to establish correlations	5
Trend line	To present statistical trends (and clarify patterns of data)	5

Table 1.2: Choosing the right chart (continued)

TYPE OF CHART	USE	CHAPTER
Histogram	To show frequency distribution for two or more series	5
Logarithmic	To demonstrate the percentage or rate of change	5
Free-form graphic	To illustrate a sequence of procedures or a system design	10
High/low/close	To show ranges, changes, and values within one time period, such as stock and bond prices	7
Area	To show cumulative totals of several series and changes in volume over time	7
Area with 3D	To emphasize general volume comparisons; not for exact comparisons	7
Gantt or PERT	To present work schedules or plans	7
Organization	To show structure or breakdown of responsibility in an organization	8
Map	To present geographical maps	10

To get you going on using graphs, I will introduce some of the more basic charts—text, pie, line, bar, and organization—in this section. You will learn how to identify which of these graphs best suits your needs.

TEXT CHARTS

Most of the data that you'll probably work with are numbers, which are easily graphed. However, you'll need to use a *text* chart for nonnumerical data. Figure 1.6 shows a text chart that is easy to make.

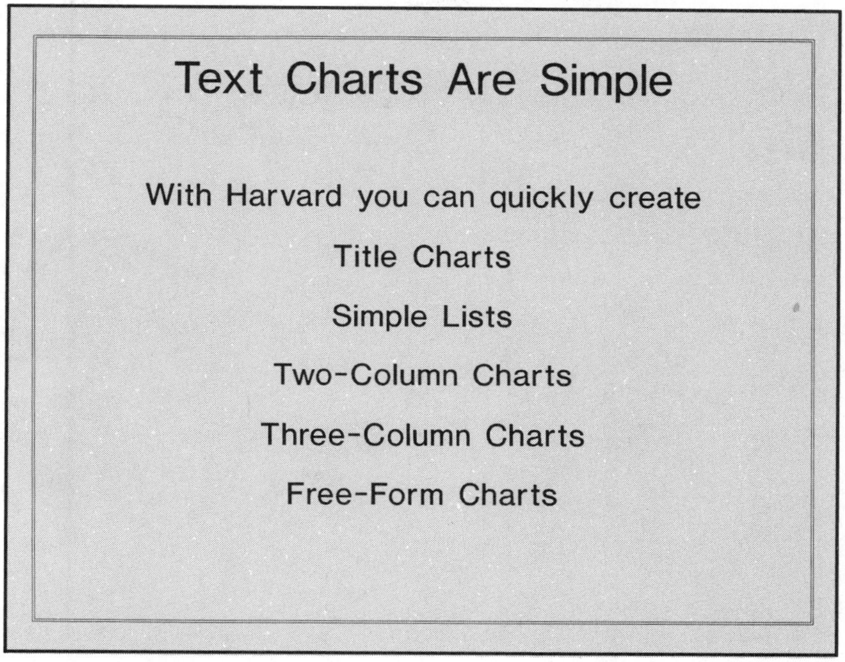

Text Charts Are Simple

With Harvard you can quickly create

Title Charts

Simple Lists

Two-Column Charts

Three-Column Charts

Free-Form Charts

Figure 1.6: A sample text chart

With text charts you can introduce or summarize your presentation to reinforce your main points. By interspersing text graphs in your graphics presentations, you can also provide more variety for your audience, which helps to keep them interested in what you have to say.

The best text charts are simple. Keep your lines short by highlighting only main ideas. If you want to write complete sentences that thoroughly explain your ideas, write a report. Limit your text charts to fewer than ten lines, with no more than seven words to a line. If you try to cram too much into a text chart, your audience will become confused and lose interest.

PIE CHARTS

When you are dealing with simple numerical data, a *pie* chart is one of the easiest graphs to make and understand (see Figure 1.7). Each slice represents an individual part of a particular group. The larger the slice, the greater the percentage of the whole group. In Figure 1.7, for example, the whole pie is the total number of accidental

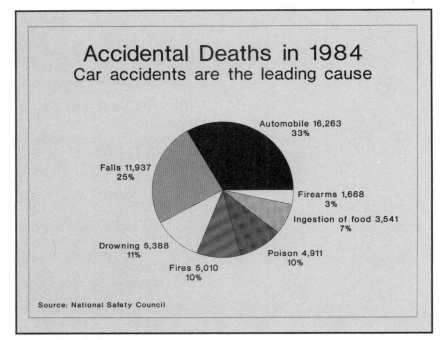

Figure 1.7: A sample pie chart

deaths, and its slices are the causes of death, with the corresponding data value for each cause. Harvard also lets you effortlessly change the data values to percentages.

A good pie chart is both easy to read and graphically appealing. Although Harvard lets you designate 12 slices, restrain yourself and use 8 slices at most. If necessary, combine some of your smaller slices into one. When there are too many slices, labels run together, and it gets increasingly difficult to compare the sizes of the pie slices.

A useful pie only displays one point in time. For example, you can't use a pie chart to display two years of corporate financial conditions. The chart just wouldn't make sense. You could, however, use one pie for each time period. A time period can be anything from a minute to a day to a year.

Unlike a pie chart, a *line* chart shows trends and changes over time. They're also commonly used to compare frequency distributions, population studies, and ranges. For example, Figure 1.8 contains a line chart that is a *frequency distribution*. When you use a frequency distribution, you are counting how many times an event occurred. For example, if you want to chart a group's exam scores, you create a frequency-distribution chart. Here you might have 4 people scoring 60, 5 people scoring 62, and so on. (You'll learn to use statistics in your graphs in Appendix C.)

Notice that the line in Figure 1.8's chart *zigzags*. This chart's sharp angles emphasize major magnitude differences. In contrast, the *curved* line graph in Figure 1.9 has a smoother, more continuous line, which is better for showing trends. When choosing between zigzags and curves, think of what you're trying to say. If you want to show a gradual trend, use the curve. If you're trying to dramatize fluctuations in your data, however, use the zigzag.

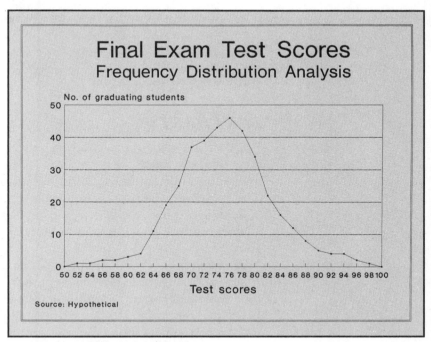

Figure 1.8: A frequency-distribution chart

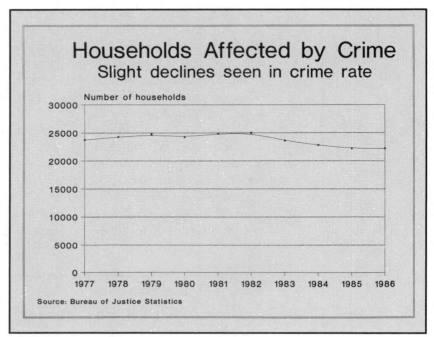

Figure 1.9: A curved line chart

BAR CHARTS

Like a line chart, a standard *bar* chart shows change over time. However, it is easier for an audience to understand. In fact, it's the first graph students learn to draw in elementary school. Use the standard bar chart when you want to show growth over time and at the same time emphasize differences in mass or size (see Figure 1.10). As with any chart, you don't want to clutter your bar chart—use at most 15 bars.

A *cumulative bar* chart is simply a bar chart with running totals. For example, in Figure 1.11, January's bar displays the sales for that month, while February's bar presents the sales for both January and February. Since the data are cumulated month by month, the last month, December, shows the sales for the entire year.

Cumulative bars are excellent for comparing targeted objectives with the actual results. Thus, they're often used in graphs showing

Figure 1.10: A sample bar chart

fund-raising activities and sales goals. As you can see in Figure 1.11, you can use Harvard to highlight goals with illustrative graphic symbols and text.

ORGANIZATION CHARTS

One of the first things a business student learns in college is how to make an *organization* chart like that in Figure 1.12. An organization chart breaks down a company's structure, showing who's responsible for what and to whom. This often provides insights on operations. Use these charts to show the organization's management to stockholders, creditors, customers, and other people interested in your company.

GETTING READY TO USE HARVARD

Now that you have been introduced to the types of charts you can make with Harvard, let's prepare to start using it. If you haven't

Figure 1.11: A cumulative bar chart

already installed Harvard, do so now using the step-by-step instructions in Appendix A. To use Harvard, you'll need the following hardware and software:

- One hard disk or two 720K floppy-disk drives
- A monitor and compatible graphics adapter, preferably a color system
- A mouse, preferably one with at least two buttons
- A printer, plotter, film recorder, or other output device
- DOS 2.0 or later, or OS/2
- Harvard Graphics Version 2.1 or later

If you are using DOS alone or on a computer network, I recommend that you have at least 640K (kilobytes) of memory. If you are using OS/2's DOS mode, make sure your system has at least 2Mb (megabytes) of memory.

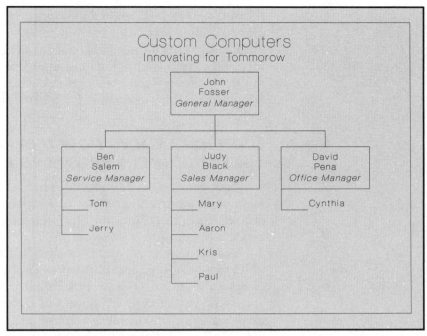

Figure 1.12: A sample organization chart

Before buying a mouse, monitor, or printer, read the sections in Chapter 2 on working with these devices.

When you are assembling a shopping list for a graphics system, keep in mind that working with graphics is processor intensive. This means that you might have to wait a long time while your computer tries to catch up to you. To minimize the wait, consider buying a PC/AT, PS/2, or other PC-compatible computer that uses an 80286 or 80386 microprocessor.

USING HARVARD ON A NETWORK

Networks allow a group of computer users to share computer programs and files. If you plan on using Harvard on a network, make sure your computer has at least 640K of memory installed and you're using DOS 3.1 or later. Also check to make sure you're installing the network edition of Harvard. With Harvard's network edition, you can have up to five people simultaneously using the program without fear of file crashes. If you use the nonnetwork version in the network, two people may attempt to open the same file simultaneously and destroy it. However, you can also install the nonnetwork edition of Harvard in a separate, private directory of the network that no one else can get to. You must also put the data files in the private directory. This keeps your files and computer safe from crashes caused by multiple access. Read your network's manual or ask your network administrator how to do this. Each network works differently.

UNDERSTANDING HOW HARVARD USES SUBDIRECTORIES AND PATHS

When you install Harvard on a hard-disk system, it is placed in *subdirectories*. Subdirectories store computer files much like a filing cabinet stores files of papers. This helps keep Harvard's program files away from conflicting software.

Harvard uses two subdirectories, \HG and \HGDATA. The \HG directory contains all the program files that run the Harvard Graphics program. The other subdirectory, \HGDATA, is where you save your graphs, symbols, and other files. It is also the directory you work in whenever you use Harvard. Both the \HG and \HGDATA subdirectories are conventions that Harvard's manual and I use. You can, however, install Harvard and your data files on any subdirectory you choose.

To work in the \HGDATA directory, you'll need to establish a path using DOS's PATH command so your computer can find the Harvard program files. Once the path is set, you can begin using Harvard.

RUNNING HARVARD GRAPHICS

You can run Harvard Graphics in one of two ways. First, you can type the commands in step 3 every time you want to run Harvard. Second, you can create a DOS batch file that includes these commands; you can then invoke this file to run Harvard automatically. Since it's quicker to use a batch file, here's how to make one. Turn on your computer and then follow these steps:

1. Type

   C:
   CD\

pressing Enter after each line. These two commands make sure that you're creating the new file in the root directory.

2. Type **COPY CON: HG.BAT** and press Enter. Everything you type now will be sent to the HG.BAT file.

3. Type

```
CD \HGDATA
PATH C:\HG;C:\DOS
HG
```

pressing Enter after each line. The first command will put you in the \HGDATA directory, the second will tell DOS where to find the Harvard program files, and the third will start up Harvard.

4. Type **CD** and press Enter. By including this command in your batch file, you will automatically return to the root directory when you exit Harvard.

5. Press the F6 function key and then Enter. This puts an end-of-file marker in your file and saves the file, returning you to the DOS prompt.

After making this batch file, you can run Harvard from anywhere in your directory system by simply typing **C:\HG** and pressing Enter.

INTRODUCING THE MAIN MENU

You'll find *A Quick Reference to Harvard's Menus* on the pages inside the back cover of this book.

Using Harvard is easy. Since Harvard is a menu-driven system, working in it is almost like ordering from a restaurant menu. Start Harvard by typing **C:\HG** at the DOS prompt if you haven't done so already. Harvard's Main Menu then appears, offering a list of options for you to choose from (see Figure 1.13). Many of these options lead to submenus that you'll work with later. To select a menu option, you type the number or letter that is to the right of the option. For example, you would type **6** to choose Produce output or **E** to choose Exit.

In addition to the ten options on the Main Menu, there are five function keys listed on the bottom of the screen. Table 1.3 describes their use. Each menu screen displays the function keys that can be used from that menu.

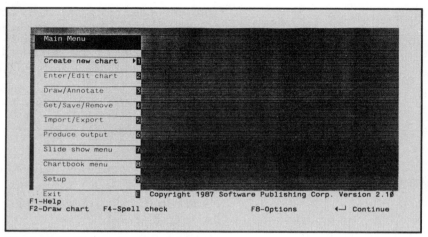

Figure 1.13: Harvard's Main Menu

Table 1.3: The Main Menu's function-key selections

KEY	FUNCTION NAME	USE
F1	Help	Provides help screens showing the courses of action available to you.
F2	Draw chart	Displays your current chart.
F4	Spell check	Checks the spelling on your chart. Available only in Versions 2.1 and later.
F7	Size/Place	Changes the size and placement of your chart's text.
F8	Options	Establishes your current chart's settings, including its orientation, border, and font.

CUSTOMIZING HARVARD GRAPHICS

Now that you are familiar with the Main Menu, you can explore using one of its options. Select Setup by pressing **9** at the Main Menu. Figure 1.14 shows the Setup menu. Its options let you customize and configure Harvard for your system. Let's begin by adjusting the default settings, which are the settings Harvard automatically provides for you.

CHANGING THE DEFAULT SETTINGS

Harvard comes with default settings for its options so that you can work with it initially. Since these defaults are set for a typical system, some of them may meet your needs. However, you can change those that don't quite easily. By choosing the Defaults option from the Setup menu, you can change any of the following settings for all your graphs:

- Data directory
- Chartbook
- Import directory and import file
- Orientation

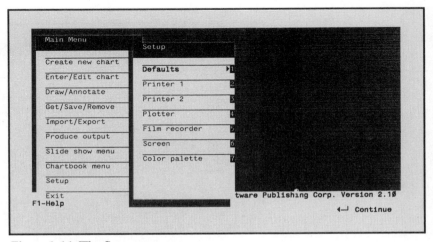

Figure 1.14: The Setup menu

- Border

- Font

- Menu colors

Some of these options are readily understandable, while the discussion of others will have to wait until you are more familiar with Harvard. For now, you'll make two changes. To make sure Harvard knows where to find your files, you'll set \HGDATA as the data directory. In addition, you'll select a frame for your graphs by choosing a single border.

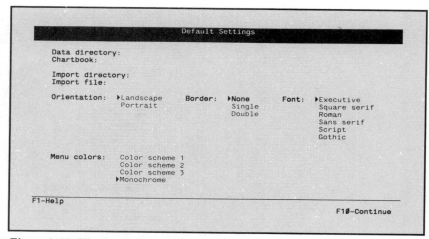

If you make a mistake, don't panic. You can use Setup as many times as you like.

1. Press **1** to display your current default settings. The Default Settings screen will resemble the one shown in Figure 1.15.

2. Type

   C:\HGDATA

   and press Enter. This lets Harvard know that you'll be using the \HGDATA subdirectory to store your data files.

3. Press the down-arrow key three times to skip the next few settings and proceed to the Border options. Press Tab once and then the down-arrow key once. This highlights the Single option for borders.

Figure 1.15: The Default Settings screen

4. Press the space bar to move the pointer to the left of Single. Harvard will now place single-line frames on all the charts you create.

5. Notice that the bottom of your screen displays the F10 key. Press F10 to return to the Setup menu.

CONFIGURING YOUR PRINTER, PLOTTER, AND FILM RECORDER

You need to configure Harvard to work with your *output device,* which can be a printer, plotter, or film recorder. To do that, you need to know the answers to these questions:

- Is the device a printer, plotter, or film recorder?
- What is its brand name and model?
- Is the device connected to a LPT or COM port?
- If you are using a COM port, what is your communications protocol? Is the Baud rate 9600, 4800, 2400, 1200, or 300? Is parity odd, even, or none? Does it use seven or eight data bits, and does it use one or two stop bits?
- Is the device supported by Harvard?

To answer these questions, refer to your computer, output device, and Harvard Graphics manuals. You can also check the list of supported devices in Appendix B. If you don't know which port is which, perhaps the following will help guide you.

Computers can have a variety of configured ports and assigned device names. For example, a computer's first *printer port* is LPT1, the second LPT2, and the third LPT3. A computer's first *communication port,* also known as a serial or RS-232 port, is COM1, and COM2 is the second.

To determine whether your device is attached to a LPT printer port or a COM serial port, remove the device's cable from the computer. Now look closely at your computer's port. If you see 25 little holes on the port, then it's probably a LPT port. If you see either 25 or 9 little pins or wires, then you probably have a COM port.

If it is a LPT port and it is attached to the same board as your monitor, it's probably LPT1. You may need to experiment with several port configurations to find one that the device responds to.

To configure your device, follow these steps:

1. At the Main Menu, press **9** to display the Setup menu.

2. Select the device you want to configure by choosing one of the following:

   - Press **2** to configure a printer (if you only have one printer)

   - Press **3** to configure a second printer

   - Press **4** to configure a plotter

   - Press **5** to configure a film recorder

3. Find your device's brand name and model on the Setup screen.

4. Use the Tab and arrow keys to move to and highlight your device's name. Press the F10 key to configure the highlighted device.

5. A listing of the possible port configurations then appears on the screen. Use the Tab and arrow keys to highlight the port name connected to your device.

6. If you selected a COM port in step 5, you'll also have to check and highlight the communications settings for the baud rate, parity, data bits, and stop bits. The device will only function properly if these settings are correct.

7. Press the F10 key to tell Harvard which port you selected for the device. This returns you to the Setup menu.

If you have a VGA graphics monitor and can't see your charts, configure Harvard to EGA. Some VGA cards don't work well with Harvard.

CONFIGURING THE SCREEN AND COLOR PALETTE

Harvard is intelligent enough to configure your screen automatically. If you change your video configuration, however, you need to configure it, which is similar to configuring a device. To do this, you press **6** from the Setup menu to select Screen, highlight the type of screen you're using, and press F10 to return to the Setup menu.

The Setup menu's Palette Setup option lets you change how your monitor and film recorder display color. It's of little use if you are working with the black and white values of a laser or dot-matrix printer. You should experiment with Harvard first before changing its palette settings.

RECONFIGURING HARVARD

You can reconfigure Harvard any time you need to make a change. If your system changes or if you buy a new output device, simply use the Setup menu and select the device to reconfigure. You can also use this procedure if you made an error in your initial configuration.

Another system configuration that Harvard uses, the international configuration, cannot be changed through Harvard's menu system. Let's examine this configuration now.

USING AN INTERNATIONAL CONFIGURATION

The date and currency formats you use depend on your configuration. By default, Harvard uses the US.CFG file for the American configuration. It displays $ as the currency value and uses a date format of *mm/dd/yy*, where *mm* is the month, *dd* the day, and *yy* the year. You can select any of the configuration files listed in Table 1.4. Notice that the CANADA.CFG and AUSTRAL.CFG files share the same currency and date formats.

Table 1.4: The available currency and date options

CONFIGURATION	CURRENCY VALUE	DATE FORMAT
US.CFG	$	mm/dd/yy
UK.CFG	£	dd.mm.yy
CANADA.CFG	$	dd.mm.yy
AUSTRAL.CFG	$	dd.mm.yy

To change from an American to an international configuration, follow these steps:

1. Exit from Harvard using the instructions in the next section, "How to Exit Harvard."

2. At the DOS prompt, type **CD\HG** and press Enter to change to the \HG subdirectory.

3. Type

   COPY *filename*.CFG HG.CFG

   Replace the word *filename* with the international driver you want to use. Choose either UK, CANADA, or AUSTRAL.

4. Type **HG** and press Enter to start up Harvard again.

HOW TO EXIT HARVARD

Now that you've installed and configured Harvard, you may want to take a break and exit the program. If you don't want to take a break, read through the instructions for exiting so you'll know how to quit Harvard and then continue with Chapter 2. To exit Harvard, do the following:

1. Press the Esc key until you see the Main Menu.

2. Press **E**.

Harvard will then end and return you to the DOS prompt. You can now shut your computer off.

SUMMARY

You've covered a lot of ground in this chapter. Not only have you learned the advantages of graphic presentations, but you've seen how to maximize those advantages by using Harvard Graphics.

You've learned how to read and interpret charts. You understand the anatomy of a chart and can show its elements, series, and axes. You're familiar with the differences between pie, line, bar, and organization charts.

You have run Harvard Graphics, have become familiar with its Main Menu, and have customized Harvard Graphics for your system. Finally, you've learned how to exit Harvard.

In the next chapter you'll learn how Harvard works with a mouse, monitor, and output devices. You'll learn firsthand how to use Harvard Graphics and create the following types of charts:

- Title
- Simple list
- Pie
- Bar
- Line

You'll also learn how to save your charts and print them for others to see.

2

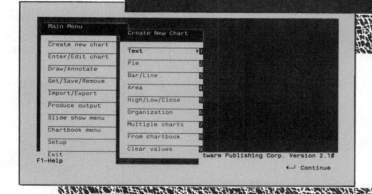

GETTING STARTED

CHAPTER *2*

HARVARD IS AN EXCEPTIONALLY EASY PROGRAM TO work with and understand. As you'll see in this chapter, you can create simple graphs within minutes. Although these graphs are simple, they serve as the building blocks to more complicated graphs. Before you work through the "Hands-on" sections in this chapter, let's examine how Harvard works with a mouse, monitor, and output devices.

HOW TO USE A MOUSE WITH HARVARD

Working with Harvard is easiest when you use both a mouse and the keyboard. Like your keyboard, a mouse is an *input device*. They both send information to the computer. This is different from an output device such as a printer, which receives information from the computer. To use a mouse, simply push or drag it along your desk and press the buttons to initiate a particular action. For example, you can drag the mouse until you've highlighted a menu option you want and then select it by pressing the left mouse button.

Moving a mouse is a more intuitive movement than typing at the keyboard. When you move the mouse, the pointer on the screen moves in the same direction. Gesturing with a mouse is like moving a piece of charcoal or a pencil to draw a picture. For example, if you're using Harvard's Draw/Annotate option, you can illustrate your chart with a quick movement of your wrist. In contrast, using the keyboard slows you down since it takes a lot of key punching to move the cursor from one point to another.

BUYING A MOUSE

There are three classes of mice that you can buy:

- IBM PS/2 direct-connect mouse

- Bus mouse
- Serial mouse

If you use a PS/2 computer, select the IBM mouse. It plugs directly into your computer without requiring a separately installed board or a serial port. Reserve your ports for other devices such as film recorders, plotters, and printers.

Don't buy a one-button mouse since it doesn't offer enough selection capabilities.

If you're not using a PS/2, you'll need to choose between a bus and a serial mouse. A serial mouse plugs into your computer's serial port, while the bus mouse connects to a special board that you install in one of your computer's expansion slots. The type of mouse you select depends on whether you need your expansion slots or your serial ports for other devices. Carefully evaluate potential equipment upgrades. For example, if you only have one serial port and plan on installing a plotter, get a bus mouse (providing you have an extra expansion slot in your computer).

When you buy a mouse, make sure it has two or more buttons so it'll provide all the selection capabilities you'll need. With a two-button mouse, you can simulate a third button by pressing the two buttons simultaneously.

An alternative to the mouse is the track ball, which is a pointing device that is becoming popular. The track ball acts like a mouse but looks like a ball housed in a box. You simply spin the ball in the direction that you want the pointer to move. It's just like the track ball used to shoot down missiles in video arcades. Its advantage is that you don't need space on your desk for moving the mouse.

INSTALLING THE MOUSE

A *mouse driver* is a software program that tells your computer to check your mouse's input. You install a driver by typing its file name without the extension. For instance, if your driver's file name is MOUSE-.COM, you would type **MOUSE** before running Harvard or place the command in your AUTOEXEC.BAT file. Alternatively, you can include the MOUSE command in the HG.BAT file you created in the last chapter. Do this by following these instructions:

Use your word processor to edit files and save them as ASCII or DOS text files. Word processors are often easier to use than EDLIN.

1. Type

   EDLIN C:\HG.BAT

and press Enter to run DOS's editor program. An asterisk and an underscore should then appear on the screen. If it doesn't work, make sure you have the editor program (EDLIN.EXE) on your disk. Then change to the directory it is in and repeat the command.

2. Type **1I** and press Enter to use EDLIN's insert line mode. You'll know you can add a line to the beginning of your HG.BAT file when 1: appears several spaces to the right.

3. Type

   C:*subdir*\\MOUSE

   and press Enter. Replace *subdir* with the name of the subdirectory that your mouse driver is in. If your system uses a driver other than MOUSE.COM, substitute its file name as well.

4. Press Ctrl-C by pressing your Ctrl key and the C key simultaneously. This gets you out of the insert line mode.

5. Press **E** to save the file and return to DOS. If you have trouble with EDLIN, consult your DOS manual.

WORKING WITH THE MOUSE

Start up Harvard by typing **C:\\HG** so you can practice using the mouse. First, highlight the Main Menu option you want to look at. As the mouse moves across the desk, the cursor or mouse pointer moves across the screen highlighting different options. If you run out of room on your desk, just pick your mouse up, reposition it, and continue to move it in the desired direction. You select a highlighted option by pressing the first, or left, button on the mouse.

Pressing the second, or right, button returns you to the previous menu or screen. As you may recall, in the previous chapter you used the Esc key to leave the Setup menu. You could have also pressed the second mouse button to accomplish the same thing.

To select a function key using a mouse, first press both mouse buttons. A menu of the available function keys will open at the bottom of the screen so you can then move to a function-key option and press the left button to select it. Choosing a function key sometimes brings several pages of options. To move from one page to another, simply move your mouse past the top or bottom of the page. See Table 2.1 for a quick reference of mouse commands and their keyboard equivalents.

Table 2.1: Using the mouse and keyboard

ACTION	KEYBOARD	MOUSE
Select menu option	Enter or F10	Left button
Select setting	Space bar	Left button
Return to previous menu or screen	Esc	Right button
Select function keys	F1 to F10	Press both buttons, then left button
Move to next page	PgDn	Move pointer past bottom of screen
Move to previous page	PgUp	Move pointer past top of screen

Throughout this book, I give instructions for keyboard users. If you're using a mouse, substitute the appropriate mouse commands for the keyboard instructions. Once you've finished practicing with the mouse, you can exit Harvard for the moment by pressing Esc or the right mouse button to return to the Main Menu and then selecting the Exit option. You can now examine how your monitor's display affects Harvard.

HOW YOUR MONITOR INTERACTS WITH HARVARD

Your monitor uses a video card to display your graphs. A video card, which is an electronic board that you install in your computer, lets your computer send video signals to your monitor. Some video configurations show the graphs in a better light than do others. It's important for you to understand what to expect on your monitor.

Use a monitor that matches your video card. If you're using a Video Graphics Array (VGA) card, you should also be using an analog monitor. If you're using a monochrome or Hercules Graphics Adapter, then you should have a monochrome monitor. The Color

Graphics Adapter (CGA) uses a low-resolution RGB monitor, while the Enhanced Graphics Adapter (EGA) uses a high-resolution RGB monitor. Video cards aren't interchangeable. For example, you can't use a monochrome video card on a color monitor—it will burn your monitor, video card, or both. The most common video cards are the following:

- Monochrome provides text but no graphics, 720 × 350
- Hercules Graphics Adapter provides graphics without color, 720 × 385
- CGA displays 320 × 200 in 4 colors
- EGA displays 640 × 350
- VGA displays 640 × 480 in 16 colors or 320 × 200 in 256 colors

The numbers after each adapter are the resolution that it can display. Thus, the EGA video card's resolution, which is 640 × 350, means your monitor can show 640 dots, called *pixels,* across the width of the monitor and 350 pixels down the length. The letters and graphs that appear on your screen are composed of pixels. The more pixels your screen displays, the sharper its image.

The IBM PS/2 comes with VGA circuitry already installed. VGA produces a superior screen resolution that you'll enjoy working with. Other computers can have almost anything in them as video cards are purchased and installed separately. If you don't like the video card (and monitor) you're using, think about having your dealer upgrade it for you. Whatever you do, though, don't use a monochrome card.

If you use a monochrome card besides Hercules Graphics, you won't see graphics. This also applies to full-screen desktop publishing monitors such as Genius. Since you can only see text with these configurations, you'll have to send your graphs to the printer just to see them. In addition, you can't design your custom graphs with the Draw/Annotate option—you can't illustrate a graph you can't see.

If you need color, configure your system with an EGA or VGA video card and color monitor. As some inexpensive film recorders plug directly into your monitor, the quality of your video configuration has a direct bearing on the quality of your slides. You don't need

⊙ If you're using OS/2's DOS mode, you'll find that Harvard's VGA screen configuration doesn't work. Either use DOS instead of OS/2 or reconfigure Harvard to use an EGA screen.

⊙ The Color Graphics Adapter (CGA) card doesn't display Harvard graphs in color when you are using Draw/Annotate. Even though you're using a CGA card and a color monitor, Harvard displays charts in black and white.

to worry about screen resolution if you plan on using a high-quality film recorder, which does not connect to your monitor. Quality recorders are independent of other system devices and can produce images with 2,000 to 8,000 lines of resolution.

Unlike film recorders, printers aren't affected by a monitor's resolution. In fact, printed output, especially from laser printers, is often better than what you see on your screen.

Now that you are familiar with your monitor and how it affects your printed output, let's explore the output options available to you.

WHICH OUTPUT DEVICE SHOULD YOU CHOOSE?

Usually your choice of output is easy to make. If you have only a printer, you haven't much choice. However, when you have access to a printer, a plotter, and a film recorder, the decision becomes harder.

WHEN TO USE A PRINTER

Use printers to produce reports, handouts for your presentation, and something for your audience to make notes on. Give your audience a copy or outline of your presentation. Printouts are also useful when you are presenting facts or statistics to small groups of two to ten people. Printing your data is fast and easy. If you want to print 3D charts, use a printer since plotters ignore 3D settings.

WHEN TO USE A PLOTTER

Transparencies lack resolution and clarity for large audiences.

Although plotters can't produce 3D charts, they do create a better quality of output than printers do for most types of charts. However, a plotter can take from 3 to 15 minutes to plot a single graph. Thus, if your presentation contains 12 charts, your plotter (and you) will be busy for up to 3 hours producing them. Because a plotter is so slow, you don't want to use it for long presentations to a few people—it simply isn't time efficient. Nevertheless, a plotter is ideal for making transparencies for overhead projectors. If you will be addressing an audience of 10 to 25 people, you might consider plotting your graphs on transparencies for your presentation. You will then be able to project your graphs onto a wall or a screen, and everyone will be able to see them easily.

WHEN TO USE A SLIDE RECORDER

For presentations, slides are even better than plotted transparencies. They can be used for an audience of almost any size. The problem with slides, though, is that they're expensive. Outside slide services can cost about $10 per slide. If you try to make your own slides, they then cost about $1 apiece, not including the cost of the equipment, which itself is expensive. An inexpensive slide recorder, such as the Polaroid palette, runs for about $2,000 and has a resolution that matches the video screen's. The quality of its output is only suitable for small audiences. High-resolution film recorders cost about $8,000.

PRINTING SYMBOLS

In its list of symbols, the Harvard manual displays asterisks next to those that can't be produced on plotters.

Symbols present you with a unique problem because they require a color or PostScript printer. Some symbols won't produce on plotters, and other printers simply display colored symbols in solid black. PostScript printers come with the programming sophistication necessary to automatically convert color instructions into shades of gray.

Chapter 10 shows you how to get around the silhouette problem by modifying the symbol.

If a symbol uses solid colors instead of patterns, it might appear as one black glob on your dot-matrix or laser printer. For example, if you use the symbol that Harvard provides for the United States, you'll see each state marked in a different color on the screen. However, when you print it, all you will see is a silhouette since all the states will be black.

Since you now know how to use a mouse with Harvard, and understand how your monitor and output devices will affect your charts' appearance, you are ready to create some charts.

CREATING QUICK AND SIMPLE TEXT CHARTS

Now you'll get to see for yourself just how easy Harvard is to use. Restart Harvard by typing **C:\HG** if you exited it after practicing with your mouse. Once you see the Main Menu, select the option to create a chart by pressing **1**. The Create New Chart menu then appears as shown in Figure 2.1. Let's use the first option, Text. (You'll learn about the other options on this menu when you use them in subsequent ''Hands-on'' sections.)

Start by pressing **1** to select Text from the Create New Chart menu. Figure 2.2 shows the new menu you'll see, the Text Chart Styles menu. It lists six different types of text charts you can create.

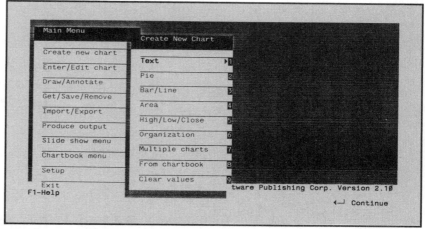

Figure 2.1: The Create New Chart menu

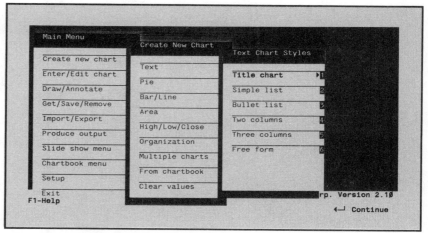

Figure 2.2: The Text Chart Styles menu

HANDS-ON: CREATING A TITLE CHART

Let's begin with a title chart since presentations themselves usually start with them. Title chart screens are divided into thirds. In general, use the top third of the chart for the title and the center for presenting your topic, message, or name. Use the bottom third for the time, date, and/or location of the presentation. To create a title chart, follow these steps:

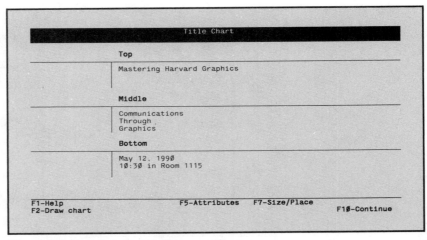

To get help when using Harvard, press the F1 key. After viewing the help menu, simply press Esc to return to your chart.

1. Press **1** at the Text Chart Styles menu to select the Title chart option. Your cursor should be positioned on the first line of the top section.

2. Type **Mastering Harvard Graphics**.

3. Press Enter three times to move the cursor to the first line under Middle. This line will then be highlighted.

4. Type **Communications** and press Enter.

5. Type **Through** and press Enter.

6. Type **Graphics** and press Enter. Your cursor will now leave the middle section and go to the bottom of the chart.

7. Type **May 12, 1990** and press Enter.

8. Type **10:30 in Room 1115**. Your computer screen should now resemble the one shown in Figure 2.3.

Figure 2.3: Entering the text for your chart

You won't see the chart's border when you view the chart on the screen. You'll see it, however, when you print or plot the chart.

9. To view your completed chart, press the F2 key. Your graph will then appear on the screen (see Figure 2.4). When you've finished admiring your graph, press Esc. You'll be returned to where you were in the chart when you pressed F2.

10. Press the F10 key to finish working in your title chart and return to the Main Menu.

You've now created your first chart and have viewed it on your screen. Although pressing F10 told Harvard that you finished entering your chart's data, you still need to save it.

HANDS-ON: SAVING YOUR CHART

Since you are now at the Main Menu, you can save this chart for the future presentation you'll give on Harvard. Do this as follows:

1. From the Main Menu, press **4** to select the Get/Save/Remove option. Its menu will then be displayed on your screen.

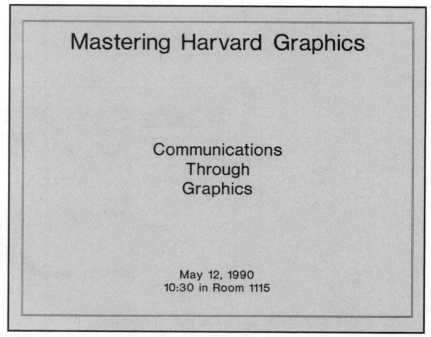

Mastering Harvard Graphics

Communications
Through
Graphics

May 12, 1990
10:30 in Room 1115

Figure 2.4: The completed title chart

2. Press **2** to select the Save option. You'll now see the Save Chart box appear on your screen (Figure 2.5). The cursor will be blinking on the line that prompts you to give a file name for your chart.

3. Type **MYTITLE** as the name you want to give to this file, then press Enter. The cursor advances to the next line where Harvard has already entered the description for you. By default, Harvard uses your chart's title as the description. You can change the description by simply typing over it. (This will not affect the chart's actual title, however.)

4. Press Enter again to keep the default description. Within a few seconds, the file will be saved and you'll return to the Get/Save/Remove menu.

5. Press Esc to return to the Main Menu. Now that you have saved your file, you can recall it at anytime to modify it.

HANDS-ON: CREATING A SIMPLE LIST CHART

Now that you've created your first chart and saved it, create the simple list chart. This chart can list several items, names, or short phrases on separate lines that are automatically centered. As with all

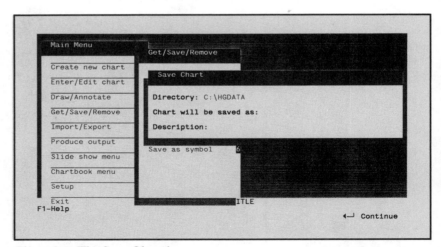

Figure 2.5: The Save Chart box

Harvard charts, you can include a title, subtitle, and footnote. Create a simple list chart by following these steps:

1. Press **1** at the Main Menu to select the Create new chart option.

2. Press **1** at the Create New Chart menu to choose Text.

3. At the Text Chart Styles menu, which then appears, press **2** to select the Simple list option. Since you've just finished creating the title chart, Harvard is wondering whether to insert its text into your list chart. It displays the Change Chart Type box, which contains the message

   Keep current data: ►Yes No

4. Highlight the No setting and press Enter. Since you want to create a new chart, you don't want to keep the old data. The Simple List data-entry screen then appears. The cursor, which is currently an underscore, is in the Title field at the top of the screen.

5. Type **Simple List Charts** and press Enter.

6. In the Subtitle field, type **Pointers for effective chats** and press Enter. Oops, I think we made a mistake. We dropped the *r*, typing *chats* instead of *charts*.

7. Move the cursor to the *t* in *chats* using the arrow keys to correct the error. Press the Ins, or Insert, key. Notice that the cursor has changed to a full-height cursor telling you the insert mode is on. Press **r**, then turn the insert mode off by pressing the Ins key again.

8. Press Enter twice to skip the Footnote field and place the cursor on the first line of the list-entry area.

9. Type **Titles are large and bold** and press Enter.

10. Type **Double space for readability** and press Enter.

11. We goofed again by not following our own advice. We've used single-spacing instead of double. Press the up-arrow key once so that you're on the last line you typed. Press Ctrl-Ins (press the Ctrl and Ins keys simultaneously) to insert a blank

line between your first and second list items. If you want to delete the line and start over, you would use Ctrl-Del.

12. Since your cursor is still at the beginning of your second list item, press the down-arrow key once and then Enter to start your next double-spaced line.

13. Type **Keep the chart simple** and press Enter twice.

14. Enter the following lines, remembering to press Enter twice after each line:

> **Use subtitle when required**
>
> **Use plain text styles**
>
> **Abridge your sentences**
>
> **Use less than eight lines**

Your screen should now look like Figure 2.6.

15. Press the F2 key to view your completed chart and then press Esc to return to the data-entry screen. If you are satisfied with the way your chart looks, press Esc four times to return to the Main Menu. Your chart should look like Figure 2.7.

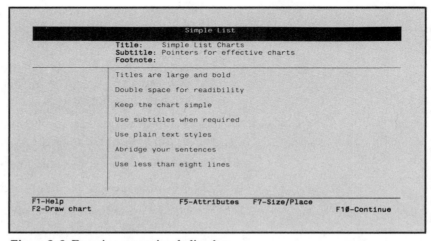

Figure 2.6: Entering your simple list data

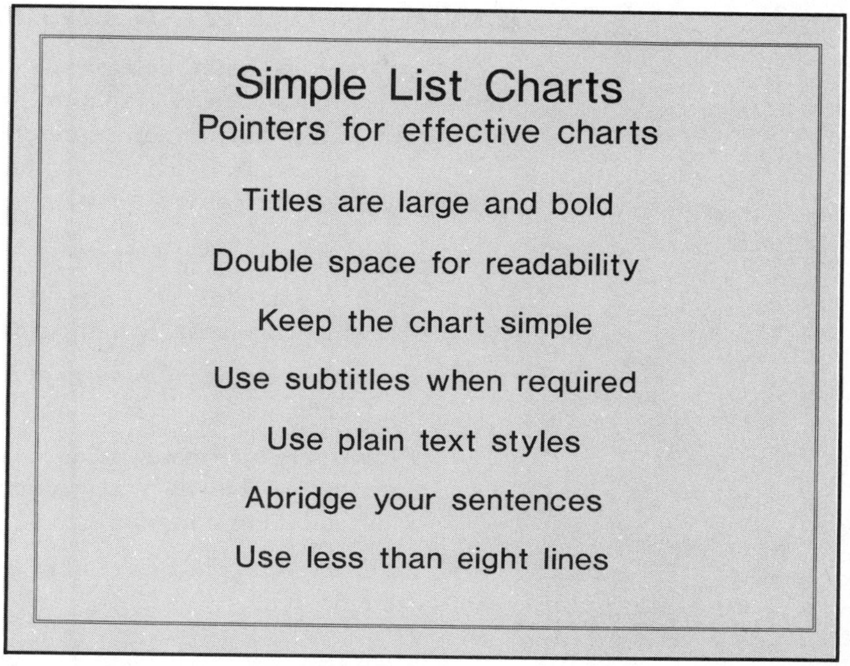

Simple List Charts
Pointers for effective charts

Titles are large and bold

Double space for readability

Keep the chart simple

Use subtitles when required

Use plain text styles

Abridge your sentences

Use less than eight lines

Figure 2.7: The completed simple list chart

Notice that you got out of the data-entry screen this time by pressing Esc instead of F10. There are often several ways in Harvard to execute the same option. Whenever possible, I'll show you both ways. You can then choose to use whichever you like best. Using the steps presented to you earlier, save your simple list chart as MYLIST with the Main Menu's Get/Save/Remove option.

CREATING PIE, BAR, AND LINE CHARTS

Now that you have created several text charts, let's look at numerical charts. First, you'll learn how to create a pie chart and retrieve it after you have saved it. Then you'll use the third item on the Create New Chart menu, Bar/Line, and the pie chart's data to create bar and line charts.

HANDS-ON: CREATING A SIMPLE PIE CHART

The pie graph is one of the easiest graphs to create and understand. Suppose you want to graph how your friend distributes his income. Since this distribution represents everything he spends, you'll create a pie chart to divide his total spending into identifiable sections. Follow these steps:

1. Select the Create new chart option and then press **2** at its menu. A data-entry screen entitled Pie Chart 1 Data Page 1 of 2 will then appear, with the cursor in the Title field.

2. Type **Monthly Spending** for your pie chart's title and then press Enter.

3. Type **Where's the money going?** in the Subtitle field and press Enter twice. This will place your cursor in the first slice's row under the column headed Label Name.

4. Enter all your pie slice names by typing each label. For example, type

   Housing

   Food

   Utilities

   Miscellaneous

   Clothing

   Savings

   remembering to press Enter after each line.

5. Move your cursor to the next column to enter the values for the labels you just typed by pressing the Tab key. Move to the first line next to the Housing label by pressing the up-arrow key several times.

6. Add these elements to the Value Series 1 column by typing each number and pressing Enter:

   1250

   439

210

185

135

55

Since you're only creating one pie, you won't need to enter data on the second page of the data screen.

7. Double-check your screen, making sure it resembles the one shown in Figure 2.8. Display the pie chart by pressing F2 (see Figure 2.9). After you have finished looking at it, press Esc and then F10 to return to the Main Menu. When you save this pie chart using the Get/Save/Remove option, give it the name **MYPIE**. You'll need this file for creating your next graph.

You probably created this pie graph quicker than you did your first text chart. You'll find that the more you use Harvard, the more proficient you get.

The next chart you'll learn about is the bar chart, which is the most flexible pictorial chart you can use in Harvard. For example, you can modify the bar chart to create vertical bars, percentages, stacked bars, overlapped bars, and even line graphs, as you'll see shortly.

Slice	Label Name	Value Series 1	Cut Slice Yes No	Color	Pattern
1	Housing	1250	No	2	1
2	Food	439	No	3	2
3	Utilities	210	No	4	3
4	Miscellaneous	185	No	5	4
5	Clothing	135	No	6	5
6	Savings	55	No	7	6
7			No	8	7
8			No	9	8
9			No	10	9
10			No	11	10
11			No	12	11
12			No	13	12

Figure 2.8: Entering data for your pie chart

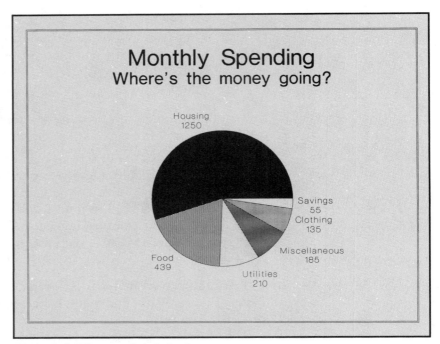

Figure 2.9: The completed pie chart

Because the bar graph also has more available options than do the text and pie charts, it may take you longer to become familiar with its many variations.

The bar graph that you'll create will borrow its data from your pie graph named MYPIE. By getting the data from the pie chart, you are saved from having to retype all that information.

HANDS-ON: RETRIEVING A SAVED CHART

To get a saved chart, simply follow these directions:

1. At the Main Menu, press **4** to choose Get/Save/Remove. This is the same menu you use to save a file.

2. Press **1** to select the Get chart option. A directory appears, showing the files that you saved on the disk. Notice the sub-directory's name above the file names. This tells you where Harvard is looking for your files.

3. Press the down-arrow key until the MYPIE.CHT file is highlighted. Notice that Harvard automatically added the .CHT extension to the file name. This way you'll know that any file ending with a .CHT extension is a chart file.

4. Once MYPIE.CHT is highlighted, press Enter or F10. You'll now see this graph displayed on your monitor. To get to the Main Menu, press Esc twice.

As you've just experienced, selecting a chart is easy since each chart's name, creation date, type, and description appear in the directory. HG.DIR is the name of the file where this directory is stored. Should you ever copy all your chart files to another subdirectory, make sure you include HG.DIR. Otherwise, you won't have the convenient descriptions of your charts when you go to select them.

After you have retrieved a chart and returned to the Main Menu, Harvard automatically uses it when you select a menu option that requires a chart. You can tell Harvard not to use it, however, if you want to create a chart from new data. You did this when you created a simple list chart. In this case, you do want to use it.

HANDS-ON: CREATING A BAR CHART

Creating the chart will be a little easier since you're borrowing data from the pie chart. Press **1** to select Create new chart, then **3**, the Bar/Line option, to create a bar chart. You'll then see the Change Chart Type box, which contains the message

Keep current data: ►Yes No

Since you want to use the pie graph's data, just press Enter to accept the default Yes. The Bar/Line Chart Data screen then appears, containing the data from the pie chart's screen. The labels for the pie slices are now the names of the X axis points. The value for each point is listed in the Series 1 column, which is the third column. You can add three more series in the remaining columns. Press the F2 key to see how your pie graph's data looks now. When you have finished viewing your new bar graph, press Esc. Now modify this graph by naming your first series and adding a second series containing budget data to help your friend save enough money to buy a computer.

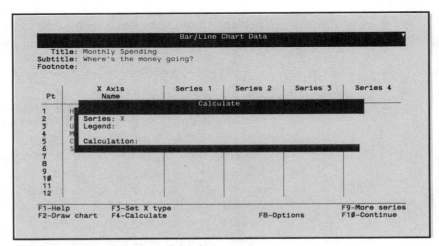

Use the F4 key, which is labeled Calculate on the screen, to save time and quickly label your series.

1. Move your cursor to the Series 1 column using the arrow keys.

2. Press the F4 key. The Calculate box will then appear, with the cursor in the Legend field (see Figure 2.10). Although you use the Calculate box to do statistical computations on your series, you can also use it to name your series.

3. Type **Spent** and then press the Del key three times to replace the default Series 1 label. Press Enter twice to return to the Bar/Line Chart Data screen.

4. Move to the Series 2 column by pressing the Tab key. Then press F4 so you can enter a label for your new second series. This time though, type **Budget**, delete the extra characters, and press Enter twice.

5. Move to the first row in the Budget column.

6. Type the following budget figures for your friend, remembering to press Enter after each number:

    1000

    420

    200

    200

Figure 2.10: The Calculate dialog box

120

334

Each number is the second series data for the X axis point in the same row. For example, 120 is the budgeted amount for Clothing, which is the fifth X axis point (see Figure 2.11).

7. Press the F2 key to view your graph. It should look like Figure 2.12. Save your chart with Get/Save/Remove option using the name MYBAR.

HANDS-ON: CREATING A LINE CHART

Harvard's line chart is derived from the bar chart: the only difference is that you display the X axis points of a series as a connected line instead of as separate bars. Let's save time again by using the previous bar chart's data. Modify these data to create a line chart by following these directions:

1. From the Main Menu, press **2** to select the Enter/Edit chart option. You'll see the same Bar/Line Chart Data screen that appeared in Figure 2.11.

2. Press the F8 key and the initial Titles & Options screen will appear (Figure 2.13). There are four pages of options you

```
                          Bar/Line Chart Data                              ▼

        Title: Monthly Spending
     Subtitle: Where's the money going?
     Footnote:


              X Axis
     Pt       Name              Spent        Budget       Series 3     Series 4

     1        Housing           1250         1000
     2        Food              439          420
     3        Utilities         210          200
     4        Miscellaneous     185          200
     5        Clothing          135          120
     6        Savings           55           334
     7
     8
     9
     10
     11
     12

     F1-Help         F3-Set X type                              F9-More series
     F2-Draw chart   F4-Calculate              F8-Options       F10-Continue
```

Figure 2.11: The Bar/Line Chart Data screen

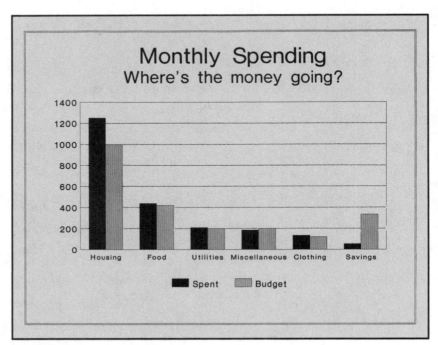

Figure 2.12: A completed bar chart

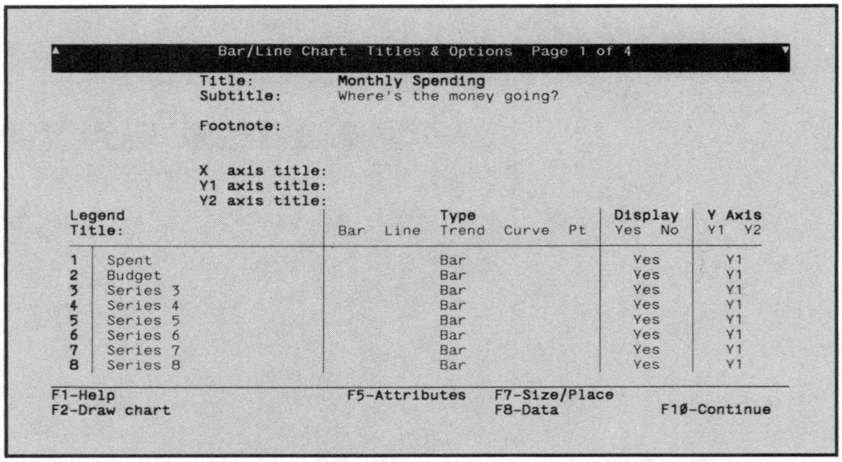

Figure 2.13: The first page of the Bar/Line Chart Titles & Options menu

can choose from. You'll only use some of these options for your line chart.

3. Using the Tab and arrow keys, move the cursor to the first row in the Type column. Since you are using the bar chart's data, the column lists all of the series as bars. You want to change the type of display from bar to line.

4. Press the space bar to set the Spent series to Line. Press it again and notice that it changed to Trend. Press the space bar four more times until the Line option reappears.

5. Press Enter to move to the Budget series' row in the Type column.

6. This time press **L**. The Type setting instantly changes to Line.

7. Press PgDn to move to the second page of the Titles & Options menu (Figure 2.14). Press End to move to the bottom of the screen. Highlight the Legend frame's Shadow option and press the space bar. This will enclose your legend in an artistic shadow box.

8. Press PgDn to go to the third Titles & Options page, which looks like Figure 2.15.

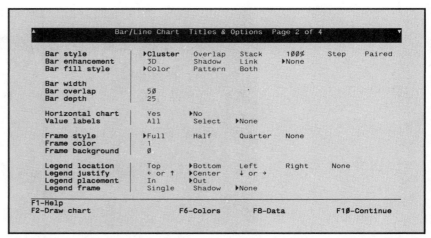

Figure 2.14: The second page of the Bar/Line Chart Titles & Options menu

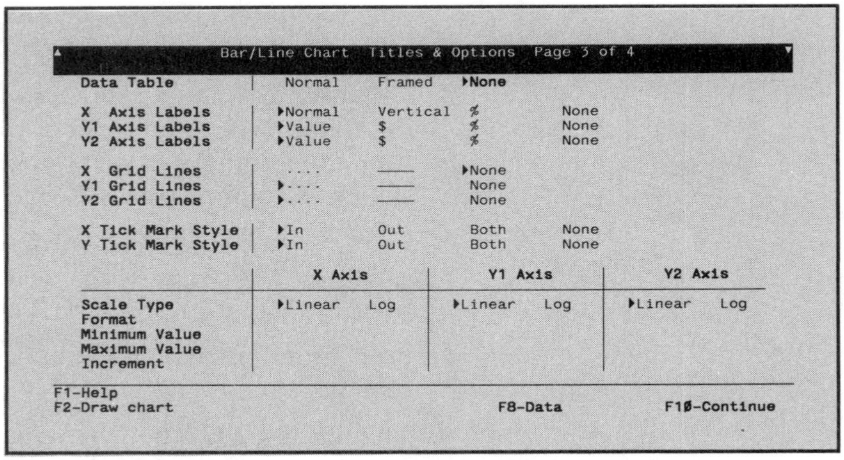

Figure 2.15: The third page of the Bar/Line Chart Titles & Options menu

9. Press Enter twice and the right-arrow key once to highlight the Y1 Axis Labels $ option. Press the space bar to select it. This will place the dollar sign on the scale for the Y axis.

10. Press PgDn again to display the fourth page of the Titles & Options menu (Figure 2.16). Press Enter six times to reach the X axis title field.

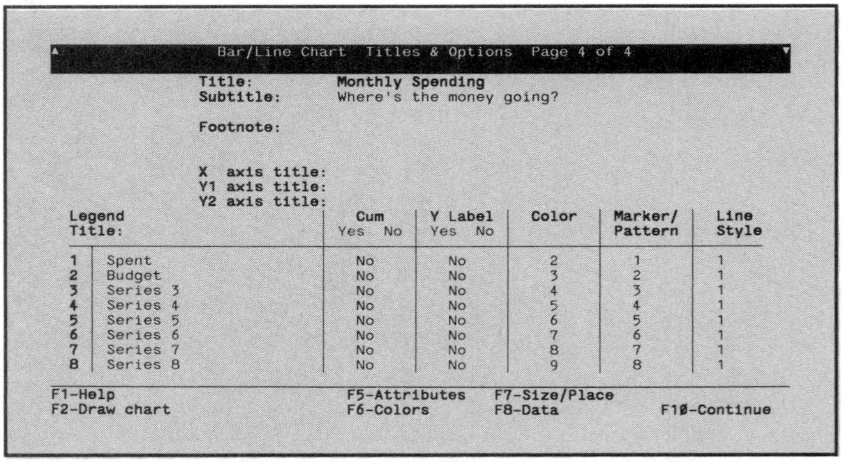

Figure 2.16: The fourth page of the Bar/Line Chart Titles & Options menu

11. Type **Expense category** and press Enter to add a title for the X axis. The cursor will then move to the Y1 axis title field.

12. Type **Dollars spent** and press Enter to add a title for the Y axis.

13. To view your completed line chart, press F2. Your chart should resemble Figure 2.17.

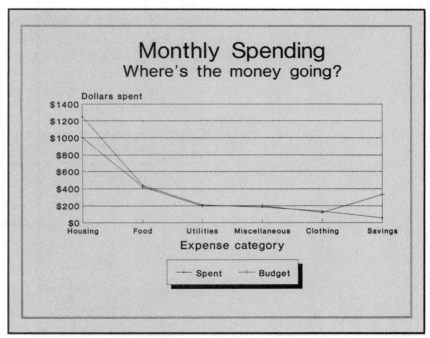

Figure 2.17: Your completed line chart

When you have finished looking at your chart, press F10 to return to the Main Menu and save it by using the Get/Save/Remove option. Don't use the previous MYBAR file or you will replace your bar graph. Use MYLINE, instead.

CORRECTING YOUR ERRORS

When you use Harvard, it's likely you will make mistakes. As you saw when you made your simple list, it is usually simple to correct errors, provided you know which keys to press. Error correction is a simple two-step process: you move the cursor to the error and then correct it by deleting, replacing, or inserting characters. You use the Tab, Shift-Tab, and arrow keys to navigate a graph just as you would a menu. Harvard uses the keystrokes common to many word processors to be consistent with programs you might be using. Table 2.2 summarizes the keys you will need to correct your errors. You can also correct spelling errors automatically, as you'll see in Chapter 3 when you take a closer look at text charts.

Although it is not included in Table 2.2, you can use the left-arrow (←) key on the first character of your line to move to the end of the previous line. Similarly, if you press the right-arrow (→) key at the end of a line, you'll move down to the beginning of the next line.

Table 2.2: The cursor-movement and editing keys

KEY	ACTION
↑	Moves cursor up one line
↓	Moves cursor down one line
←	Moves cursor one space to the left
→	Moves cursor one space to the right
Tab	Moves cursor to the next item
Shift-Tab	Moves cursor to the previous item
Home	Moves cursor to the screen's first item
End	Moves cursor to the screen's last item
Ctrl-←	Moves cursor one word to the left
Ctrl-→	Moves cursor one word to the right
Backspace	Deletes the character to the left of the cursor, moving the cursor back one space
Del	Deletes the character at the cursor
Ins	Switches character insertion on and off
Ctrl-Del	Deletes a line on the screen or clears a chosen selection
Ctrl-Ins	Inserts a line on the screen

Whenever you see two keys connected by a dash (-), it means you must press both keys simultaneously. For example, Ctrl-Del means that you should press both the Ctrl key and the Del key at the same time. I'll use this convention throughout this book. The term *item* in Table 2.2 signifies an option, selection, or a line of text; I'll also use this convention in the rest of the book.

HOW TO PRINT YOUR CHARTS

Now that you have created and saved several charts, you will want to print them to use in your presentations. As you know, you can choose between sending your charts to a printer, a plotter, and a film recorder. I'll show you how to do all three.

DOUBLE-CHECKING YOUR CHART

Regardless of which output device you choose, always look your graph over before printing it. Doing this is time efficient and saves money. Each mistake you make can cost you up to $10 just for the materials, let alone the extra time you waste reprinting the chart.

Before printing your graph, check the following:

- Is all the text there? (Long lines may be truncated.)
- Is your spelling correct?
- Check your message and title. Are they clear?
- Is the chart simple and easy to understand?

Remember that you retrieve a chart by using the Main Menu's Get/Save/Remove option. When you return to the Main Menu and choose the Produce output option, Harvard uses the chart you just retrieved.

PRODUCING PRINTER OUTPUT

Since you used the Main Menu's Setup option in Chapter 1 to configure Harvard Graphics to your printer, it should be ready to be used. To begin printing your charts, press **6** at the Main Menu to choose the Produce output option; its menu will then appear (see Figure 2.18).

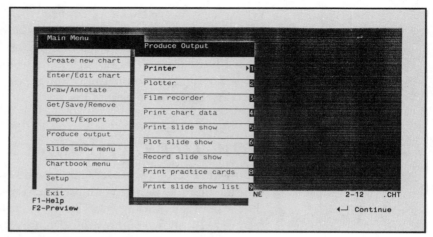

Figure 2.18: The Produce Output menu

Press **1** to choose the Printer option. You'll now see the Print Chart Options box on your monitor, listing the available options for a printer (see Figure 2.19). The default settings for each of the six options is marked by ►. If you want to accept all the defaults, all you have to do is press Enter six times and your chart will be printed quickly. Instead of doing that, however, let's examine the settings for these options. When an option has several settings, you use the arrow keys to highlight the setting you want and press the space bar to select it.

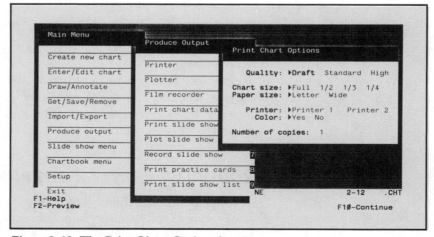

Figure 2.19: The Print Chart Options box

Quality This option allows you to choose between three printing modes: Draft, Standard, and High. If you choose Draft, your charts are printed quickly but have a rough appearance. If you use Standard, your graphs look better but take longer to print. If you select High, printing is painfully slow but makes distinguished-looking graphs. However, some printers can only work in one or two printing modes. For example, your printer may only be able to print in Draft or High. If so, it will use the High mode when you select Standard.

Chart size This option determines the size of your graph and the position it will occupy on your paper. Of course, Full size takes the entire $8\frac{1}{2} \times 11''$ sheet of paper. Figure 2.20 shows how the chart is placed on the paper when you select one of the other sizes. If you select anything smaller than $\frac{1}{2}$, make sure you set the output quality to High. Otherwise, the text will be unreadable.

Paper Size You change this option to Wide only if you have a large printer such as a wide carriage dot matrix. This will then print your graph on a $14 \times 11''$ sheet of paper. To fill the entire sheet, set the Chart size option to Full.

Printer If you have more than one printer, you use this option to choose which one you want to send output to.

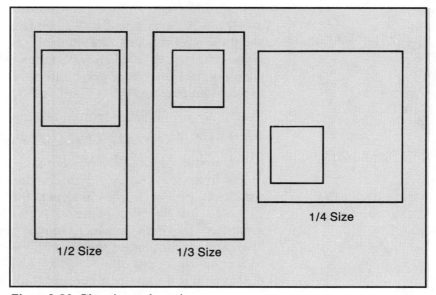

Figure 2.20: Choosing a chart size

Use color paper to get an inexpensive color effect with a black and white printer.

Color This option is only of value when you're using a color printer. If you set it to No, the color printer will only use black ink. Your Color selection is ignored if you're using a black and white printer.

Number of copies You center the number of copies you want with this option. Harvard will make as many as you like. When you press Enter at this option, Harvard begins to print your chart.

However, if your printer isn't ready when you press Enter, you will see the following error message:

Output device is not ready
Press ◄─┘ to continue; Esc to Cancel

Check to make sure you've turned your printer on and that its online light is lit. Also check that the printer cables are attached properly and that you're not out of paper. If you're still having problems, press Esc to cancel and try reconfiguring your printer as discussed in Chapter 1. Otherwise, press the left-arrow key to continue once your printer is ready.

You'll know that Harvard is busily working on your printing job when it displays the Printing box, containing the message "Press Esc to cancel." Depending on your choice of printing options and printer, your graph will finish printing in between ten seconds and three minutes, and the Printing box will remain on your screen. If you change your mind and decide against printing the graph, simply press Esc. Once your graph finishes printing, you'll be returned to the Main Menu.

PRODUCING PLOTTER OUTPUT

When you select a plotter, you have four options that you can choose from. By pressing **2** at the Produce Output menu, you'll see the Plot Chart Options box as shown in Figure 2.21.

Quality Just like using a printer, you have three Quality settings available. Unlike the printer's settings, however, the Standard and High settings for plotters use proportional spacing. This means that each letter has a particular width assigned to it. For example, the letter *M* might make up five proportional spaces, while the letter *i* might

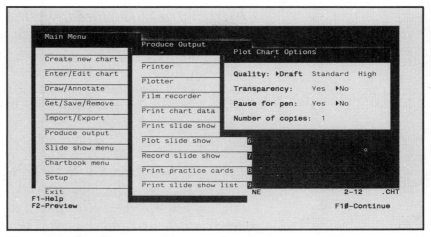

Figure 2.21: Sending your output to a plotter

only use one space. Proportional spacing yields charts that are easier to read. Choose from

- Draft—no proportional spacing, patterns instead of solid colors, stick-like lettering only, no text attributes

- Standard—proportionally spaced, stick-like lettering, colors filled in, color text appears when set

- High—WYSIWYG (what you see is what you get) plotting

Transparency To make transparencies, set this option to Yes. Since transparencies use special oil-based pens (make sure you have these on your plotter), Harvard plots the graph slower to make sure the ink has ample time to dry. It also puts more space between the plotted colors so they don't run together.

Pause for pen Choose this option if you have a simple one- or two-pen plotter. This tells your plotter to pause between colors to let you insert a different color pen. After changing pens, press Enter to continue plotting.

Number of copies As with printers, this sets the number of plotted charts you want to make. If you choose more than one copy, the plotter will pause between copies to let you change the paper. Your chart will be sent to the plotter after you set this option.

PRODUCING FILM RECORDER OUTPUT

When you choose Film Recorder from the Produce Output menu, you are only presented with one option, Number of copies. Simply choose the number of 35mm slides you want. If you're using the Polaroid Palette or Palette Plus film recorder, Harvard pauses between copies to let you change the film. Harvard automatically advances the film on other 35mm recorders.

PRODUCING CHART DATA

The Produce chart data option prints out the values you used to create the graph. When you select this option, you are prompted to send the output to printer 1 or 2. The selected printer prints the X data labels, the names of the series, and the elements used in the series. For example, if you retrieve the bar chart you created in this chapter and select the Print chart data option, you will get the report shown in Figure 2.22.

```
        X Data              Spent            Budget
--------------------  --------------   --------------
Housing                   1250              1000
Food                       439               420
Utilities                  210               200
Miscellaneous              185               200
Clothing                   135               120
Savings                     55               334
```

Figure 2.22: Printing your bar chart's data

SUMMARY

You now have a basic understanding of how Harvard works, and you have practiced using it. You learned how Harvard works with a mouse and your video display, and have explored your output options. You've also created the following charts:

- Title
- Simple list

- Pie
- Bar
- Line

You can now start producing your own graphs and experimenting with the options that are available.

In the next chapter, you will examine more complicated charts. You'll learn how to create artistic text charts, using bullets and graphics. You'll also learn how to change the size, style, and colors of your text characters, check your spelling automatically, and how to use text charts in presentations. You're well on your way toward mastering Harvard.

3

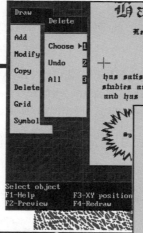

Draw / Delete

Draw
Add
Modify
Copy
Delete
Grid
Symbol

Delete
Choose ▶ 1
Undo   2
All   3

Select object
F1-Help   F3-XY position
F2-Preview   F4-Redraw

Harvard Master

Let it be known and proclaimed that

Your Name

has satisfactorily and honorably completed the
studies and works of Mastering Harvard Graphics
and has demonstrated superior graphic abilities.

Use Harvard Graphics
for better presentations

- Use lowercase letters for readability
- Use borders for a polished look
- Use a minimum of words
- Double space
- Include your message
- List related topics with bullets
- Emphasize with *italics*, not capitals

Text Attributes in
Select from a variety of

- Fill and Bold are default at
  Fill off
  Bold off

- *Italic on looks like this*

- <u>Underline on looks like this</u>

- Use color on with color output devices

- *Mix* attributes on a <u>line</u>

CREATING TEXT CHARTS

CHAPTER *3*

AS YOU LEARNED IN CHAPTERS 1 AND 2, PICKING THE right chart to convey your message is essential. You'll want to use text charts to convey nonnumerical messages, break repetitive displays of graphs, and build anticipation. Remember that your text chart must be able to stand on its own merit without the benefit of illustrations.

USING TEXT CHARTS

Since I have already discussed using text charts to convey nonnumerical messages and to vary your graphics presentations, let's see how text charts can build up an audience's anticipation.

When you present the charts well, you can create suspense in your presentations by using a technique where the text charts build on each other. For example, you can use this method for presenting a new car's features. Start by showing a chart that contains just one of your car's features, as shown in Figure 3.1.

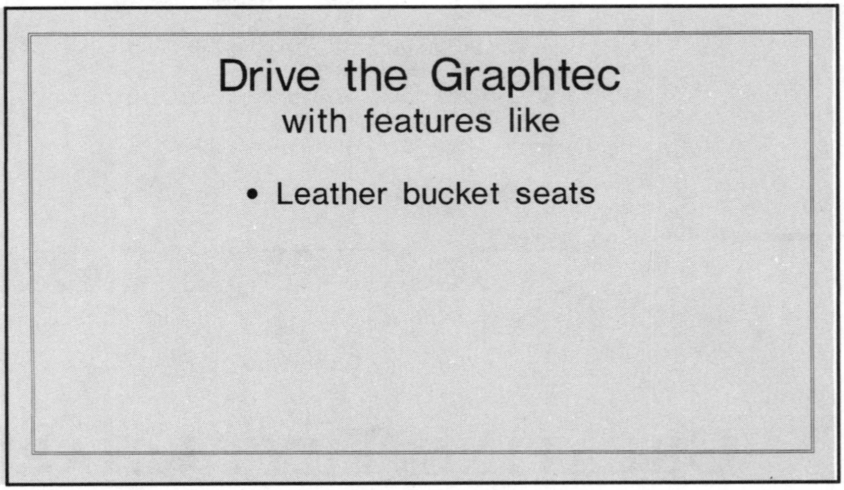

Remember, if you can't break your message into several short phrases, you're probably better off getting your word processor going and writing a report instead.

Drive the Graphtec
with features like

- Leather bucket seats

Figure 3.1: Your initial chart in the chart-building sequence

After you discuss the first feature, present a second chart that lists the first feature plus an additional feature (see Figure 3.2). Continue showing your other features one at a time by building off the previous charts. For example, you can create a third chart to add your parachute ejection seat feature. By using text charts in this way, you keep your audience in suspense while they await your next feature.

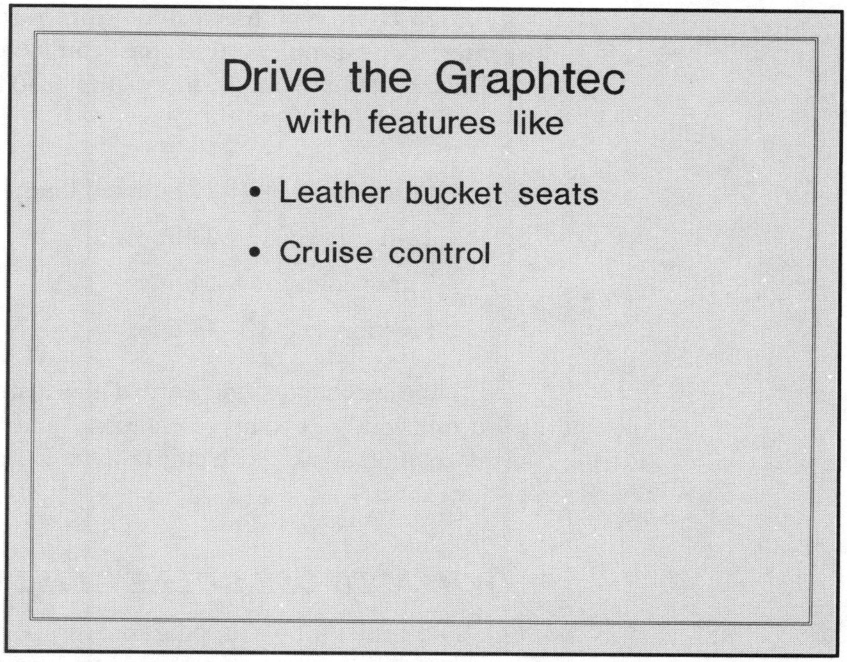

Drive the Graphtec
with features like

- Leather bucket seats
- Cruise control

Figure 3.2: Building on your first chart

UNDERSTANDING
YOUR TEXT CHART CHOICES

You invoke the Create New Chart menu by pressing **1** at the Main Menu. You invoke the Text Chart Styles menu when you press **1** again. Use this menu to specify the type of text chart you want to create. You can choose from the following style options:

Use Title chart to create presentation title charts.

Use Simple list to make single-column lists.

- Use Bullet list to group and emphasize related items.
- Use Two columns to create two-column lists.
- Use Three columns to create three-column lists.
- Use Free form for almost any textual chart, including four or more columns, signs, and illustrations.

Each chart type has a maximum number of lines that you can enter. For example, a title chart can have at most nine lines of text. Other charts let you use more lines as follows:

Simple list	48 lines
Bullet list	24 bulleted lines
Two columns	23 lines
Three columns	14 lines
Free form	48 lines

In the last chapter, you learned how to make a title chart, which introduces or outlines your presentations, and a simple list, which provides information quickly with little fanfare. Let's examine the remaining text chart styles.

WHEN TO USE BULLET LISTS

The bullet's bold appearance grabs your audience's attention, emphasizing the items in your list. You use bullets to group related information. Don't overuse bullets in your presentations, or your text charts (and your presentation) will become monotonous.

WHEN TO USE COLUMN LISTS

Don't use a column list when you want to include decimals in a text chart, because the decimal points don't always align. Instead, use a free-form chart.

Both two- and three-column charts are ideal for displaying short phrases or phrases mixed with numerical values, such as financial figures. Consider carefully, however, whether a pictorial graph might be better for your numerical data. Often, you can use a column list to present alphanumerical data and then follow it with a pictorial chart showing the data's relationships.

WHEN TO USE FREE-FORM CHARTS

Use free-form charts to make signs and posters.

When used with Harvard's Draw/Annotate option, the free-form chart is the most powerful and versatile of the text charts. The free-form chart can replicate any of the other text charts without their restrictions. For example, you can mix different sizes of text on the same line, or use wide columns. You can also create new styles of charts, such as four-column charts.

The free-form chart's versatility brings with it a minor disadvantage. Whereas it might take three minutes to make a simple bullet chart, it would take five minutes to make a free-form chart showing the same data. Thus you should use a free-form chart only when the other text chart styles are too confining for your message; you'll learn how to make this distinction in this chapter.

DESIGNING EFFECTIVE TEXT CHARTS

Besides choosing the right type of text chart for your message, you also need to design it well. You chart's design affects your audience's perception of you and your organization.

There is a lesson to learn from the mail-order industry. The next time you sift through your junk mail, look at those with quality stationery, illustrative brochures, and professional designs. Although the company might operate from a garage, the effective design of its literature may suggest a large, efficient organization. Similarly, if your chart is neat, orderly, and intelligible, your audience will perceive you, your organization, and your presentation more favorably.

Consistency is the most important element of a design. If you use a border in one chart, then all of your charts in the presentation should have borders. Likewise, use the same font for all your graphs. Your presentation, particularly its logo and graph design, should also be consistent with your organization's other presentations. Frequent changes give viewers the impression of a disorganized and inconsistent organization.

USING BORDERS

As you know, I recommend using borders for all presentation graphs. In the first chapter, you configured Harvard to give your graphs a single border by default. To temporarily change this default for your next chart, press F8 at the Main Menu. The Current Chart Options menu will then appear (Figure 3.3). The first option is Orientation, which we'll discuss shortly. The second option, Border, has three settings: None, Single, and Double. As with all Harvard menus, you use the Tab, Shift-Tab, and arrow keys to highlight one of these settings and then press the space bar to select it. If you want to use a double border for your charts, choose this setting now. While you are at this menu, let's examine the Orientation option, which also influences the effectiveness of your charts' design.

CHANGING THE ORIENTATION

All the charts you've created so far have a landscape orientation, which is Harvard's default. Just like landscape paintings, these charts are wider than they are long. Conversely, portrait-oriented charts are longer than they are wide. Use the Portrait setting for long lists, forms, or detailed flow or organization charts. Since the next chart you will make will be the bullet chart, leave the Orientation option set to Landscape for now. The remaining option on the Current Chart Options menu is Font. When designing your charts, consider how the font style affects a chart's readability and its appeal to an audience.

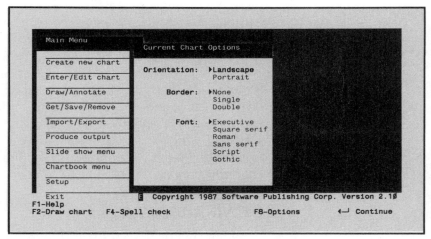

Figure 3.3: The Current Chart Options menu

SELECTING FONT STYLES

Harvard lets you choose from six fonts. Figure 3.4 compares these font styles and their attributes. Executive and Square serif, which are on the left in Figure 3.4, are probably your best choices for presentations. Since both fonts are normally boldfaced, they can be easily seen. The debate over which is the best font style has become fierce. The Executive style is a no-frills, sans serif font that is predominant in Europe. The Square serif style uses the more traditional serif look, which dominates literature in the United States. Choose whichever you prefer.

All your text changes when you select a different font. This means that you can't mix font styles in a chart. The second you pull a symbol into a chart, its text takes on the chart's font settings. This is a blessing in disguise, however, since it keeps your chart consistent in its design.

When you have finished making your selections in the Current Chart Options menu, you press F10 to return to the Main Menu. All

You can't make Roman, Sans serif, Script, and Gothic fonts boldfaced. The illustration in Appendix F of the Harvard manual errs in showing these fonts as bold.

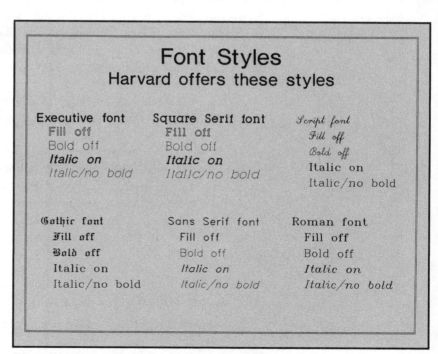

Figure 3.4: Examples of the available font styles

You can mix Roman with the Script or Gothic font by italicizing it—they both substitute the Roman font for their italic attribute.

of your selections are then set for all the charts you create in this work session—unless you call up the menu again and change them.

EMPHASIZING WITH TEXT ATTRIBUTES

Although you want to keep your chart consistent in its design, you also want your audience to focus on key parts of your chart's message. Often, you can do this by changing those words' appearance. For example, you can emphasize a word by italicizing or underlining it. To change the appearance of your text, you use the F5 key, which is labeled Attributes on the bottom of data-entry screens.

Suppose you want to change a single word's attributes. You first move the cursor to the word's initial letter and press F5. The following attributes will then be displayed on the bottom of your screen:

▶Fill   ▶Bold   Italic   Underline   Color 1

Now use the right-arrow key to highlight the text to be changed. Since Fill and Bold are the default attributes, deselect them by moving to them and pressing the space bar. Then use the Tab and Shift-Tab keys to move to Italic, Underline, or Color 1 and press the space bar to select the attribute you want. When you have finished selecting your attributes, press Enter.

If you want to change an entire line of text, move the cursor to it and press Shift-F5 instead of F5. Then select the attributes you want. Be careful, however, when you are changing attributes in your text charts—you don't want to have too much differently styled text in your chart, or your audience will become distracted and may have trouble reading your chart easily. In general, I recommend changing individual words or short phrases rather than long lines and using only two or three attribute styles in your chart. For example, select Fill and Bold as one style and then deselect them and choose Italic for a second style.

MAKING YOUR CHARTS READABLE

The font and its attributes are not the only factors that affect your chart's readability. How you place the text on the chart is equally important in designing charts. For example, Figures 3.5 and 3.6

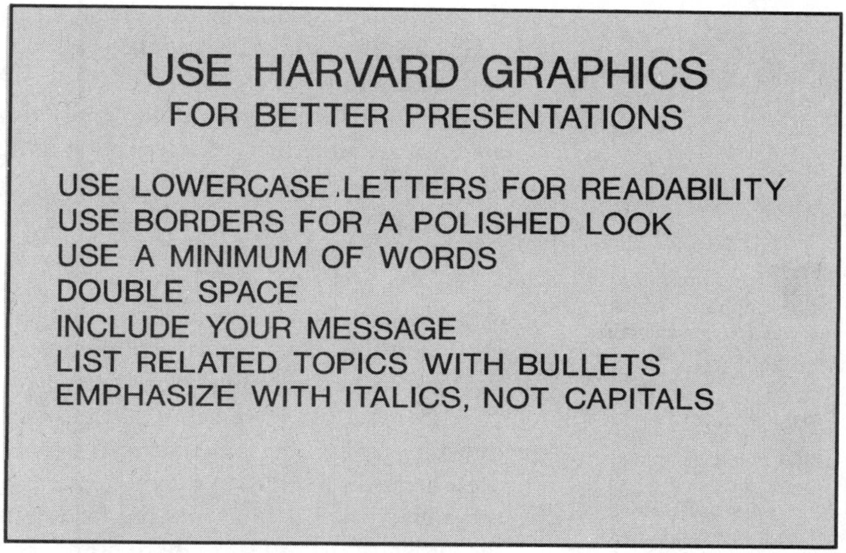

USE HARVARD GRAPHICS
FOR BETTER PRESENTATIONS

USE LOWERCASE.LETTERS FOR READABILITY
USE BORDERS FOR A POLISHED LOOK
USE A MINIMUM OF WORDS
DOUBLE SPACE
INCLUDE YOUR MESSAGE
LIST RELATED TOPICS WITH BULLETS
EMPHASIZE WITH ITALICS, NOT CAPITALS

Figure 3.5: A poorly designed text chart

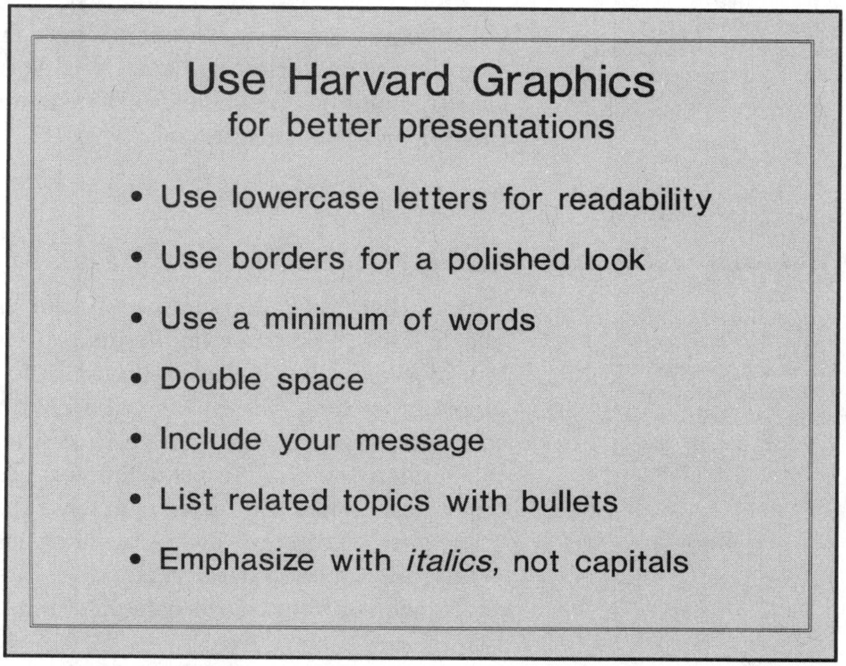

Use Harvard Graphics
for better presentations

- Use lowercase letters for readability
- Use borders for a polished look
- Use a minimum of words
- Double space
- Include your message
- List related topics with bullets
- Emphasize with *italics*, not capitals

Figure 3.6: A well-designed text chart

show two charts with the same text. Even though they use the same text, one is ugly and unreadable, while the other is more appealing and is easy to read.

There are three errors in the chart shown in Figure 3.5. First, it uses all capital letters, which gives it a harsh, angular look. Second, the lines aren't double-spaced, which makes them run together. Third, because the chart isn't enclosed in a frame, the viewer's attention is more likely to wander.

On the other hand, Figure 3.6 is readable because it uses both uppercase and lowercase letters and the text is double-spaced. Its border and bullets also focus the audience's attention on its contents.

When you're creating color charts, you need to consider the colors you use. Almost ten percent of the population is color blind or has difficulty in distinguishing between red and green. Refrain from using these colors as more than minor elements in your design. For example, don't create a chart that uses red for negative numbers, or someone in the audience may mistake those numbers as being positive.

Charts aren't the place to flaunt your vocabulary. Charts should be short and precise in meaning. This isn't, however, an excuse for abbreviating terms your audience isn't familiar with. You probably won't cause confusion by using NASA, but you might cause confusion by using DPM instead of Department of Personnel Management for a nongovernmental audience.

If you need to emphasize a letter or word, don't capitalize it, use *italics*.

For effective presentations, I recommend you use the Executive or Square serif font, upper- and lowercase letters, a single or double border, and well-spaced lines. Also avoid using red and green, since many people can't distinguish these colors.

HARNESSING SPECIAL CHARACTERS

Special characters may disappear or change if you use a font other than Executive. Always double-check your graphs for accuracy.

Now that you understand how your chart's design influences its effectiveness, you can examine its contents. In addition to entering text by typing the characters on the keyboard, you can enter special characters that are not on your keyboard. Figure 3.7 lists the special characters that you can include in a chart when you use the Executive font. This list includes bullet, currency, mathematical, and international character symbols. You can use these characters anywhere in both text and pictorial charts.

Entering a special character is simple. First place the cursor in the correct location on your chart's data-entry screen. For example, if you want

Special Characters
in Executive Font

7	•	135	ç	145	æ	156	£	173	¡
15	*	136	ê	146	Æ	160	á	174	«
16	-	137	ë	147	ô	161	í	175	»
128	Ç	138	è	148	ö	162	ó	225	ß
129	ü	139	ï	149	ò	163	ú	230	µ
130	é	140	î	150	û	164	ñ	231	T
131	â	141	ì	151	ù	165	Ñ	232	c
132	ä	142	Ä	152	ÿ	166	ª	233	R
133	à	143	A	153	Ö	167	º	251	√
134	å	144	É	154	Ü	168	¿	254	■

Figure 3.7: Harvard's special characters

the English pound sign (£) to be the second word in your title, type the first word in the Title field and then follow these steps:

1. Look up the number that represents your character in Figure 3.7. For example, the number 156 represents the English pound sign.

2. Press down on the Alt key and keep it down. Don't take your finger off the Alt key yet.

3. Using your keyboard's numerical keypad, which is on the right side of your keyboard, press **156**. Don't use the numerical keys that are above your letter keys.

4. Release the Alt key. Your special character will then appear in the chart's title.

WORKING WITH A BULLET CHART

Bullet charts are as easy to create as simple list charts are. In this section you'll learn how to create a bullet chart and change its text attributes. You'll also learn how to change the bullet itself.

HANDS-ON: CREATING A BULLET CHART

To create a bullet chart, press **1** at the Main Menu and press **1** again to select the Create New Chart menu's Text option. Once you see the Text Chart Styles menu, follow these steps:

1. Press **3** to choose the Bullet list option. The data-entry screen you'll use for the bullet chart will then appear, displaying the cursor in the Title field (see Figure 3.8).

2. Type **Text Attributes in Harvard** and press Enter. The cursor then advances to the next line, where you'll enter the subtitle.

3. Type **Select from a variety of attributes** and press Enter twice to move the cursor to the body of your chart. You'll now see a bullet on the screen with the cursor a few spaces to the right of it. You're ready to enter your first bulleted item.

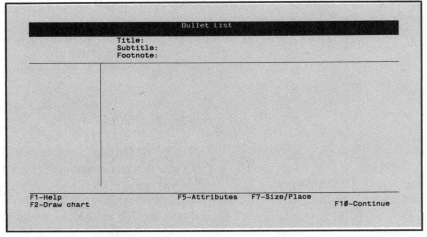

Figure 3.8: The Bullet List data-entry screen

4. Type **Fill and Bold are default attributes** and press Enter. You won't see a bullet appear on the next line because you only pressed Enter once. (Harvard requires bulleted lines to be double-spaced.)

5. Type **Fill off** but don't press Enter, leaving the cursor on this line.

6. To change the attributes for the line, press Shift-F5. Harvard's text attributes will then be displayed at the bottom of your screen and the entire line will be highlighted.

7. Press the space bar once to turn the Fill attribute off. Notice that it is no longer marked by ►.

8. Press Enter twice. The first time you press it, you confirm the attribute settings for the line. The second time you press it, the cursor advances to the next line in your chart.

9. Type **Bold off**.

10. Press Shift-F5 and deselect the Bold attribute. Do this by pressing the Tab key once and then pressing the space bar.

You can add bullets to your chart's subentries. Use the instructions in the ''Harnessing Special Characters'' section.

11. Press Enter three times. When you press Enter the third time, you skip a line and a bullet appears on the following line. By default, Harvard only places a bullet in front of double-spaced items, which ensures that you space your charts well. Since you didn't double-space the previous two lines, they're subentries of the first bulleted item.

Keep the Bold default for steps 12–19 so that you can see the differences between the attributes better.

12. Type **Italic on looks like this**.

13. Press Shift-F5 and select the Italic attribute. Then press Enter three more times to leave the attribute settings, move down two lines, and create another bullet.

14. Type **Underline on looks like this**.

15. Press Shift-F5 and select the Underline attribute to change this line. Then press Enter three times to move to the next bulleted line.

16. Type **Turn color on with color output devices**. (You don't need to follow this step and the next if you don't have a color monitor and printer.)

You can change the color of a bullet by leaving the first space blank and selecting the Color attribute for it. Bullets use the color of the first character on the line.

17. Press Shift-F5 and select the Color attributes. Press the space bar several times and notice that the number for the Color attribute changes each time. Keep pressing the space bar until you see Color 2 appear. Then press Enter to select it and create another bulleted line.

18. Type **Mix attributes on a line**. You'll now change the words on this line so each has a different attribute.

19. Using the left-arrow key, move the cursor to the *M* in *Mix*. Press F5. Press the right-arrow key several times until the word *Mix* is highlighted. Then select the Italic attribute for *Mix* and press Enter.

20. Continue setting the attributes for the other words in this line. Following the procedures in the previous step, deselect Fill for the word *attributes,* deselect Bold for the word *a,* and select Underline for the word *line.*

21. Save your bullet chart using the Get/Save/Remove option on the Main Menu and then print it using the Produce output option. Refer to this chart, which should resemble Figure 3.9, to see what the text attributes look like. Because this chart provides examples of all the attributes you can select, it contains more attributes than you would normally use in one graph.

CHANGING BULLET SHAPES

In addition to modifying your text's appearance in your charts, you can change the bullets as well. To do this, press F7 at the Bullet List screen. The possible bullet styles are then displayed under the Bullet Shape option in the upper-left corner of the data-entry screen (see Figure 3.10).

To select a different bullet style, simply press the Tab key until you've highlighted the row of bullet shapes and then press the space bar until the bullet shape you want is highlighted. If you select #, you'll see a number for an item in your list instead of #. For example, the first bullet on your chart will be 1, the second 2, and so on. Remember that a bullet uses the same attributes that you give to the first character or space in its line.

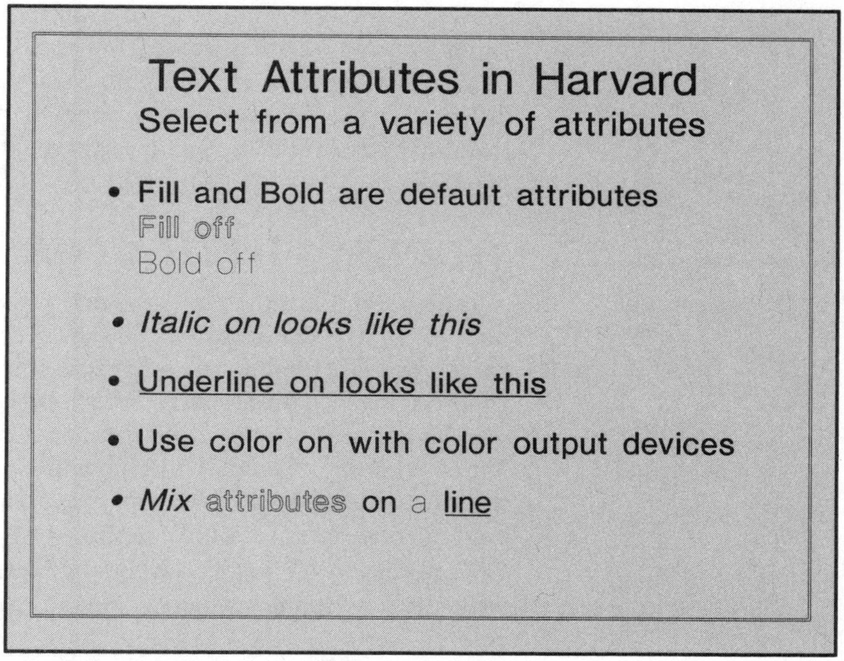

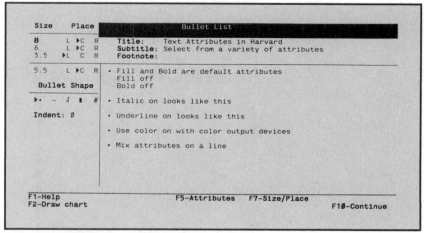

Figure 3.9: A bullet chart showing text attributes

Figure 3.10: Selecting a bullet shape

After selecting a bullet shape, press Tab to move down to the Indent option. To designate how many spaces an indent will be, replace the 0 with a larger number. Your bullets and text will then be indented to the right by that number when you press Tab. Press F10 to confirm your selections and return to the Main Menu.

WORKING WITH A COLUMN CHART

Building a column chart is a quick and easy way to arrange text in neat columns. The steps you follow to create this type of chart are similar to those for creating other text charts. In this section, you will create a three-column chart. To create a two-column chart, choose the Two columns option from the Text Chart Styles menu instead of Three columns. Figure 3.11 shows the Three Columns data-entry screen. Notice that each column has a blank header area where you type the description for the column.

Columns are left justified when they contain text and right justified when they contain numbers. Thus, to align decimal numbers in a column chart, use the same number of decimal places. For example, if your column has the numbers 5.67 and 3.4, you should enter the latter as 3.40. In general, only use whole numbers in column charts. Round fractional numbers so they'll look better in the columns and be easier to read.

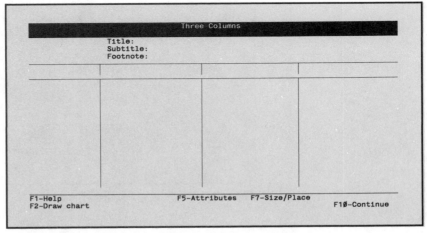

Figure 3.11: The Three Columns data-entry screen

HANDS-ON:
CREATING A THREE-COLUMN CHART

Let's create a three-column text chart. You'll find them simple to make.

1. At the Main Menu, press **1** to select Create new chart, then press **1** to choose Text, and press **5** at the Text Chart Styles menu to select Three columns. The Three Column data-entry screen then appears (Figure 3.11).

2. Type **Ocean Areas and Depths** for the title and press Enter.

3. Type **for the world's largest bodies of water** for the subtitle and press Enter.

4. Type **Depth in feet** for the footnote and press Enter.

5. You'll now see your cursor in the first column's header area. Type **Name** as the column's header and then press Tab to move to the next header.

6. Type **Sq. Miles** and press Tab.

7. Type **Avg. Depth**, and press Enter once and Shift-Tab twice to move to the first column's data area.

8. Type these values into your Name, Sq. Miles, and Avg. Depth columns. Don't worry about aligning your numbers because Harvard does it for you.

Pacific Ocean	64,186,300	12,925
Atlantic Ocean	33,420,000	11,730
Indian Ocean	28,350,500	12,598
Arctic Ocean	5,105,700	3,407
South China Sea	1,148,500	4,802
Caribbean Sea	971,400	8,448
Mediterranean Sea	969,100	4,926
Bering Sea	873,000	4,926
Gulf of Mexico	582,100	5,297
Sea of Okhotsk	391,100	3,192

9. Press F2 to see your chart; it should resemble Figure 3.12. When you're finished, press Esc to return to the data-entry screen. You'll now modify your columns' spacing.

HANDS-ON: *MODIFYING YOUR COLUMNS' SPACING*

Suppose that after viewing your chart, you decide you need to adjust its spacing. To do this, use the F7 key. Although you used this function key when you selected a new bullet shape, pressing it in the column chart's data-entry screen displays different options (see Figure 3.13).

You can now use the Column Spacing option to fix your columns' widths. Follows these steps:

1. From the data-entry screen, press F7. The Size/Place menu will appear, displaying the Column Spacing option. Notice that the default spacing for your column is M for medium.

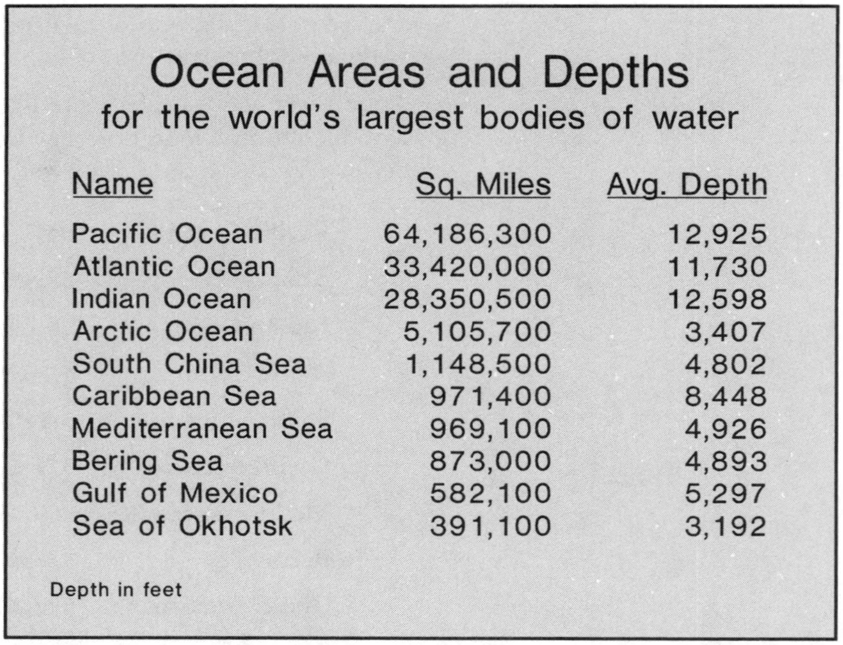

Ocean Areas and Depths
for the world's largest bodies of water

Name	Sq. Miles	Avg. Depth
Pacific Ocean	64,186,300	12,925
Atlantic Ocean	33,420,000	11,730
Indian Ocean	28,350,500	12,598
Arctic Ocean	5,105,700	3,407
South China Sea	1,148,500	4,802
Caribbean Sea	971,400	8,448
Mediterranean Sea	969,100	4,926
Bering Sea	873,000	4,893
Gulf of Mexico	582,100	5,297
Sea of Okhotsk	391,100	3,192

Depth in feet

Figure 3.12: A completed three-column chart

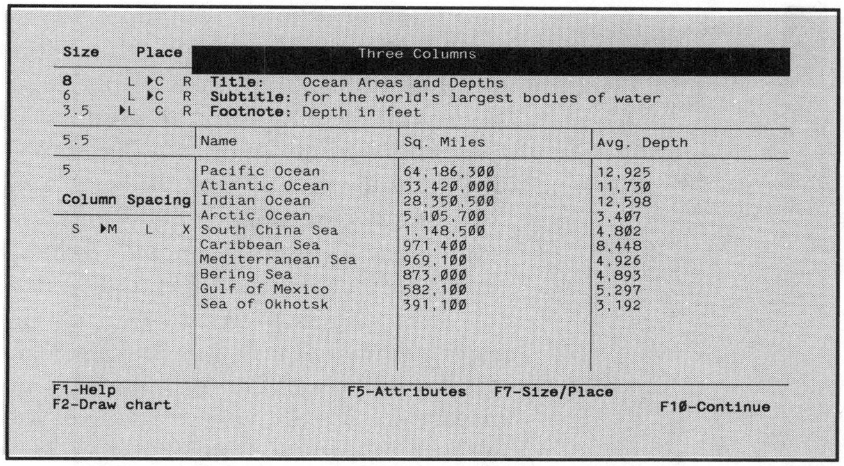

Figure 3.13: Spacing the columns in your chart

2. Move your cursor to the Column Spacing field and press **S** for small. This spaces the columns closer together. Press F2 to check its effect on your chart. Press Esc when you're done to return to the Main Menu.

3. Press F7 again and set Column Spacing to L for large. Press F2 to see how your chart looks now. You've lost some of the numbers on the last column.

4. Set Column Spacing to M again, press F10 to return to the Main Menu, and then save your chart as MYCOLUMN.

Always check your chart's appearance after setting its spacing by pressing the F2 key. You may need to readjust it as some of the phrases in the right column may be cut off, or truncated, when you print the chart. In other words, your columns' combined widths may exceed the size of your paper.

CHANGING YOUR CHART'S TEXT SIZE

Sometimes the text in your chart will be truncated even if you have chosen the smallest setting for the columns' spacing. In this case, you may want to change your text's size so it will fit in the columns. To do this, use the F5 Size/Place key.

Use the Text option of Draw/Annotate to mix text sizes in your chart's body text. Refer to the ''Hands-on: Customizing Text with Draw/Annotate'' section in this chapter.

Don't use text sizes smaller than 4, or your audience won't be able to read the chart.

When you press F7, you'll see Harvard's default size and placement settings for your chart's title, subtitle, footnote, and body text (see Figure 3.13). To change placement, move the cursor to the alignment you want and press the space bar. Understanding placement is easy. L means text is aligned on the left, C means centered, and R means right aligned. Because Harvard only allows one setting for the body of your text, all the body text in your column chart must be the same size and alignment. To change the size of your text, place the cursor on the old number and type the new size. You can choose text sizes ranging from 1 to 99, including decimal numbers. Compare the different text sizes listed in Figure 3.14. Because the actual text sizes vary slightly depending on your output devices, differences in text sizes are relative. For example, size 8 is always twice the height of size 4, regardless of which output device you use.

Try changing your chart's body text size from Harvard's default of 5.5 to 5 and then press F10 to leave the Size/Place Options menu. Press F2 to draw your chart and see whether all the text fits in your

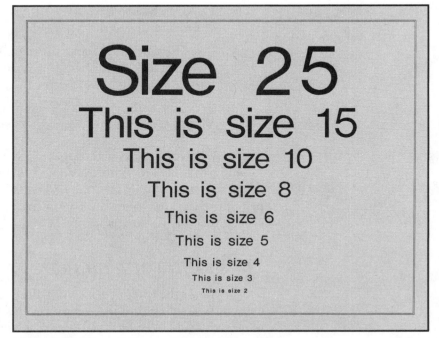

Figure 3.14: The relative text sizes in Harvard

For maximum readability, double-space your text if it is smaller than size 8.

columns. You can also use Table 3.1 to determine the right size for your chart's text. Table 3.1 is only an approximate guide since Harvard uses proportional spacing, which can vary the number of characters per line. In this table, I have given you text sizes that are good starting sizes if you use upper- and lowercase letters. The smallest size matches Harvard's limit of 48 lines and 60 characters.

To use this table, count the number of characters (including spaces) in your longest line and count the number of lines in your chart. Then, using Table 3.1's columns for your chart's orientation, find the size that fits both your chart's spacing and number of characters and set the Size option to it. If your lines are still too long for the type size you need, consider splitting them into two lines. If you have

Table 3.1: Chart size guide

LANDSCAPE				PORTRAIT		
NUMBER OF CHARACTERS	SINGLE SPACING	DOUBLE SPACING	SIZE	NUMBER OF CHARACTERS	SINGLE SPACING	DOUBLE SPACING
6	2	1	35	5	3	2
7	2	1	30	6	3	2
10	3	1	25	7	4	2
12	3	2	20	9	5	3
17	3	3	15	12	6	4
25	6	4	10	18	9	6
32	8	5	8	23	11	7
42	11	6	6	29	15	9
48	13	8	5	36	18	11
58	16	10	4	43	22	13
60	21	13	3	60	30	18
60	32	18	2	60	44	24
60	48	24	1	60	48	24

> If you are not using a subtitle in your chart, you can capture that additional space at the top of your chart by changing its line size to 0.

too many lines, consider creating a second chart or paring your current chart's contents.

Not all the space on the chart is printable. Because Harvard reserves a margin of about one inch around your graph, all your text may not be printed even though you see some additional space on the paper.

WORKING WITH A FREE-FORM CHART

The free-form chart is my favorite, because it's almost limitless in what it lets you do. For example, you can type multicolumn data into the chart and align them yourself. You can also use different sizes of text in the chart's body, even on the same line.

To maximize the flexibility of your free-form chart, you will type only the chart's title and subtitle in its data-entry screen and then continue to create the chart using the Draw/Annotate menu's Add option.

HANDS-ON: CREATING A FREE-FORM CHART

Although you probably didn't know it when you first bought this book, you also get a free certificate of accomplishment as a Harvard Master without any additional cost—all you have to do is design it.

At the Main Menu, press **1** to display the Create New Chart menu. Then choose Text to display the Text Chart Styles Menu and begin to create your certificate by following these steps:

1. Press **6** to choose Free form. The Free Form data-entry screen, which then appears, looks just like the Simple List data-entry screen.

2. Type **Harvard Master** in the Title field and press Enter.

3. To change the size of the title line, press the F7 key and type **15** in the first line, replacing the title's default of size 8. By default, the title is also centered, which is what you want.

If you just set an option at the top or middle of the Current Chart Options menu, pressing Enter will move you to the next option. Keep pressing Enter to advance through the options. When you press Enter at the last option, you return to the Main Menu.

4. Press F10 twice, once to leave the Size/Place menu and the second time to leave the data-entry screen and return to the Main Menu.

5. Press the F8 key to display the Current Chart Options menu. Make sure that orientation is set to Landscape and that Border is set to Single. Then select Gothic for the Font option by highlighting Gothic and pressing the space bar.

6. Press Enter to confirm your settings for your free-form chart and return to the Main Menu.

Now that you have set up your free-form chart, you are ready to add its body text with the Draw/Annotate menu options.

HANDS-ON:
CUSTOMIZING TEXT WITH DRAW/ANNOTATE

Adding customized text to your free-form chart is simple. You can add text, letters, and special characters anywhere you like and in whatever size or attribute you desire. Follow these steps to continue working on your certificate:

1. From the Main Menu, press **3** to display the Draw/Annotate menu.

2. Press **1** to select the Add option. The Add menu will then appear (see Figure 3.15).

3. Press **1** to select Text. A new screen containing your free-form chart and the Text Options menu will appear (see Figure 3.16). The cursor will be at the bottom of the chart next to the Text prompt.

4. Move to the Text Options menu by pressing F8. Since the cursor is in the Size field, change the text size to 5 by pressing the Delete key twice.

5. Press the F8 key again to return to the Text prompt at the bottom of the chart.

6. Type **Let it be known and proclaimed that** and press Enter. It's rather stuffy, but wait until you see the finished product.

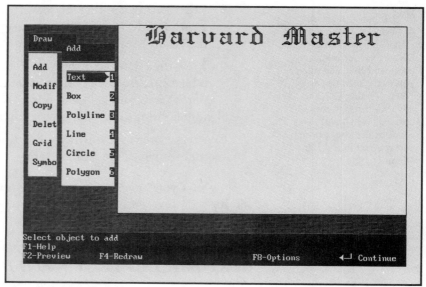

Figure 3.15: The Add menu

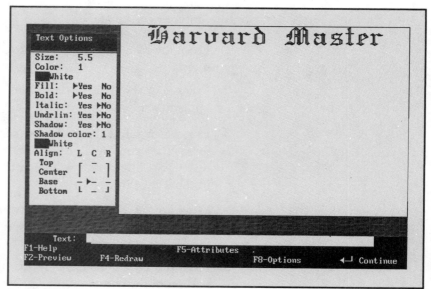

Figure 3.16: Adding text to your free-form chart

When you press Enter, a rectangle appears on your chart, showing you how much space your text occupies.

7. Use the arrow keys or mouse to position the rectangle below your chart's title. After you have placed it correctly, press Enter and you'll see text replacing the rectangular box.

If you placed the text in the wrong spot, simply press Esc until you see the Draw menu. Select Modify; then select Move, move the cursor to the text you want relocated, and press Enter. The text will be transformed back into a rectangle. When you see the rectangle reappear, reposition it in the correct spot and press Enter.

8. Press F8 to switch to the Text Options menu and then type **10** to change the text size of your next line. Press F8 again to return to the Text prompt. (Free-form charts provide the only way of mixing text sizes within the body of a chart.)

9. Type your name on this line and press Enter.

10. Move the rectangle to the middle of the chart under the last line and press Enter. Use the completed chart shown in Figure 3.17 as a guide for placing it and the remaining lines.

11. Change your text size back to size 5. Then type each of the lines

> **has satisfactorily and honorably completed the studies and works of Mastering Harvard Graphics and has demonstrated superior graphic abilities.**

placing each line under your name after you type it.

12. Change the Size option back to the default size of 5.5 for the next lines.

13. Type

> **Signed and sealed this 10th day of January, 1990 by Glenn Harold Larsen**

replacing the listed date with the date you plan on finishing this book.

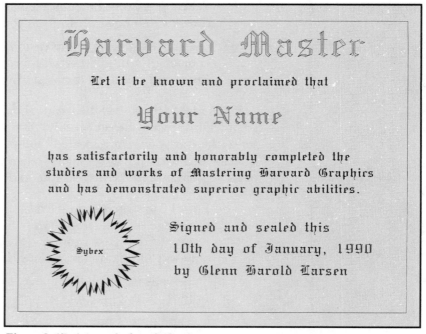

Figure 3.17: A sample free-form chart

14. Move each line after you type it to the lower-right side of the chart. Using Draw/Annotate's Text option lets you place text in ways that you normally couldn't. In this chart you've centered, indented, and left aligned differently sized text. Now you'll add a symbol to this chart.

HANDS-ON: ADDING SYMBOLS TO YOUR CHART

Adding a graphic symbol to your chart is easy. You'll use the Draw/Annotate option to help make an official seal.

1. Press **6** to select the Symbol option from the Draw menu.

2. At the Symbol menu, press **1** to access Harvard's symbols. When the directory appears, highlight the file called STARS.SYM; it contains a starburst that you can use as a seal.

3. Press Enter to use the highlighted file. Your screen should now look like Figure 3.18.

4. Move the cursor to the box on the second row with the round starburst (seal) in it and press Enter. The box that then appears on your chart is where Harvard is proposing to place the symbol.

5. Press the Backspace key to reposition the box. It will then disappear, and you'll see a cross-hair cursor that looks like a large plus sign.

6. Move the cross-hair cursor to the bottom corner where you want the symbol to appear. Press Enter to anchor its bottom corner. Then use the arrow keys to position the box exactly. After boxing in your symbol's position, press Enter. The symbol should show on your graph.

7. Return to the Text Options menu, so you can add text to the starburst symbol you just added. Change the text size to 3.5, type **Sybex**, and press Enter. Move the positioning rectangle to the center of your starburst and press Enter.

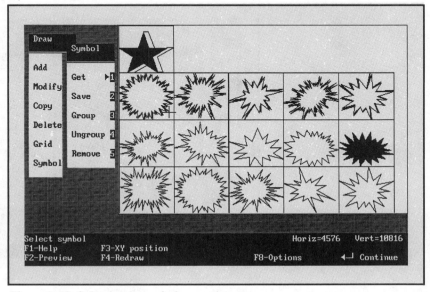

Figure 3.18: Selecting a symbol

MODIFYING YOUR COMPLETED TEXT CHART

If you find a mistake when you check your chart, don't worry; it can be easily fixed. Suppose you added the wrong symbol or a line of text that doesn't belong in your chart. Since you remove it by using the Delete option from the Draw menu, you need to press F10 to return to the Main Menu and then select Draw/Annotate. The Draw menu then appears. To remove the incorrect symbol or text, follow these steps:

1. Press **4** at the Draw menu. You'll then see the Delete menu (Figure 3.19).

2. Press **1** so you can choose what you want to delete. (Alternatively, you could press **3** to delete all your text and symbols.)

3. You'll see the cross-hair cursor on the screen. Press your arrow keys until the cursor is on the object you want to delete and then press Enter. You'll see four small circles around the object marking it for deletion. You're now asked to confirm your deletion.

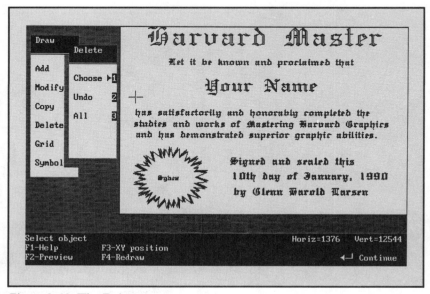

Figure 3.19: The Delete menu

4. Press Enter to accept the default, Choose this option, and your selected object will be deleted. If you made an error, you can select the next object on the graph, or start the whole procedure over again. If you didn't intend to delete anything, just press Esc until you see the Main Menu.

If your text or symbol is correct but is in the wrong place, you can move it instead of deleting it. To do this, choose Modify from the Draw menu and then select the Move option. Move the cross-hair cursor to the object you want moved and press Enter. The text or symbol reverts back into a movable rectangle. Using the Tab and arrow keys, relocate the rectangle to the text's new position and press Enter.

CHECKING YOUR SPELLING

You're not finished with your chart yet. You should always check to see if your spelling is correct. If there is anything in life you can count on besides paying taxes, you can bet your audience will catch your spelling errors. It's better to let Harvard find them instead. Follow these steps to use Harvard's spell check:

1. From the Main Menu, press the F4 key to start the spell check.

2. If you've misspelled any words, Harvard will display them one at a time on the screen. Even if you spell everything correctly, Harvard will present my name and tell you it's not in the dictionary (see Figure 3.20).

3. If Harvard presents a word that is correct but is also one you probably won't use again, simply press Enter to continue the spell check.

4. If you're sure the word is correct, you can add it to Harvard's dictionary by highlighting that option and pressing Enter. The spell check will continue, and Harvard will never flag this word again in any of your charts.

5. If the word is misspelled, highlight the Type correction option and retype it correctly. If the correct word is one of Harvard's suggested spellings in this box, you can highlight it and press Enter instead of retyping the word.

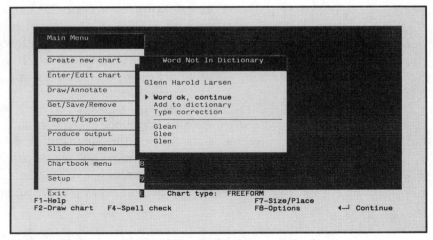

Figure 3.20: Harvard's Word Not In Dictionary dialog box

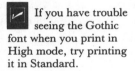 If you have trouble seeing the Gothic font when you print in High mode, try printing it in Standard.

6. Repeat steps 2 through 5 until you see the message "Spell check complete." Then press Enter to return to the Main Menu.

7. Save and print your chart using the Get/Save/Remove and Produce output options.

SUMMARY

You can now create all of the text charts. You have learned how their design affects you, your organization, and the charts' contents.

In addition to creating bullet, column, and free-form charts, you have also learned to add graphic symbols to your text charts. Finally, you learned how to check the spelling of your documents, which helps ensure that your completed chart is professional.

In Chapter 4, you'll learn how to master the creation of pie charts. You'll find many of the techniques you learned in this chapter of value in pictorial charts, since you'll often find occasion to add text to these charts.

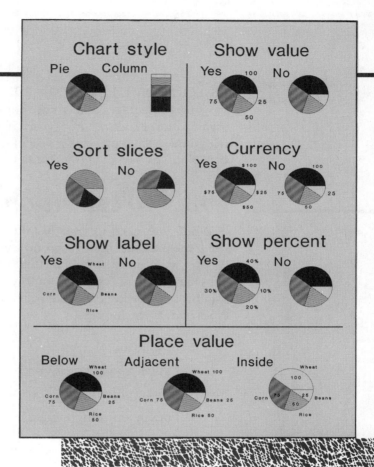

CREATING PIE CHARTS

CHAPTER *4*

AS YOU HAVE LEARNED, PIE CHARTS ARE IDEAL FOR showing percentages of a whole. For example, take the sales that an organization generates in a year. If several divisions comprise this sales total, each represents a slice of the whole. Remember that each slice of the pie is a data element of the series—the whole pie.

WHEN TO USE PIE CHARTS

When you need to express your data as percentages, consider using the pie chart first. A second choice is the percentage bar chart. (In fact, you can even use Harvard's Pie option to create percentage bar charts, as you'll see later in this chapter.) Because pie charts are suitable for showing parts of a whole, you can display many different types of data, including

- Sales income
- Expense and budget breakdowns
- Market share
- Population compositions
- Ratios

Once you decide to create a pie chart, consider whether several pies will better present your data. Remember that you can't have more than one series in a single pie. For example, you can show two years of financial data in two separate pies. You will then be able to identify easily any changes in a data element's percentage from one year to the next. Although you can use as many pie graphs as you like within a single chart, the simpler the chart, the better.

After you choose the number of pies you want, you need to decide which type of pie chart to use. You have almost as many choices as a car dealer has models. For example, you can choose between a cut, proportional, linked, or 3D pie chart. Let's look closer at these variations.

FOCUSING ATTENTION
ON A PARTICULAR SLICE

You can cut a slice from a pie to emphasize its data. For example, if you are making a pie for a company's sales, you may want to pull out the slice for the division with the highest sales percentage. Only pull out one or two slices because too many cut slices make it difficult to compare elements and create a messy looking graph.

LINKING PIES AND PERCENTAGE BARS

Sometimes, you want to use a pie chart but find that you have too many data elements—the sizes of the resulting pie slices would be difficult to compare, and their labels would run together. To get around this problem, you can create a chart within a chart by treating a cut slice as both part of the whole series and as its own series. As you can see in Figure 4.1, the cut slice links the pie's elements to the data elements on the percentage bar.

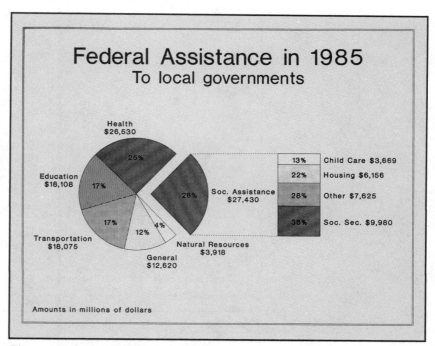

Figure 4.1: A sample linked pie chart

When linking charts, you can choose to have the cut slice's chart displayed as either a pie or percentage bar. I prefer using a bar to display the linked graph, because otherwise it could take your audience a while to figure out that two pies aren't two separate series. Your information will be clearer if you use a pie and a percentage bar.

BEWARE OF PROPORTIONAL PIE CHARTS

Although you can use two or more pies in your graph to show their relative value, you may unintentionally deceive your audience. For example, Figure 4.2 contains a proportional pie chart showing the relative sales of a bakery's pies. On a daily basis, it markets and sells twice as many apple pies as it does blueberry. Thus the apple pie in Figure 4.2 should be twice as big as the blueberry pie. Do you think it is?

If your answer is no, you're mistaken but not alone. For many people, it's difficult to determine circular proportions because they

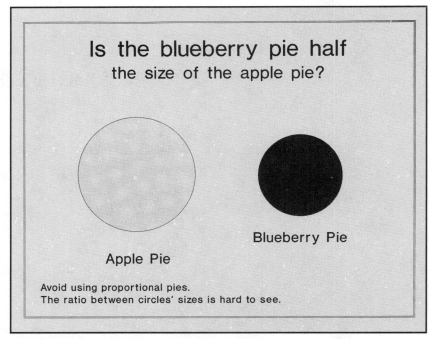

Figure 4.2: A proportional pie chart

think in terms of linear distance. Mathematically, the apple pie is twice the area of the blueberry pie, just what it should be. As always, you want your charts to be easily understandable, so avoid comparing pie sizes.

WORKING WITH 3D EFFECTS

You can't cut a slice from a 3D chart.

Like proportional pie charts, 3D pie charts can throw your audience, even though they are interesting to look at. Figure 4.3 shows a pie that is evenly divided in half. However, because the closer half is lighter than the other half (a trick for showing perspective), it may look larger. As if this weren't enough, the cherry slice uses vertical lines, which give the impression of added length.

Don't let artistic style distort your charts. A chart's primary function is to inform. Style is always secondary to meaning.

Because a 3D perspective can result in misleading charts, refrain from using it. Otherwise, your chart's and your credibility may be questioned.

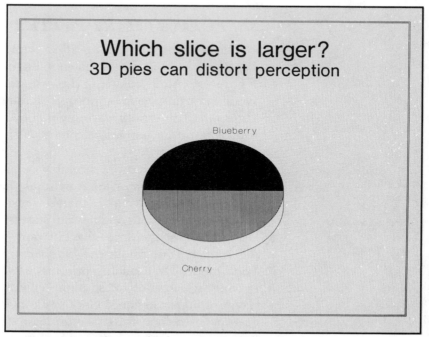

Figure 4.3: Creating a 3D effect in your pie charts

DESIGNING EFFECTIVE PIE CHARTS

Ideally, your charts should be both accurate and artistically appealing. Your audience will be captured by an attractive graph and will, therefore, understand its message quicker—provided its message is clear.

Always use percentage figures in your pie charts. Adding dollar amounts is optional.

PLACING THE ELEMENTS

Your most important elements should start at the 3 o'clock position on the pie and progress counterclockwise, with each subsequent slice a lighter color. Because Harvard does this for you automatically, you only have to worry about it if you rearrange the slices using Harvard's Sort slice option.

Arrange your data from the largest element to the smallest unless you want to emphasize a particular element.

SELECTING CHART PATTERNS

The patterns you use can affect the legibility of your chart even more drastically than was shown in Figure 4.3. For example, look at Figure 4.4. After looking at the two Harvard patterns for a while, you'll think that the lines waver. You may even see little circles moving about. This watery wavering is known as the moiré effect. You'll usually see it on pop-art calendars or posters, which are about the only places it belongs.

If you use at most seven slices in your pie graph, which is the limit I recommend, you can choose patterns that don't create this effect. However, if you have more than seven slices, you'll run out of good pattern combinations and have to start using pop-art patterns.

Avoid the moiré effect in your printed charts by selecting the High mode. Its better quality makes finer lines, minimizing the pop-art look.

Figure 4.5 shows the twelve Harvard patterns that you can use to differentiate your pie slices. This chart shows the patterns printed in High mode. Draft-quality printing shows wider lines with greater spacing, which adds to the moiré effect. Your most important elements should be assigned black or dark gray values, such as patterns 1, 4, or 7. In contrast, give your least important elements white or light gray patterns such as 3 or 6.

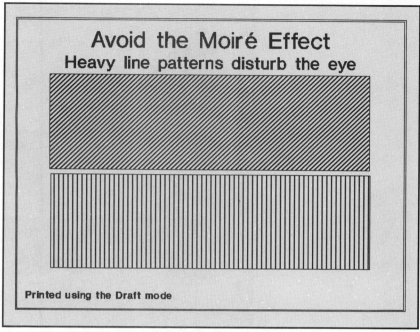

Figure 4.4: A pop-art chart

By setting a slice to 0 in the Color column, you can hide that slice. Use this technique to create a sequence of charts for one pie, hiding all of the slices except one for the first chart. Then display an additional slice in each subsequent chart, with the last chart showing the completed pie.

Don't place red and green next to each other as people who are color blind can't distinguish them.

SELECTING COLORS

When you display graphs on your color monitor or print them on a color printer, plotter, or film recorder, you have up to 16 colors to choose from in addition to the twelve patterns. Although Harvard automatically assigns a color for each slice, you can select another color by typing its corresponding number in the Color column on the Pie Chart Data screen. (You used this data-entry screen in Chapter 2; we'll examine it in more detail shortly.) The numbers for Harvard's colors are listed in Table 4.1.

Like patterns, the darker colors dominate the chart and should be reserved for elements you want to emphasize. Use lighter colors for the less important elements. Rather than displaying many colors, consider using one or two colors with patterns in your charts. Combining colors and patterns also helps differentiate colors that don't show enough contrast.

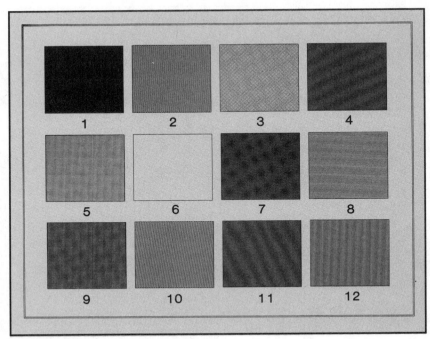

Figure 4.5: Harvard's pattern choices

Table 4.1: Harvard's selection of colors

NUMBER	COLOR	NUMBER	COLOR
1	White	9	Royal Blue
2	Cyan	10	Gold
3	Magenta	11	Violet
4	Green	12	Pink
5	Blue	13	Grey
6	Red	14	Crimson
7	Yellow	15	Dark Green
8	Orange	16	Black

USING THE
PIE CHART DATA SCREEN

Creating a pie chart is a little different than creating a text chart. When you chose Text from the Create New Chart menu, you were given another menu so you could select the type of text chart you wanted. Because you can mix several variations in one pie chart, you create the chart first and then choose enhancements such as the Link option.

To create a pie chart, simply press **2** from the Create New Chart menu. The first page of the Pie Chart Data screen then appears. Since you created a simple pie chart in Chapter 2, you're already familiar with entering a title, subtitle, footnote, and labels for a pie chart. Remember that you can enter up to 20 characters for each label. The column headed Value Series 1 holds the numerical values for your labels. For instance, slice 1 might show 105,600 as the amount spent on payroll for a pie chart on expenses. When you set the Cut Slice column to Yes for a slice, it will be extracted from the pie. The two remaining columns, Color and Pattern, contain Harvard's default values. Since you now know how these two features affect your chart's readability, you can reset them for your charts.

If pie slice labels run together, omit the labels on the data-entry screen and create them with the Add Text option of Draw/Annotate. Sometimes thin pie slices, which run labels together, can be combined into one slice labeled Other.

CHANGING SLICE COLORS AND PATTERNS

Because Harvard's default is for color slices, you need to set the Fill Style option on the Pie Chart Titles & Options menu to Pattern or Both to display the pattern values you choose on the Pie Chart Data Screen. (The Both option will display colored patterns.) If you want to use patterns for your slices, first press the F8 key to access the Pie Chart Titles & Options menu and reset Fill Style.

To change the color and pattern of your pie slices, follow these steps:

For the best color or pattern effect, work from dark to light. Fluctuating between dark and light patterns makes it difficult to see pie shading differences.

1. Use the arrow keys and move the cursor to the row for the slice you want to change. Then press the Tab key to get to either the Color or Pattern column.

2. Replace the color or pattern number with the number you want to use. You can choose a pattern number from those

Even though the F6-Color Option label is always on the pie chart's data screen, you can only select this function when your cursor is in the Color column.

shown in Figure 4.5 or a color number from the list shown in Table 4.1.

3. Press Enter.

Should you need help with your selection, move to the Color column and press the F6-Color Option key. When you're in the Color column, a listing of available colors appears on the Pie Chart Titles & Options screen. To use this listing, highlight the color you want and press Enter.

DELETING, INSERTING, AND MOVING PIE SLICES

Press F2 to check your pie chart's readability after you modify it. You will need to reassign your slices' colors or patterns if they conflict in their new order.

You can easily edit and rearrange slices on the data-entry screen. With the cursor on a slice's row, press Ctrl-Del to remove the slice or Ctrl-Ins to insert a slice on that row. To move a slice to a new position, move the cursor to its row and then press Ctrl-↑ to move the slice up a row or Ctrl-↓ to move the slice down a row.

CREATING TWO PIES WITH ONE SERIES

You can enter nine series' worth of data by pressing the F9-More series key. Because you can only display two pies at a time, the best use for this feature is showing two pies that use one series. For example, you can have a chart with a single series where the first pie shows data values and the second pie shows percentages. By setting up a graph this way, you only need to edit a series once for both pies to reflect your changes.

To do this, create a single pie chart. Then press the PgDn key to get the Pie Chart 2 Data screen. (This is the screen you'll use to create a two-pie chart in this chapter's "Hands-on" section.) Press the F9 key several times until the Series 1 Data screen appears. Now both pies will use the same data. You can then customize each pie differently by using the Pie Chart Titles & Options menu.

CUSTOMIZING YOUR PIE CHARTS

When you changed the Fill Style option to use patterns, you used the Pie Chart Titles & Options menu. Now let's examine the other customizing features this menu provides. To display this menu (Figure 4.6), press the F8-Options key at the data-entry screen.

ADDING AND CHANGING TITLES

The top part of the initial Pie Chart Titles & Options menu provides settings for customizing your titles, subtitles, and footnotes. For example, you can add an extra line to your subtitle and up to two extra lines to your footnote, as shown in Figure 4.6. You can also label your pies individually, which is useful if you are working with a two-pie chart.

To change the size and placement of your titles, subtitles, and footnotes, press F7 at this menu and adjust the Options settings, just as you did for your text charts.

You also use the Pie Chart Titles & Options menu to set the attributes for your pie chart's text. By choosing the attributes for your pie title, you also automatically set the attributes for the labels for that pie's slices. For example, if you have one pie on your chart and you want to boldface its labels, move the cursor to the Pie 1 Title field, press Shift-F5, and select Bold. Because you only have one pie, it

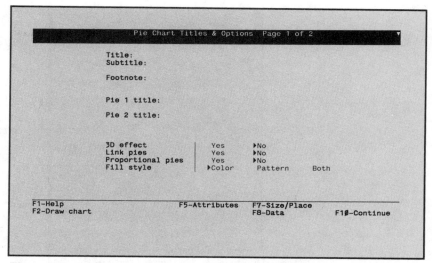

Figure 4.6: The first page of the Pie Chart Titles & Options menu

doesn't need a title of its own, so you can leave this field blank—your labels will still be boldfaced. Always set your pie title's attributes to Bold; otherwise, your text will print too lightly in High mode.

CHOOSING A PIE CHART VARIATION

As discussed earlier in this chapter, you should decide which pie variation fits your data before you create a pie chart. Once you have entered the data, you use the Titles & Options menu to select the pie chart variations you want by highlighting Yes for it and pressing the space bar. You can even combine the Proportional pies option with either 3D effect or Link pies. However, you can't use 3D effect and Link pies together. The Fill Style option, which you are already familiar with, needs to be set for every graph. If you have a black and white printer and monitor, set it to Pattern. If you have a color monitor and a black and white printer, you can set it to Both.

Since you have now explored all of the features on the first page of the Pie Chart Titles & Options menu, press PgDn to move to its second page (see Figure 4.7).

Although you can use the Proportional pie option with 3D effect, I don't recommend it.

If you need to return to the first page of the Titles & Options menu, press PgUp.

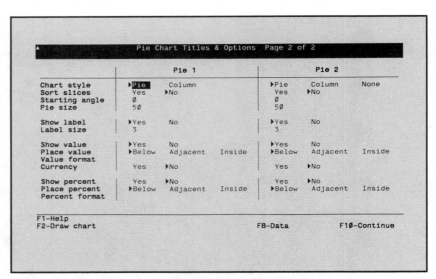

Figure 4.7: The second page of the Pie Chart Titles & Options menu

FORMATTING PIE CHARTS

In this section, I discuss all of the options on this page of the menu. You can refer to Figure 4.8 to see their effects. Remember that to select a setting for an option, you move to it with the Tab, Shift-Tab, and arrow keys, and then press Enter.

You'll notice that there are two columns, one for each pie. To customize a one-pie chart, you simply make the changes in the Pie 1 column and forget about the second column. For a two-pie chart, you use both columns. For example, if you create two pies to compare this year's and last year's expense percentages, set Show percent to Yes in both columns. If you only change the setting in one column, you might find yourself presenting data that you didn't intend to. This year's percentages compared with last year's dollar amounts doesn't tell much.

Chart style   With this option, you can display your series as either a pie or a column. Use the Column setting for Pie 2 in linked pie charts.

Sort slices   This option sorts pie slices from the largest to the smallest, which can give a degree of order to jumbled pies. However, it's better to enter the data in the order you want it presented so that you don't disrupt the gradation of the slices' colors or patterns. Because the slices are sorted by their rows on the data-entry screen, whatever values you set in their Color or Pattern column remain with them (see Figure 4.8). Of course, to keep the same order of patterns or colors, you can reassign the pattern or color values after you sort the slices.

Sometimes you can change the starting angle to prevent pie slice labels from running into each other.

Starting angle   Use this option to select a starting angle for your first slice. Choose a number from 0 to 359. Starting angle 0 is at the 3 o'clock position, angle 90 is at 12 o'clock, angle 180 is at 9 o'clock, and angle 270 is at 6 o'clock. Keep your most important pie slice between 0 and 90, as this is the area viewers will focus on.

Pie size   You can change the size of your pie by entering a number between 1 and 100. Larger numbers make bigger pies, although the larger the pie, the more likely your slice labels will become truncated. On the other hand, the smaller the pie, the more likely labels for thin pie slices will run together. Therefore, experiment with your pie's size to balance these two extremes.

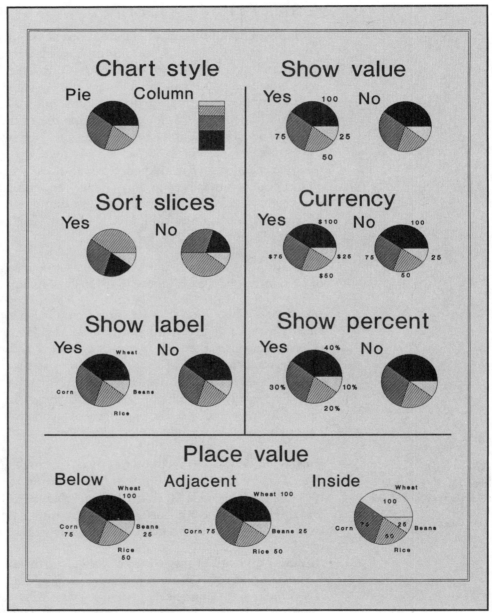

Figure 4.8: Examples of pie chart options

Show label   Use this option to hide your slice labels if your labels are running together and you want to create labels inside the slices with the Draw/Annotate Add Text option. In general, I recommend you use pie chart labels either by entering them at the data-entry screen or by creating your own Draw/Annotate labels—don't present a pie graph without any labels at all.

Place value   You can put the numerical values below or next to your label, or inside the pie slice itself. Look at the bottom of Figure 4.8 to see what the different placements look like. Notice that I had to change the pattern for the wheat slice from 1 (black) to 6 (white) when I used the Inside option. If I hadn't, you wouldn't have been able to see the black number against the black background. Remember to do this yourself when placing values inside the pie.

Value format   You can format your numerical values with this option. For example, if you want thousands and millions separated by commas, type a comma in the Value format field. Instead of showing 1000 on your chart, you'll then see 1,000. Table 4.2 shows all the formats you can select.

When you're working with thin slices, place values next to your labels to keep each slice's value and label separate from those of the other slices.

You can mix format options. Just make sure you give the number of decimal places you want first, or it will be considered as trailing text. For example, type **2** , if you want two decimal places and commas in your values.

Table 4.2: Value formatting options

FORMAT OPTION	TYPE	SAMPLE RESULT
Comma	,	25,000
Decimal places	3	7.112
Leading text*	*text*		£345
Trailing text*		*text*	46 lb
Scientific notation**	!	9.22OE + 04

* Press the space bar if you need a space between text and value
** Use for audiences familiar with format

Currency   When you select Yes for this option, Harvard will display your data as monetary values, using the monetary symbol you established when you configured your system in Chapter 1. If you're using the American configuration, you'll see the $ sign.

Show percent   Percentages will be displayed when you set this option on. It might be confusing, though, if you try showing both the values and percent. If you must, however, set either Place value or Place percent to Inside.

Place percent   As with values, you can place percentages below or next to the label, or inside the pie slice.

Percent format   The formatting options shown in Table 4.2 also apply to percentages.

HANDS-ON: CREATING A TWO-PIE CHART

You'll now create a chart with two pies using several of the options you've read about in this chapter. You're going to make a chart that compares the two parts of a financial balance sheet. Because total assets equal total liabilities and capital, you'll present the assets in one pie and liabilities and capital in the other. Start creating your chart by following these steps:

1. Press **1** at the Main Menu to select the Create new chart option. Then press **2** to select the option for creating a pie chart. The Pie Chart 1 Data screen will then appear.

2. Type the following lines in the Title and Subtitle fields:

   Warby Corporation's
   1989 Balance Sheet Analysis

3. Type these label names and values for the first pie chart

Fixed Assets	**92200**
Investments	**49800**

Current Assets	46500
Good Will	15000

in the Label Name and Value Series 1 columns.

Most financial charts compare both actual dollar values and percentages, so you'll show both in this chart. This means that for maximum readability, you'll have to put either the values or percentages within the pie slices and rearrange the patterns so that the numbers inside the pies are readable. You'll use patterns 4, 5, 3, and 6 to present your first four elements in order from darkest to lightest (see Figure 4.5).

4. Move the cursor to the first row under the Pattern column and change the first slice's pattern from 1 to 4 and press Enter. Change the Investments slice's pattern from 2 to 5. Press Enter twice to move to the fourth slice, Good Will, and change its pattern from 4 to 6.

5. Press PgDn to enter the data for the second pie. The Pie Chart 2 Data screen will then appear. Enter the following data in the Label Name, Value Series 2, and Pattern columns:

Capital	110500	4
Long Term Liab.	70000	5
Current Liab.	23000	3

6. Press the F8-Options key. The second page of the Pie Chart Titles & Options menu then appears.

7. Move to the Footnote field and type

   Total Assets = $203,500

then press Enter. Add a second line to your footnote by typing

   Total Liabilities and Capital = $203,500

8. Move the cursor to the Pie 1 title field and type **Assets**. This positions Assets below the first pie. If you wanted the title to

You had just enough spaces to type that last line. If you didn't, you could have continued typing the footnote on a third line or you could have used Draw/Annotate to add text.

be displayed above the pie instead of below it, you could press F7 and set the placement to ↑ instead of ↓.

9. To give the pie's title and labels a Bold attribute, press Shift-F5 with the cursor in the Pie 1 Title field. The attribute settings will appear at the bottom of the screen. Press Tab to highlight Bold. Press the space bar to select it and Enter to return to the Titles & Options screen.

10. Move the cursor to the Pie 2 title field and type

    Liabilities & Capital

    Leaving the cursor on that line, press Shift-F5, select Bold, and press Enter. The attribute for this title and the pie's labels will be Bold.

11. Since you have entered most of your components for the two-pie chart, see how it looks so far by pressing the F2 key.

It doesn't look very good, does it? The first pie's Current Assets label crosses with the second pie's Long Term Liab. label. To correct this, you can choose from three methods: you can shorten the labels, rotate their starting angles, or make each pie smaller. Since in this case the pie labels can't be shortened without affecting their readability, you will try to rotate the slices. If rotation doesn't work, you would make the pie chart smaller—not so small, however, that its size impairs its readability.

12. Press Esc to return to the Pie Chart Titles & Options menu and press PgDn to move to its second page. Move the cursor to the Pie 2 column and change the Starting angle setting from 0 to 13. This should rotate the second pie's starting angle just enough to prevent its text from mixing with the first pie's. Press F2 again and see if the text looks better now. Press Esc to return to the Titles & Options menu.

13. To continue modifying your chart, move your cursor to the Value format line and type a comma. This will place commas in large numbers to make them easier to read. For uniformity, don't forget to place the comma in the Pie 2 column as well.

14. Since you're working with dollar amounts, move the cursor to the Currency option and select Yes in both the Pie 1 and Pie 2 columns.

15. To help see financial ratios easily, set Show percent to Yes for both the Pie 1 and Pie 2 columns.

16. Move the cursor to the Place percent option and select Inside. This will keep the percentages away from the dollar amounts to avoid confusion.

17. Since you have finished customizing your chart, press F10 to return to the Main Menu and then press F4 to check your chart's spelling.

18. As a last double-check, press F2 to draw your chart. Figure 4.9 shows what your completed pie chart should look like. If everything is correct, save it as WARBY using the Get/Save/ Remove option and then print it in High mode using the Produce output option.

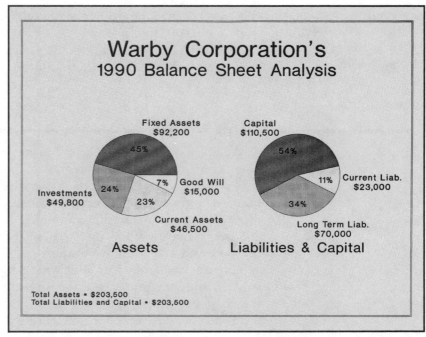

Figure 4.9: Your Two-Pie Chart

PLACING SEVERAL GRAPHS ON A CHART

Although you can only create one- or two-pie charts with the Pie Chart Data screen, you can place as many pies on a chart as you like by using symbols or by using Harvard's Multiple charts option. Using the symbol method takes a little longer, but it gives you the most control and has few limitations. With the Multiple charts option, you can create charts a little faster, but it limits you to six charts whereas the symbol technique doesn't have a limit. You'll learn more about using the Multiple charts option in Chapter 7.

Figure 4.8 shows a 15-pie chart that I created with Harvard. First, I created each set of two pies as a separate chart. (I made the three-pie group at the bottom from a single-pie and a two-pie chart.) I then saved each chart as a symbol in a file named PIEOPT using the Save as symbol option on the Get/Save/Remove menu. By doing so, all the pies I created were readily available in one special symbol file.

To put this graph together, I created a new free-form chart and left it blank. I then used Harvard's Draw/Annotate feature to add everything and change the size of the pie symbols.

If you make a multiple-pie chart using symbols, add the text separately. Don't include titles, footnotes, or pie titles in the symbols you save. You will then be able to produce a uniform character size for your chart's text.

SUMMARY

You have now explored the use of pie graphs. You learned how to emphasize important elements and choose the pie chart that will best present your data. The effective designs of charts are also starting to become familiar. You understand the importance of element placement and are familiar with combining colors and patterns in your charts. You've seen how the moiré effect distorts images and know how to avoid it in your own graphs.

You are now familiar with the wide range of custom functions you can add and have practiced using some of them by creating and customizing a two-pie chart.

In this chapter, you have only been working with one data series. In the next chapter, you'll learn how to create charts using two or more series.

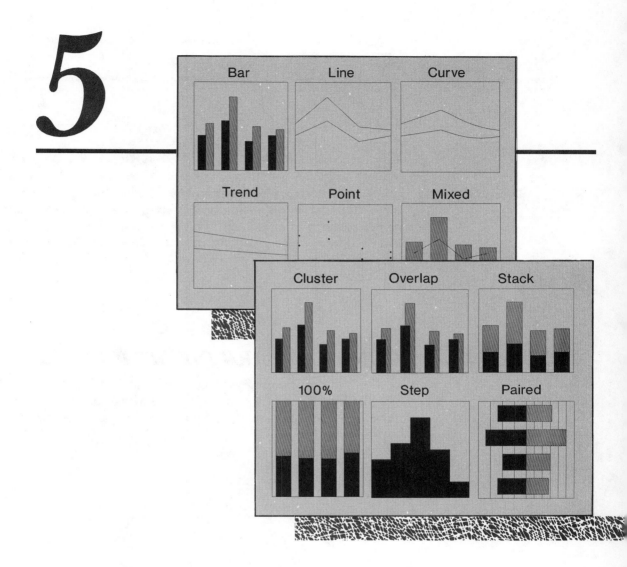

5

CREATING BAR
AND LINE CHARTS

CHAPTER 5

YOU HAVE ALREADY USED THE CREATE NEW CHART menu's Bar/Line option in Chapter 2 to create a simple bar and a simple line chart. However, you can also select this option to create many other variations, including clustered, overlapped, stacked, 100 percent, stepped, horizontal, 3D, shadow, and linked. As always, you need to examine your data and objectives carefully when selecting a chart type.

USING THE BAR/LINE OPTION

When you're choosing your chart type for the Bar/Line option, your first decision is how you want your series displayed. Figure 5.1 shows how each of the following chart types displays the same data.

- Bar
- Line
- Curve
- Trend
- Point
- Mixed

As you'll recall from Chapter 2, to select one of these chart types, you press F8 at the Bar/Line Chart Data screen, move to the Type column on the first page of the Bar/Line Chart Titles & Options menu (Figure 5.2), and press the space bar until the type you want is set for the column.

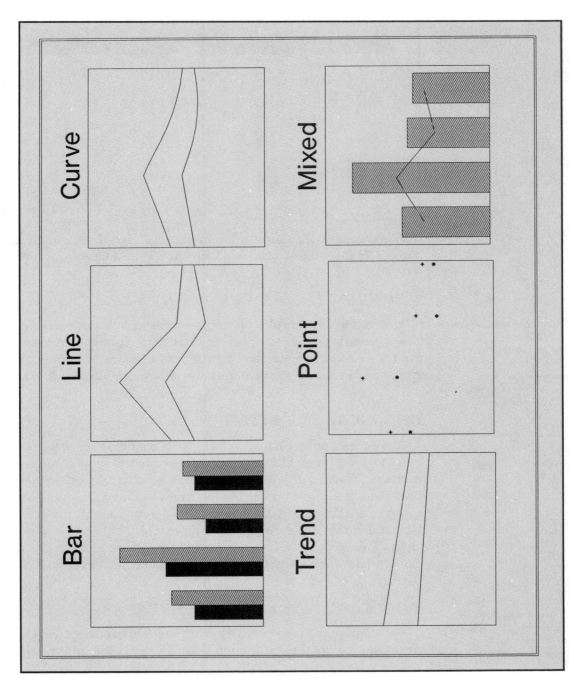

Figure 5.1: Choosing a chart type to fit your data

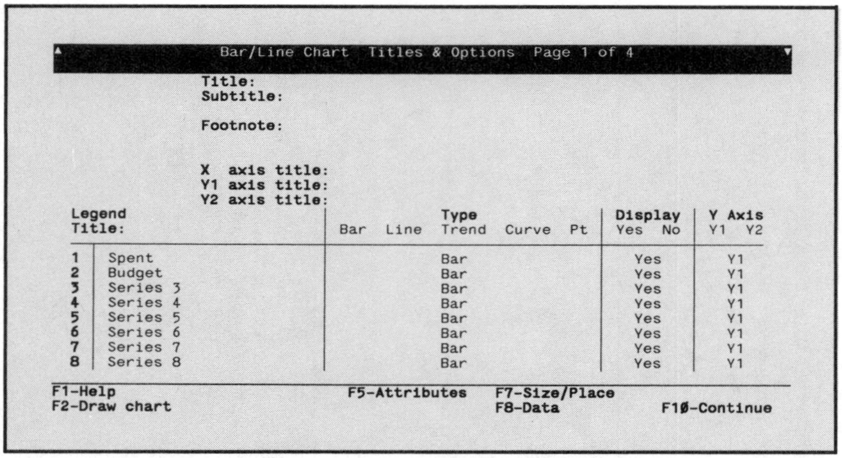

Figure 5.2: The first page of the Bar/Line Chart Titles & Options menu

KNOWING THE CHART'S LIMITATIONS

> You can also display 240 elements per series when using dates or numerical values, or 60 elements when using names—more than you should ever need.

Harvard lets you display up to eight series in a chart. (Remember that a series is composed of one or more data elements.) However, limit your chart to fewer than four series to prevent it from getting cluttered. If your data are complex, consider using several charts.

CHOOSING A BAR CHART

As you learned in Chapter 2, bar charts are the simplest for audiences to understand. Use them to show volume and simple time comparisons. You can group bars together to compare data elements of different series. For example, the bar chart in Figure 5.1 shows four groups containing a data element (bar) from each of the series. Remember that you shouldn't have more than 12 to 15 bars in your chart. This means that if you arrange your data into five series, you can compare at most three groups of data elements from those series.

CHOOSING A ZIGZAG OR CURVE LINE CHART

> An area chart also shows data fluctuations; however, it emphasizes volume (see Chapter 7).

Both zigzag and curve lines show the amount of change from one data point to another. Although you can easily identify the data

Because printing in High mode often makes it difficult to distinguish the series lines, trace over them with Draw/Annotate to darken them.

fluctuations by looking at the zigzag's angles and height, use the curve line to display gradual changes or general trends, as in frequency distributions.

You can display a large number of elements with a line chart. For example, fifty years of statistical data in a bar chart would be too cluttered, while the same data in a line chart would be perfectly understandable. Although each line, which is a series, can contain many data elements, limit the number of series you display. Using more than five series turns your line graph into spaghetti.

DETERMINING THE LATEST TREND

A trend chart shows the direction toward which the data are moving over time. Use it to make sense out of fluctuating or scattered data. When you choose this type of chart, Harvard mathematically averages the series' data to make a straight line, which is known as the *best-fit line*. Trend lines have the same advantages and limitations as curve lines.

SELECTING THE POINT CHART

Use a point chart, which is also called a scatter or dot chart, to show correlations between two or three series of values. Each series can contain at most 240 data points if you use a numerical or time-based X axis. Consider adding a trend line to show the pattern between a series' scattered points, as many people find it difficult to compare groups of dots. Often, these charts are used in statistical analyses. Make sure your audience is familiar with them before you present them.

MIXING CHART TYPES

You can also use mixed charts to help distinguish one series from another. For example, you could use bars to show sales and a line to show the cost of goods. This helps keep different types of data distinguished on the same chart. As I just mentioned with point charts, you can include a trend line with other chart types to clarify the pattern or trend for your data. For example, you could create a series of bars to show a corporation's sales over a twelve-month period and then copy the sales data to a second series to display a trend line. The bars show the changes in sales from month to month, and the trend line shows whether sales are up or down overall.

SELECTING A CHART VARIATION

Now that you've determined the type of chart you're going to make, consider whether you'll need a variation. You select a chart variation by choosing a combination of bar styles and enhancements. Following are all of the possible variations:

BAR STYLE	BAR ENHANCEMENT	OTHER VARIATIONS
Cluster	3D	Dual Y axis
Overlap	Shadow	Horizontal bar
Stack	Link	Cumulative bar
100%	None	Deviation bar
Step		Logarithmic
Paired		

Some variations distort data. For example, if you use the Overlap and 3D options together in a bar chart, the value 7 will be graphed as 6¼.

Even though Harvard refers to bar styles and bar enhancements, some of these are applicable to line charts as well. However, the Overlap, Stack, Step, Shadow, and Link variations have no affect on a line chart.

CHOOSING A BAR STYLE

Harvard designs your graph as a Cluster style by default. To change it, you choose another style for the Bar style option on the second page of the Bar/Line Chart Titles & Options menu (see Figure 5.3). (You will change these options in the "Hands-on" sessions in this chapter.) Figure 5.4 shows the six bar styles.

The Cluster and Overlap options only work with bar charts.

WHEN TO USE A CLUSTER STYLE Use the Cluster style in bar graphs to compare several series' data elements. The data ele-

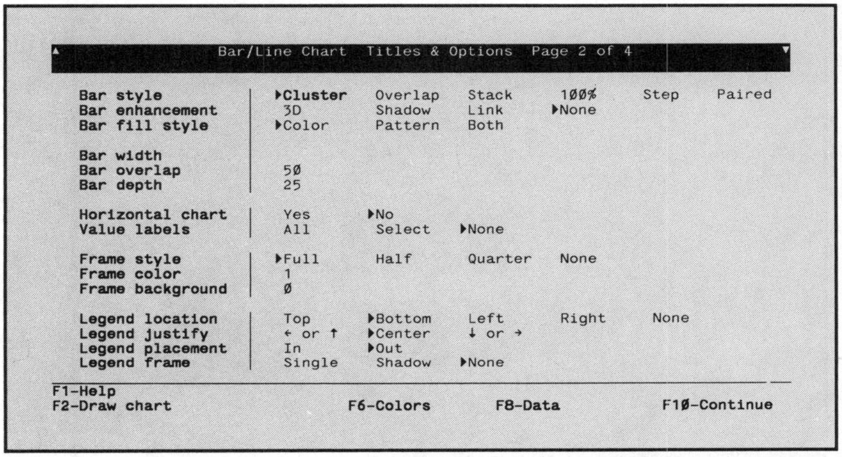

```
┌────────────────────────────────────────────────────────────────────┐
│ ▲       Bar/Line Chart  Titles & Options  Page 2 of 4            ▼   │
│                                                                      │
│    Bar style           ▶Cluster   Overlap   Stack    100%   Step  Paired │
│    Bar enhancement       3D        Shadow    Link    ▶None           │
│    Bar fill style       ▶Color     Pattern   Both                    │
│                                                                      │
│    Bar width                                                         │
│    Bar overlap           50                                          │
│    Bar depth             25                                          │
│                                                                      │
│    Horizontal chart      Yes       ▶No                               │
│    Value labels          All       Select    ▶None                   │
│                                                                      │
│    Frame style          ▶Full      Half      Quarter  None           │
│    Frame color           1                                           │
│    Frame background      0                                           │
│                                                                      │
│    Legend location       Top       ▶Bottom   Left     Right   None   │
│    Legend justify        ← or ↑    ▶Center   ↓ or →                  │
│    Legend placement      In        ▶Out                              │
│    Legend frame          Single    Shadow    ▶None                   │
│                                                                      │
│  F1-Help                                                             │
│  F2-Draw chart                   F6-Colors      F8-Data      F10-Continue │
└────────────────────────────────────────────────────────────────────┘
```

Figure 5.3: The second page of the Bar/Line Chart Titles & Options menu

ments will then be grouped together, which makes it easier to compare them. Because the Cluster style doesn't affect line, trend, curve, and point chart types, leave the setting to Cluster if you don't want one of the other Bar style options.

WHEN TO USE AN OVERLAP STYLE   With the Overlap style, the bars are also clustered into groups except they overlap one another within the groups. The choice between Overlap and Cluster is often aesthetic; choose the style you like best. If you use the Overlap option, make your series with the smaller values the first ones so that their bars won't obscure the later series' bars. In other words, the shorter bars in the overlapping groups should be in front of the larger ones.

WHEN TO USE A STACK STYLE   The Stack style works like a pie in that it shows the parts within a whole. You can choose the Stack style to show effectively the equivalent of six or seven pies in one chart.

Order your series from largest to smallest. This way the dominant elements are on the bottom of the stacks, which balances them. To emphasize the bottom elements, give them your chart's darkest color or pattern.

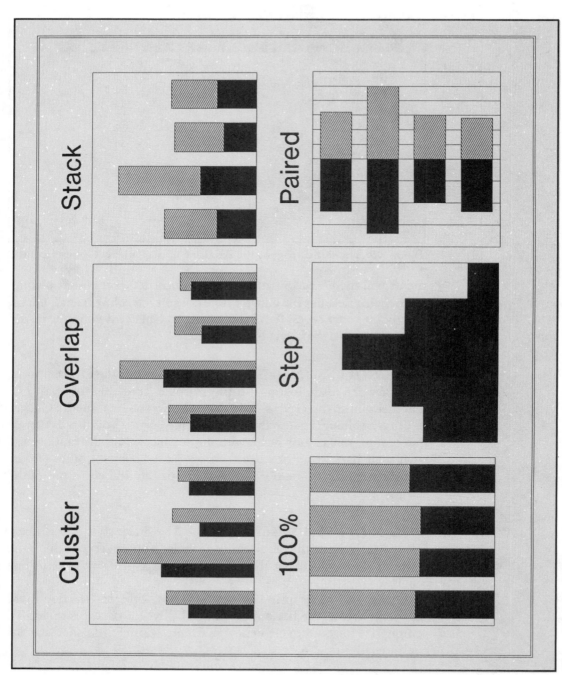

Figure 5.4: The six Bar style variations

WHEN TO USE A 100% STYLE   By using the 100% style with the Stack option, you make each stack the same size, giving it a value of 100% while showing each of its parts as a percentage. This display emphasizes the differences between the percentages within the stacks.

WHEN TO USE A STEP STYLE   Use the Step style to emphasize mass and volume in frequency distributions. Step style charts, or *histograms,* are for audiences familiar with statistical graphs. You're more likely to find them in technical than in business presentations.

WHEN TO USE A PAIRED STYLE   Choose the Paired style, or sliding bar as it is often called, to show correlations between different types of data in a dual-axis graph. For example, you can present the number of personnel working in a division on the left side of the Y axis and the dollars generated on the right side. To use this style, you will also need to create a dual-axis graph by setting the Y Axis column on the first page of the Titles & Options menu to Yes for one of your series.

Distinguish each paired element by matching the colors of the Y axis labels to those of the bars' elements.

USING A BAR ENHANCEMENT

Bar enhancements can further refine your charts by adding an extra dimension to them. Like the Bar style option, the Bar enhancement option is on the second page of the Bar/Line Chart Titles & Options menu. By selecting one of these enhancements, you can sometimes clarify your chart's message; however, they can also distort the chart's data if they are not used correctly, as you'll see shortly.

Plotters ignore the 3D option.

WHEN TO USE A 3D ENHANCEMENT   3D   enhancements emphasize the differences in your data but often misrepresent their values. Look at the 3D examples in Figure 5.5. It's difficult to identify the value for each element. With the 3D perspective, two identical data elements may seem to have different values if one is closer to the viewer than the other. Furthermore, viewers don't necessarily know to use the back edge of the bar to determine its value.

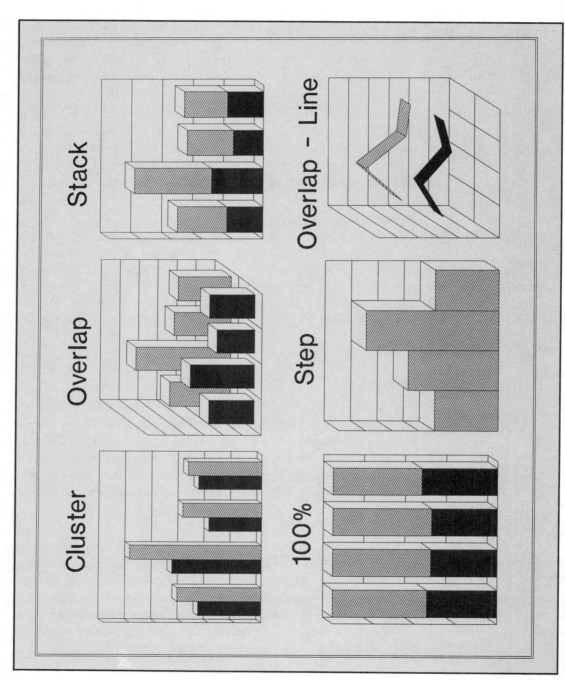

Figure 5.5: 3D effects

If you use 3D for your single series and want your audience to identify the bars' values, be sure to tell them to use the back edge of the bars.

Don't use pattern 1 (black) in your bar chart if you have selected the Shadow enhancement. You might not see the shading differences between the shadow and the black bars.

Use 3D when general relationships are of interest. Don't use 3D if you want your audience to identify the values for the data. Ideally, you should use 3D only when you want to emphasize a single series.

WHEN TO USE A SHADOW ENHANCEMENT   The Shadow enhancement also adds a dimension to your charts by placing a black edge on the right side of the bars. As you can see in Figure 5.6, the shadowed bar in the cluster is emphasized. Unlike 3D, the Shadow enhancement doesn't affect the chart's readability. The Shadow enhancement works best with the Cluster, Paired, Stack, and 100% styles.

WHEN TO USE A LINK ENHANCEMENT   The Link enhancement draws lines between bars to connect the elements in a series. The line's angle helps show how the series changes from one element to the next. Because stack and 100% bar charts focus on the changes between the elements within the bars and not between the bars, use the Link enhancement to compare the elements in a series (see Figure 5.6).

DISABLING ALL ENHANCEMENTS   The None option is the default value that disables enhancements. If you don't want to use enhancements, leave Bar enhancements set to None for all your graphs.

USING OTHER VARIATIONS

Besides selecting the style and enhancement for your chart, you can also choose to create a horizontal, cumulative, deviation, dual-axis, or logarithmic chart. Like Bar style and Bar enhancement, the option for the first variation, horizontal, is on the second page of the Titles & Options menu.

WHEN TO USE A HORIZONTAL CHART   You can use the Horizontal chart option with many types of bar and line charts. Figure 5.7 shows two groups of chart types. The top group shows default chart styles where Horizontal chart is set to No. When you set the Horizontal chart option to Yes, you'll see charts similar to those shown in the bottom group.

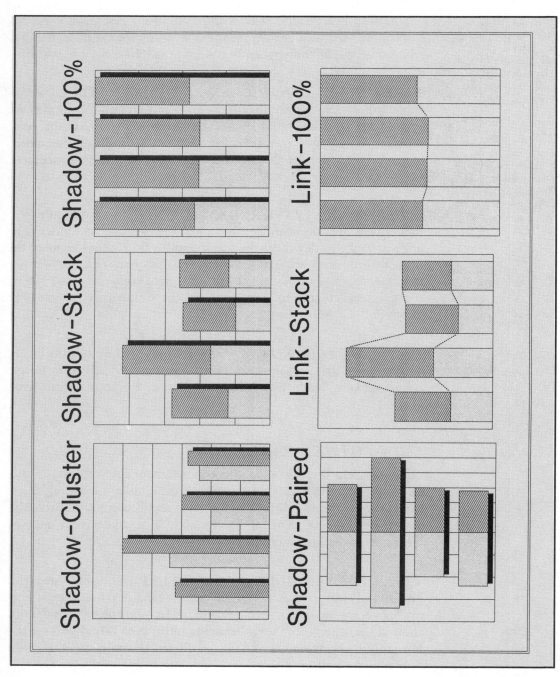

Figure 5.6: Shadow and Link effects

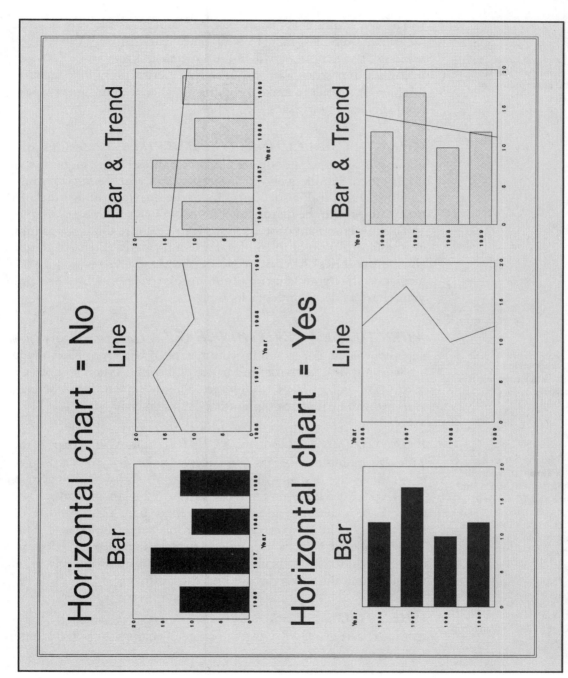

Figure 5.7: Horizontal chart variations

The horizontal line chart is difficult to read and can cause confusion. Only use the Horizontal chart option for bar charts.

The horizontal chart is an excellent choice for showing a single series containing less than 16 bars, particularly if your X axis labels are long. The long labels will not run together as they would in a vertical chart. If possible, rank the data in numerical order for a horizontal chart. It's easier to make comparisons when the bars are arranged from smallest to largest or vice versa.

WHEN TO USE A CUMULATIVE BAR CHART   Besides displaying a series as individual element values, you can choose to display them cumulatively as running totals or year-to-date amounts. The two charts in Figure 5.8 compare the display of individual element values with the display of cumulative totals.

To show cumulative totals, move your cursor to the Cum column on the fourth page of the Titles & Options menu (Figure 5.9) and change the series' label from No to Yes. Don't forget to tell your audience that your chart shows cumulative totals by changing your chart's title, subtitle, or footnote.

You can select the Stack style to present a negative and a positive series together.

WHEN TO USE A DEVIATION CHART   Deviation charts show negative values. For example, you may need negative values if you are working with temperatures or loss of income. When you place a minus sign (–) in front of any one value in the data-entry screen, Harvard will turn your graph into a deviation chart.

Use the Series 2 column for your most important series and make it the Y2 series in a paired bar chart. You can further emphasize it by giving it a dark color or pattern.

WHEN TO USE A DUAL-AXIS CHART   On the first page of the Titles & Options menu, you'll find a column headed Y Axis. You're given the choice of displaying the series as Y1 (the default value) or Y2. To display a series on the right, set it to Y2 by moving the cursor to the Y Axis column and pressing the space bar. You'll see the Y1 switch to Y2. The Y1 axis scale will be displayed on the left side of the frame, while the Y2 axis scale will be displayed on the right. Because dual-axis charts are difficult to read, always use the Paired option with it so that the two series are easier to distinguish.

Unless you're thoroughly familiar with log charts, don't change the axes to Log. Leave them set to Linear.

WHEN TO USE A LOGARITHMIC CHART   Although logarithmic charts display the degree or rate of change as opposed to the value, you should not use them in business presentations because

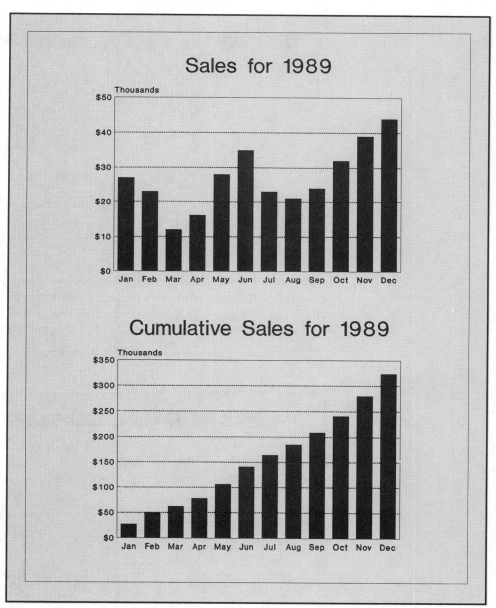

Figure 5.8: Cumulative effects

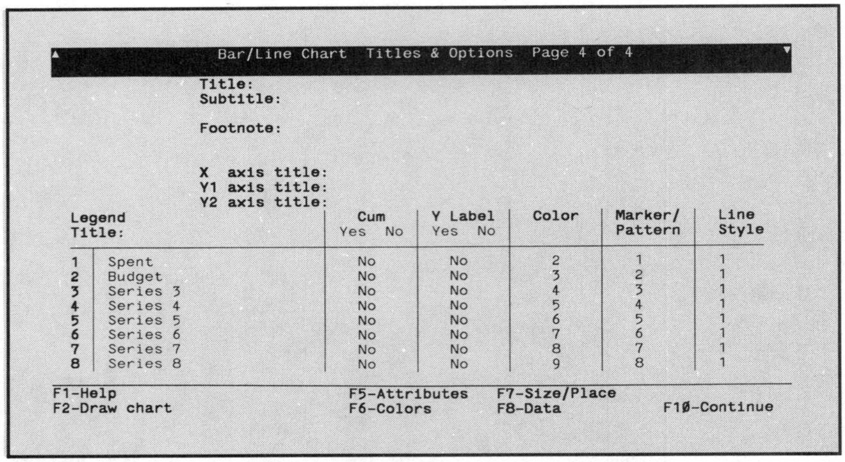

Figure 5.9: The fourth page of the Bar/Line Chart Titles & Options menu

most people aren't familiar with them. Most often, you'll find logarithmic charts in scientific and technical presentations. To make your chart logarithmic, select Log instead of Linear for the Scale Type option on the third page of the Bar/Line Chart Titles and Options menu (see Figure 5.10). For a traditional log chart, set only the Y axis to Log.

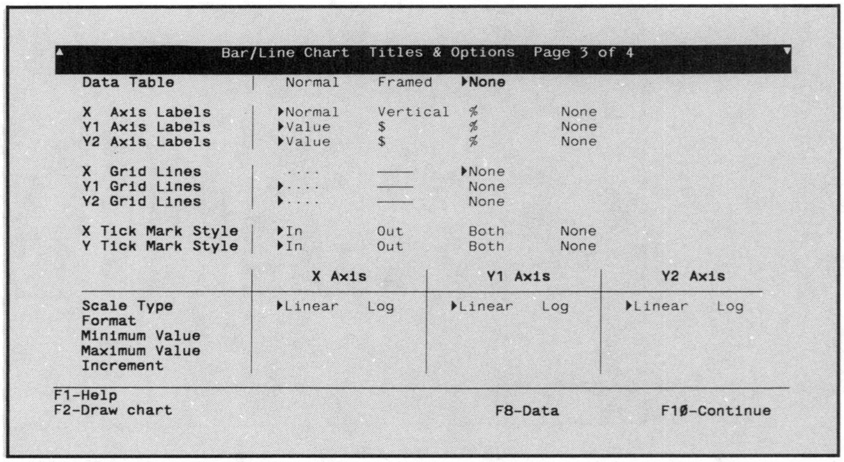

Figure 5.10: The third page of the Bar/Line Titles & Options menu

Now that you know what all the possible variations are, let's examine other changes you can make to your bar and line charts.

UNDERSTANDING YOUR X AXIS OPTIONS

After you choose Bar/Line from the Create New Chart menu, the X Data Type Menu will appear (see Figure 5.11). You'll see the cursor flashing in the X data type field, waiting for your response. Use this menu to tell Harvard what type of data you're plotting across the X axis.

SELECTING AN X AXIS DATA TYPE

Harvard is asking you for the kind of data you will use for your X axis. Enter your data type by following these steps:

If you want to use Name, just press F10. The menu will disappear, and you can begin typing your X axis labels at the data-entry screen.

1. To select a data type, highlight it with the arrow keys and then press the space bar, or type the entry in the X data type field. For example, if you want to compare yearly financial figures, you can press **Y** for Year. Harvard instantly changes

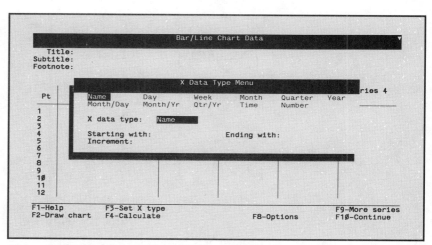

Figure 5.11: The X Data Type Menu

the X data type from Name (the default value) to Year. After selecting your X data type, press Enter.

2. Harvard now prompts you for the Starting with value for your data. Table 5.1 shows the formats you can use for the X data type you have chosen. Enter the starting value and press Enter.

3. Now Harvard prompts you for the Ending with value for your data. Type the ending value and press Enter.

Table 5.1: Valid starting, ending, and increment values

X DATA TYPE	VALID FORMATS	VALID INCREMENTS
Day	Sunday	None
Week	1	2, 3, etc.
Month	Jan	2, 3, etc.
	1	2, 3, etc.
Quarter	1	2
	First	2
	Q1	2
Year	1989	2, 3, etc.
	89	2, 3, etc.
Month/Day	Jan 1	2, 3, etc.
	1/1	2, 3, etc.
Month/Yr	Jan 89	2, 3, etc.
	1/89	2, 3, etc.
Qtr/Yr	First 89	2
	1/89	2
	1/1989	2
Time	1 AM, 12 PM	2 ... 60 (min)
	1:00, 24:00	2 ... 60 (min)
Number	1	2, 3, etc.

4. Finally, the cursor moves to the Increment field. Specify how many numbers or months to skip. If you want the complete range intact, press Enter without typing an increment. Otherwise, type a number and press Enter. The Bar/Line Chart Data screen then appears, with your X axis values already filled in.

REVISING YOUR X AXIS DATA TYPE

After entering your X axis data type, Harvard takes you to the data-entry screen. If you selected the Name data type, you can start typing your X axis labels. With other data types, you'll see the label names that Harvard automatically entered for you.

If you want to change your X data type or have noticed mistakes, simply return to the X Data Type Menu by pressing F3. You can now reenter the X data type value.

USING THE BAR/LINE DATA SCREEN

Once you return to the Bar/Line Data screen, you can enter the title, subtitle, footnote, and your data, just as you did in Chapter 2. Remember that you use the F4-Calculate key to give each series a label name. Let's look at some other chart modifications you can make from this screen.

ADDING EXTRA SERIES AND ELEMENTS

Although the Bar/Line Chart Data screen only shows columns for Series 1 to Series 4, you can add up to four more series by pressing F9. When you press F9, a second data-entry screen appears, letting you enter values for your additional series. Press F9 again to return to the first four series after you have finished with this screen.

You can also add more than 12 data elements for each series by pressing PgDn. Each time you press it, another screen appears to let you add 12 more elements, up to a maximum of 240 for each series. Move between groups of elements by pressing the PgDn and PgUp keys.

SAVING TIME WITH SCIENTIFIC NOTATION

Learn to use scientific notation as it saves time when you are working with large numbers.

If you are familiar with scientific notation, you can use it to enter large numbers quickly. For example, 5E7 equals 50,000,000. The E, which stands for exponent, tells Harvard to shift the decimal point seven places to the right. The scientific notation $-2.3E4$ equals .00023, telling Harvard to shift the decimal point four places to the left since a minus sign precedes the number.

MANIPULATING COLUMNS

After you have arranged your data into series, the type of chart you use often determines the order in which you enter them at the Bar/Line Chart Data screen. For example, you enter your series with the smallest values first if you are using the Overlap style. Just the opposite is true when you want to create a stacked bar chart. Now you need the largest values first to give a feeling of stability to your stacks. Remember that you can press F2 to view your graph and check the order of your series.

Fortunately, if you decide to reorder your series, you can use the F4-Calculate option to erase, copy, switch, and move your columns of data instead of retyping everything. To use the F4 key, you first move to the column you want to change and then press F4. Some of the functions you'll find useful are

You replace the *n* in the calculation commands with the number of the series column.

@CLR	Erases a column
@COPY(#*n*)	Copies a column
@EXCH(#*n*)	Switches two columns
@MOVE(#*n*)	Moves a column

Using these functions is simple. For example, suppose you change your 3D bar chart to a stacked bar chart. You now want to switch your largest column (Series 4) with your smallest column (Series 1). To switch columns, follow these steps at the data-entry screen:

1. Since you want the first column to receive the values in Series 4, move the cursor to the first column.

2. Press the F4 key to see the Calculate menu. Press Tab to move the Calculation field.

3. Type @EXCH(#4) and press Enter. The 4 tells Harvard which column you're switching with the current column. Since you're in column 1, Harvard exchanges column 1's data with column 4's. All other columns are unaffected.

Always start your calculation commands with @. Also remember to use the number sign (#) in front of the column number and to place parentheses around the # and column number. (To learn more about calculation commands, refer to Appendix C.)

HANDS-ON:
CREATING CHART VARIATIONS

Now that you are familiar with different chart styles and entering and modifying their data, you'll put some of this knowledge to use. You can then use the chart you create as the building block for dozens of chart variations. While constructing your graph, you'll also get to practice using scientific notation.

Your chart will show the composition of the U.S. labor force in 1986, with averages for male and female workers in the major labor groups. Your X axis will show the labor groups, while the Y axis will represent millions of people. To create the chart, follow these steps:

1. From the Main Menu, choose the Create new chart option and then select the Bar/Line option. The X Data Type Menu will be displayed on your screen, listing Name in the X data field by default.

2. Since you will be using industry names on the X axis, press F10 to accept Name as the data type. The Bar/Line Chart Data screen will then appear.

3. Type **U.S. Labor Force** for the title, **1986 Averages** for the subtitle, and **Source: U.S. Labor Department** for the footnote.

By preceding an X axis label with a vertical bar (|), you tell Harvard to display it on the second line below the X axis. Use this technique to prevent labels on your charts from running together.

4. Move to the X Axis Name column and type the following labels:

Professional

Service

Craftsmen

Industrial

Agricultural

Clerical

Sales

5. To enter the number of male and female workers in each of the seven labor groups, type the following data in the Series 1 and Series 2 columns:

15E6	116E5
58E5	9E6
123E5	12E5
129E5	44E5
29E5	6E5
35E5	143E5
69E5	64E5

Remember that Harvard will translate the scientific notation into standard notation. For example, 15E6 will be 15,000,000 on your graph.

6. Press F2 to see how Harvard plots your scientific notation. When you're done viewing the graph, press Esc to return to the data-entry screen.

7. Press F8 and you'll see the first page of the Bar/Line Titles & Options menu. Move your cursor to the first series' legend title and replace Series 1 by typing **Male.** Likewise, change Series 2 to **Female.**

8. You've now created a clustered bar chart, which is the default, and can view it by pressing F2. Figure 5.12 shows what your chart should look like.

9. Return to the Main Menu and use the Get/Save/Remove option to save this chart, naming it LABOR1.

10. To make a variation of the chart you just saved, return to the Main Menu and press **2** to select Enter/Edit chart. The Bar/Line Chart Data screen then appears, containing LABOR1's data.

11. Press F8 to display the Titles & Options menu and change the subtitle to **1986 Percentages.** Then press PgDn to move to the second page of the menu.

12. Highlight and select 100% for the Bar style option. Then press the F2 key to see your percentage chart. Figure 5.13 shows what your chart should look like now. By simply

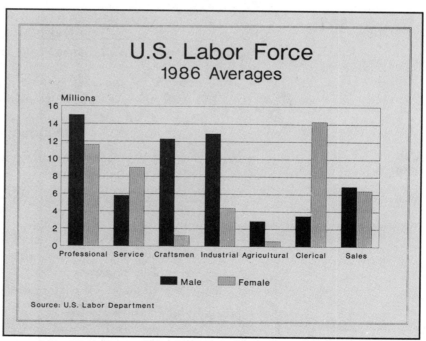

Figure 5.12: Displaying your data in a clustered bar chart

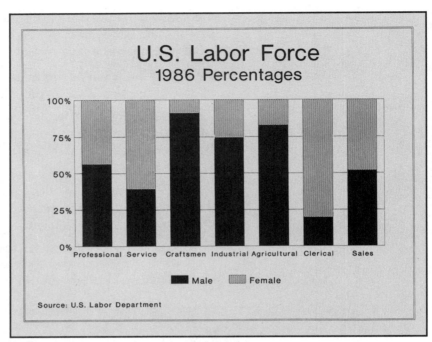

Figure 5.13: Displaying your data in a 100% chart

changing the bar style, your graph now shows the percentages of males and females in each major industry group instead of the average numbers of workers. Return to the Main Menu and save your chart.

13. For more practice, press **2** to select Enter/Edit chart. Again, you'll see the data that you previously used.

14. Press F8 to display the first page of the Titles & Options menu and then change the subtitle back to **1986 Averages**.

15. To make Female the Y2 series, move to the second row in the Y Axis column and press the space bar. (Always set the series you want emphasized to Y2.) Then press PgDn to move to the second page of the Titles & Options menu.

16. Highlight and select Paired for the Bar style option. Then set Bar fill style to Both and press PgDn twice to move to the fourth page of the menu.

Paired charts are best for showing dissimilar types of data, such as dollars and units, but you can use them for similar data types as well.

17. Move to the first row in the Marker/Pattern column and change the pattern for the Male screen series from 1 to 3. This lightens Y1's bars, which emphasizes the Y2 series.

18. Press F2 to see your paired bar chart. Figure 5.14 shows what it should look like.

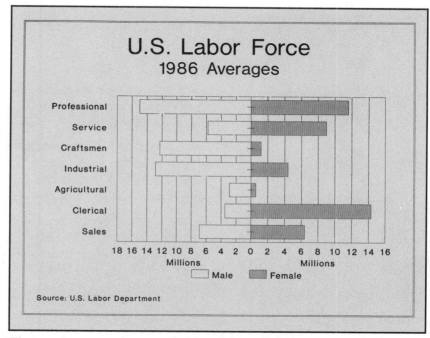

Figure 5.14: Displaying your data in a paired bar chart

You can now experiment on your own with the other styles and enhancements. Refer to the sample charts earlier in this chapter and try to duplicate their effects. There are also other variations you can create. As you experiment, you'll see that some variations present the data better than others.

HANDLING GRAPHING PROBLEMS

There is more to graphing than creating the chart variation that best represents your data. Sometimes you'll experience problems that aren't resolved by choosing a different chart style. In this section, you'll learn to identify several problems as well as how to correct or minimize their effects.

PREVENTING GARBLED X AXIS LABELS

If your X axis labels are too long and can't be shortened, there are several alternatives you can choose to prevent them from running together:

- Place a vertical bar (|) in front of every other label. The labels will then be displayed on a second X axis line instead of on the first. For example, to place Treasury on the second line, type | **Treasury**.

- If your chart is oriented vertically, set the Horizontal chart option on the second page of the Titles & Options menu (Figure 5.3) to Yes. There may then be enough room for your X axis labels.

- Change the text size of the X axis labels. To do this, press F7 from the first page of the Titles & Options menu (Figure 5.2). Using the arrow keys, move the cursor to the X labels field, which is currently blank. Type in a small type size number, such as 2.5.

- Set the Display option on the first page of the Titles & Options menu to No. Your labels will then be hidden, and you can use the Draw/Annotate option to enter new text for your labels and position them yourself.

- If you're working with numerical X axis values, you can sometimes change the increment values (depending on your data) by resetting the Increment option in the X Axis column on the third page of the Titles & Options menu (Figure 5.10). Harvard will replace the label for the increment value on your graph with a tick mark.

ADJUSTING LOPSIDED DATA

There are two viewpoints regarding data that are lopsided or show little fluctuation. One view is that this isn't a problem. The data should be left as is to accurately reflect the relationships. The second viewpoint is that charts occasionally need adjusting to provide useful information.

If one of your bars is much larger than the others, differences between the smaller bars will be harder to see because of the way Harvard plots data. For example, if one of the bars has a value of 240 and the remaining bar values are all less than 20, the Y scale will go up to 250, making the smaller bars look like they are the same size.

You can correct this by artificially giving the large bar a value of 30 in the data-entry screen. It will still be larger than the other bars, and you'll be able to see differences in the other bars. Use Draw/Annotate's Add Text option to place the real values above each bar. To make it clear that the large column doesn't show the real value, call attention to its number (240) by adding an arrow symbol to point to it.

When you need to show the precise values of all your data, set the Value labels option on the second page of the Titles & Options menu to All. The amounts will then be displayed above the bars or next to the data points on the lines.

PROCESSING DATA SHOWING LITTLE CHANGE

There are times when you need to use a Y axis that doesn't start at 0 to show a wider variation. You can change the axis's starting value on the third page of the Titles & Options menu. Enter your new starting value in the Minimum Value field on the Y Axis column.

USING CHARTS WITH MISSING DATA

When working with chronological data, you may occasionally be missing data. For example, you might have the data for 1985, 1986, 1988, and 1989 but not 1987. Obviously, the best solution is to skip the missing data and simply include a footnote to explain that 1987's figures are unavailable.

CREATING AN ACCURATE CHART

As you know, your data need the right type of chart to be presented well without being distorted. However, the data themselves must be accurate, or your graph won't tell the complete story. You may have to factor in several types of data. For example, you might conclude from a graph of your company's sales by division that the most productive division has the greatest sales. However, you might see a different story if you divide your sales data by the number of employees within each division. You might find that a smaller division generates more sales per employee than the larger division.

ADJUSTING FOR INFLATION

Suppose a manager wants to show how her firm has been doing over a period of years. It would be misleading to merely plot a line of total sales. Instead, she needs to correct her data for changes in the inflation rate for her product. This is done by using the appropriate price index published yearly by the government and dividing the firm's sales totals by the index figure called the "deflator." The resulting annual figures can then be plotted to show the real quantitative trend. In the next "Hands-on" session, you'll plot sales figures both before and after they have been deflated. You will then be able to see how inflation distorts data.

To get an idea of how the deflator rate can vary, look at Table 5.2, which shows Consumer Price Index deflators from 1967 to 1987. This table uses 1967 as the base year, meaning a 1967 dollar is worth a dollar, while later years are worth less than a dollar. You can refer to this table for your own data if its categories are applicable.

You can enter dollars and deflators directly into Harvard's data-entry screen and let it calculate the data values for you. For example, to adjust a 1986 $1,000 sales figure with the all items deflator, type **1000/3.284** at the data-entry screen. Your graph will then show 304 as the deflated dollar value.

Consult an almanac, the *Annual Economic Report to the President,* or the *Statistical Abstract of the United States* for other deflators.

HANDS-ON: GRAPHING ADJUSTED DATA

You'll now create a line chart containing unadjusted sales and sales adjusted with deflators taken from Table 5.2. Here are the steps to follow:

1. Select the Bar/Line option from the Create New Chart menu. The X Data Type menu will then be displayed on your screen.

Harvard's X Data Type default, Name, ignores increment values and includes all X axis labels.

2. Press **Y** to change the X data type from Name to Year and press Enter. Type **75** as the value for the Starting with option

Table 5.2: Consumer Price Index deflators

ALL ITEMS		FOOD		SHELTER		ALL SERVICES	
YEAR	DEFLATOR	YEAR	DEFLATOR	YEAR	DEFLATOR	YEAR	DEFLATOR
1967	1.000	1967	1.000	1967	1.000	1967	1.000
1968	1.042	1968	1.036	1968	1.048	1968	1.052
1969	1.098	1969	1.089	1969	1.133	1969	1.125
1970	1.163	1970	1.149	1970	1.236	1970	1.216
1971	1.213	1971	1.184	1971	1.288	1971	1.284
1972	1.253	1972	1.235	1972	1.345	1972	1.333
1973	1.331	1973	1.414	1973	1.407	1973	1.391
1974	1.477	1974	1.617	1974	1.544	1974	1.521
1975	1.612	1975	1.754	1975	1.697	1975	1.666
1976	1.705	1976	1.808	1976	1.790	1976	1.804
1977	1.815	1977	1.922	1977	1.911	1977	1.943
1978	1.954	1978	2.114	1978	2.104	1978	2.109
1979	2.174	1979	2.345	1979	2.397	1979	2.342
1980	2.468	1980	2.546	1980	2.817	1980	2.703
1981	2.724	1981	2.746	1981	3.147	1981	3.057
1982	2.891	1982	2.857	1982	3.370	1982	3.333
1983	2.984	1983	2.917	1983	3.448	1983	3.449
1984	3.111	1984	3.029	1984	3.617	1984	3.630
1985	3.222	1985	3.098	1985	3.820	1985	3.815
1986	3.284	1986	3.097	1986	4.029	1986	4.005
1987	3.234	1987	3.137	1987	4.244	1987	4.205

and press Enter again. Type **88** in the Ending with field and press the F10 key. You'll now see the data-entry screen. Notice that Harvard automatically filled in the X axis labels for you.

3. Type the following text for your title and footnote:

> Sales Comparisons
> Deflated $: 1967 = 1000

4. To change the Series 1 title, move your cursor to the Series 1 column, press F4, and then type **Sales $** in the Legend field. Press Enter twice.

5. Add these figures to the Sales $ column for the years 1975 to 1988, which are already entered in the X Axis Year column:

6000

28000

34000

36000

39000

52000

74000

80000

83000

84000

87000

91000

92000

94000

6. Now that you've added your first series, add the second series showing the deflated sales dollars. First, press Tab to move the cursor to the Series 2 column. Second, press the F4 key and replace the Series 2 label by typing **Deflated $** in the Legend field and press Enter once. Then copy the sales figures from the first series to the second series by typing **@COPY(#1)** in the Calculation field and pressing Enter. The Sales $ and Deflated $ Columns now contain the same data.

7. To deflate the sales figures listed in the Deflated $ column, type the division symbol (/) and the deflator after each figure as follows:

6000/**1.612**

28000/**1.705**

34000/**1.815**

36000/**1.954**

36000/**2.174**

52000/**2.468**

74000/**2.724**

80000/**2.891**

83000/**2.984**

84000/**3.111**

87000/**3.222**

91000/**3.284**

92000/**3.324**

94000/**3.364**

If you needed to enter a larger number such as 122000/3.2222, you could use scientific notation to enter it by typing 123E3/3.222.

Notice that you used every space in the column to enter most of the numbers.

8. Press F8 to display the Bar/Line Chart Titles & Options menu. Move the cursor to the Type column and set both series to Line.

9. Press PgDn to move to the second page of the Titles & Options menu. Place a legend inside your graph on the left by setting Legend location to Left, Legend placement to In, and Legend frame to Single. To place the legend in the upper-left corner, set Legend justify to ← or ↑. (Since you set Legend location to Left, Harvard ignores the horizontal directional arrow and moves the legend to the top.)

If you have only one series, a legend isn't needed.

10. Press PgDn again to move to the third page of the Titles & Options menu. Set the Data Table option to Framed. Your graph will now display a data table below your X axis that shows your series and element values.

11. Move your cursor to the Y1 Axis column at the bottom of the page and enter **0** for the Format option. This sets the number of decimal places displayed to zero.

The X axis title option's text size is also the data table's size. To change the size, move to the X axis title field on the first page of the Titles & Options menu and press F7.

12. Save your graph as DEFLATED using the Get/Save/Remove option and then print it using the Product output option. Figure 5.15 shows what your chart should look like.

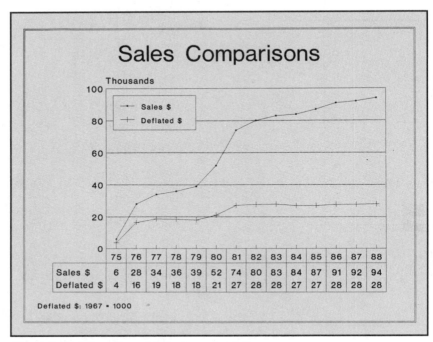

Figure 5.15: The effect of deflating sales dollars

SUMMARY

In this chapter, you learned about the variations of charts that the Line/Bar option offers. You now know how to make Harvard enter the axis labels for you. You also learned how to manipulate and move your series columns to show your data in their best light by using the F4-Calculate commands.

The problems of graphing are now familiar to you as well as the steps you can take to correct them. You know how to separate X axis labels, adjust lopsided data, and handle missing data. You have also practiced creating accurate charts by incorporating variables such as inflation into your data.

In the next chapter you'll learn how to refine your bar and line charts to get the exact impact you want.

6

Legend Positions

| Top ← or ↑ | Top Center | Top → or ↓ |

| Left — or ↑ | | Right — or ↑ |

Set legend placement to "In" when positioning legend within frame.

| Left Center | | Right Center |

| Left → or ↓ | | Right → or ↓ |

Sales   Leases

Bo

Full

Half

Quarter

None

FINE-TUNING YOUR BAR AND LINE CHARTS

CHAPTER 6

WHEN YOU VERIFY THE ACCURACY OF YOUR DATA
and choose the best chart type, style, and enhancements, your chart
conveys your message effectively. Although you have already used
the Bar/Line Chart Titles & Options menu to choose some of the
available options, there are several others you can use to refine your
charts further, making their message even more memorable.

REFINING BAR CHARACTERISTICS

You can customize the bars in your chart by changing the Bar
width, Bar overlap, and Bar depth options on the second page of the
Titles & Options menu. These three options let you enter a number
from 1 to 100, which represents a percentage of the available space.
The amount of space is determined by the number of series and elements your chart has. For example, if you choose Overlap for the Bar
style option and set the Bar overlap option to 50, 50% of the bar will
overlap onto the next bar.

ADJUSTING THE BAR WIDTH

You can't change
the Bar width
option for a step bar chart
since the step bar doesn't
have spaces between its
columns.

When you change the width of the bars in your chart, choose a number that will make your bars wider than the space separating them. This
makes your chart more attractive and emphasizes the data.

If you have many elements, your bars will end up looking like
sticks, no matter how much you adjust the Bar width option. In this
case, choose another type of chart, such as line, or split the bars
between two charts.

CHANGING THE BAR OVERLAP

The Bar overlap style stresses differences between bar lengths. To
emphasize further differences, you can change the amount of space

that the bars extend into one another by setting the Bar overlap option to a number between 60 and 75. You'll need to experiment with this setting because you don't want to overlap the bars so much that they are hard to distinguish. You can also use this option to change the spacing in 3D bar charts.

SETTING THE BAR DEPTH

The Bar depth option lets you change the 3D distance between series. As you will recall from the previous chapter, the first series is displayed as a row of bars in front of the second series. When you set the Bar depth to a high number, you increase the spacing between the rows of bars. This lets you see bars that may be hiding behind larger ones. Unfortunately, this also tends to distort your graph.

REFINING THE FRAME STYLE, FRAME COLOR, AND BACKGROUND COLOR

Frames place a border around the pictorial part of your chart. By default, Harvard uses a full frame. However, you can change the frame's style and color, and background color with the corresponding options on the second page of the Titles & Options menu.

CHANGING THE FRAME STYLE

Figure 6.1 shows the effects of setting the Frame style option to Full, Half, Quarter, and None. The type of frame you select depends on your personal viewpoints about graphics. Many graphic artists prefer to use a full frame. They feel that a full frame around the pictorial part of the graph focuses the viewer's attention on it, just as a border keeps the viewer's attention on the entire chart. Other artists consider frames unnecessary frills that distract from the data and purpose of the chart.

If you subscribe to the "no-frills" viewpoint, set Frame style to Half or Quarter. Don't select None, however, as the Frame style; otherwise, your bars will look as though they are ready to fly off.

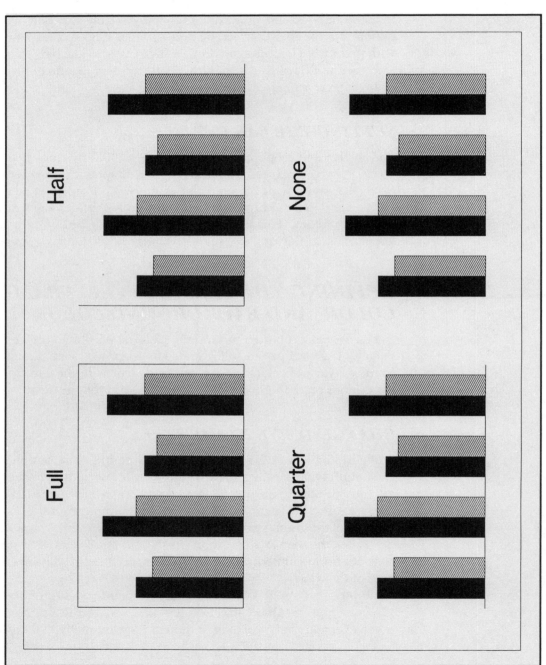

Figure 6.1: Customizing Frame styles

CHANGING FRAME AND BACKGROUND COLORS

If you are working with color printers, slides, or plotters, changing the frame and background color can help create captivating graphics. You can change these colors by resetting the option whose color you want replaced, either Frame color or Frame background. For example, if you want to change the frame's color, move the cursor to the Frame color setting and replace the number that is there with the number of the new color.

To change the background color, move the cursor to the Frame background option and reset it to the number of the new color that you want. You can press the F6 key if you forget the available colors for either option. A menu will then appear showing you a listing of colors and their corresponding numbers. Simply use the arrow keys and press Enter to select the color, or type the color number and press Enter.

Contrasting colors can be quite effective. For example, use light foreground colors such as white, yellow, green, or light blue for bars and lines against dark background colors like black or dark blue. You can also use dark foreground colors against a light background.

Grid lines and tick marks use the same color as assigned to the frame.

REFINING THE LEGEND

When you have more than one series, a legend helps keep your chart readable. Although you selected some of the settings for the Legend options in the previous chapter, you still have many other choices. As you may recall, the Legend location, Legend justify, Legend placement, and Legend frame options are all located on the second page of the Titles & Options menu.

POSITIONING THE LEGEND

The Legend location and justify options work together to provide you with 12 positions for the legend, as shown in Figure 6.2. Each small rectangle represents a potential location for your legend. Within each rectangle you'll see the two settings for that position. For example, find the rectangle containing Left on its first line and ← or ↑ on its second line. To choose this position, set Legend location to left and Legend justify to ← or ↑.

Set Legend location to None and directly label the series within the graph using Draw/Annotate. Your audience will then absorb the information more quickly and won't have to search for the legend.

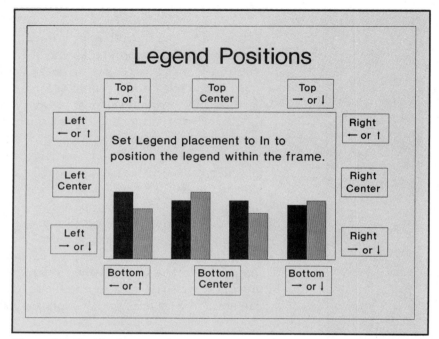

Figure 6.2: Positioning your legend

When you choose Left or Right for the Legend location, your graph's frame changes from rectangular to square so that the legend box will fit on the chart. Figure 6.3 shows how this change emphasizes the length of bars, making them appear longer. The only other drawback is that your X axis labels are more likely to run into one another.

You can also duplicate these 12 positions within your graph's frame. To do this, choose the appropriate settings for Legend location and Legend justify and then set the Legend placement option to In. (By default, Harvard displays legends outside the frame.) If you do put the legend inside the frame, make sure it doesn't distract from your data, or cover important bars or lines.

CREATING A LEGEND FRAME

Choose a frame for your legend to give it an attractive border. Select Single for the Legend frame option to place a single line around your legend. If you put the legend outside of the graph's

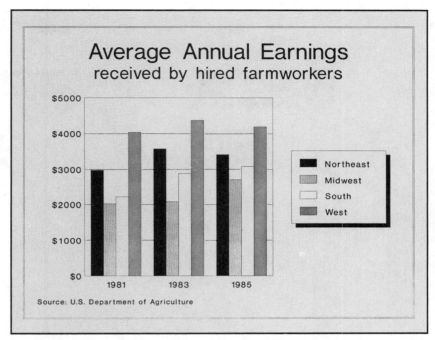

Figure 6.3: Effect of placing the legend on the side of the graph

frame, choose Shadow to give your legend an attractive border like the one shown in Figure 6.3. You can also forgo a legend frame by selecting None.

REFINING GRID LINES AND TICK MARKS

Grid lines and tick marks help your audience identify the values of your chart's elements. You change grid and tick effects by using the three Grid Lines options and the two Tick Mark options located on the third page of the Titles & Options menu.

USING GRID LINES

Consider using dotted grid lines instead of solid ones, as dotted lines are less distracting.

Although you can tell Harvard to create grid lines for the X, Y1, and Y2 axes, only do so when they are absolutely necessary for determining the values of elements. Notice that the first graph in Figure 6.4 doesn't have grid lines because the elements are labeled directly.

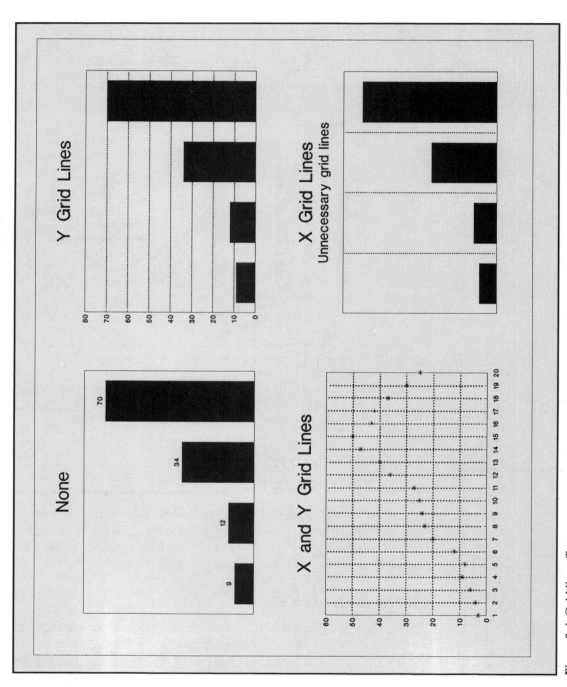

Figure 6.4: Grid line effects

Some plotters draw grid lines through bars.

Use Y grid lines when you're not labeling elements. Figure 6.4 demonstrates how horizontal Y grid lines make it easier to read bar and line values when the Y axis scale covers a wide range of numbers. Use both X and Y grid lines when both axes contain wide ranges of numbers; the dual grids in the lower left chart in Figure 6.4 help pinpoint values. However, X axis grid lines by themselves usually have little value, as you can see in the bottom right chart.

USING TICK MARKS

Tick marks are short, thick lines along the X and Y axes that can protrude from either side of the frame. Use them by themselves or with grid lines to help your audience determine the data elements, values. Figure 6.5 shows the Tick Mark Style options.

If you have many X and Y labels, select Out for the X and Y Tick Mark Style options. Ticks along the outside edge of the frame help by pointing to the labels they represent.

You should try to maintain a consistent style in your charts. For example, set the X Tick Mark Style and Y tick Mark Style options to In, Out, or Both for all your charts.

REFINING YOUR SCALE

As you know, the scales and ranges of values you select help determine how informative your chart will be. The Scale Type, Format, Minimum Value, Maximum Value, and Increment options, which are on the third page of the Titles & Options menu, all affect the scales for your axes.

As you saw in Chapter 5, you set the Scale Type option to Log when you want to create a logarithmic chart. Normally, you will want to leave it set to Linear, which is the default.

You can change measurements with the Format option. For example, to change data from inches into feet, type **12 | ft**. in the Format field. A value of 36 on the data-entry screen will then be displayed as 3 ft. on your graph, because the vertical bar tells Harvard to divide all values by 12.

You already used the Format option in Chapter 5 to tell Harvard the number of decimal places to use on the scale. Remember that when you set Format to 0, Harvard also will not display fractional numbers. Although you quickly set the values for your scale in the previous chapter's "Hands-on" section, let's examine this in more detail now.

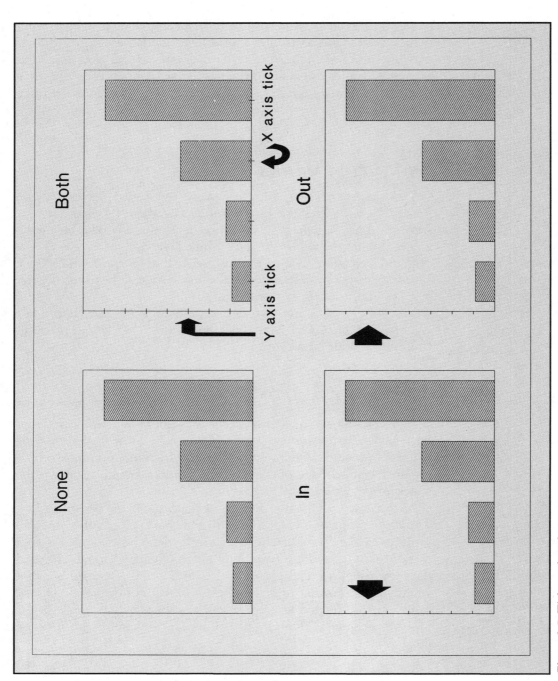

Figure 6.5: Tick mark styles

ADJUSTING THE Y AXIS RANGE

By increasing the minimum value of the Y axis, you change a graph's message. For example, you can alter a graph that seems to show nearly stable element values into one that focuses on their differences (see Figure 6.6). The top chart presents all the data, while the bottom chart shows a close-up of the differences. Just the opposite happens when you set a high maximum value without resetting the minimum—your data appear to be more unchanging.

Most charts' scales should start at zero. Think twice before you reset the Minimum and Maximum Value options for your axes, as scale changes may be confusing. If you have a good reason for changing the minimum or maximum value, make it clear in a footnote or explain it when you present the chart.

ADJUSTING THE X AXIS RANGE

As you are working with your bar or line chart, you may find that you have too much data to fit their labels on the X axis. You can choose which labels to display with the Increment option. For example, it would be difficult to label every year on a chart that shows sales over the past 50 years. You could make this chart more readable by skipping every other label; to do this, simply set the Increment option to 2 for the X axis. The skipped years will then be marked by tick marks and their data will still be graphed.

You can also select a range of X axis values by changing the Minimum and Maximum Value options for the X axis. For example, if you only want to graph the elements in rows 5 to 15 of your data-entry screen, enter **5** for the Minimum Value and **15** for the Maximum Value.

SHOWING VALUE LABELS

Grid lines, tick marks, and scales aren't always precise enough for your data. Although the chart shows a scale along the frame, it's often difficult to determine the exact value of a bar or a point on a line, especially when you are working with a wide range of values. For example, a $100,000 bar might appear to be somewhere between $80,000 to $120,000. A $20,000 difference can be disastrous for some

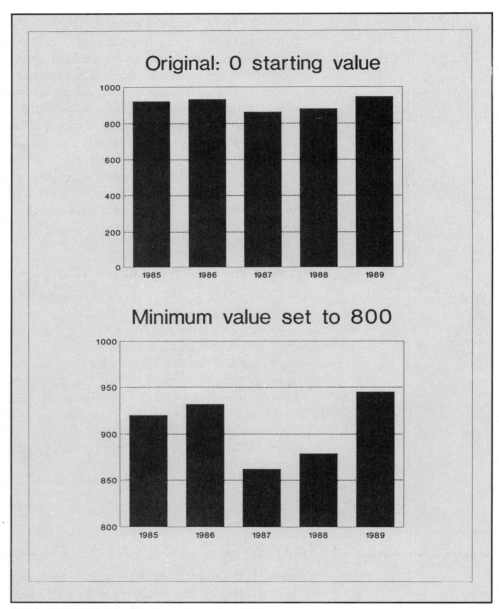

Figure 6.6: Effect of changing minimum values

presentations. In this predicament, simply show the data values to avoid any ambiguity.

When you add value labels in your graph, you do not need grid lines. You can even remove ticks, scales, and full style frames to create an effective, uncluttered chart. You'll make this type of chart in a "Hands-on" session later in this chapter.

The Value label option on the second page of the Titles & Options menu gives you three choices: you can show the numbers for all, none, or some of the series whose values you want displayed. Choose All to display values for all the elements or data points in your chart. If you need greater control over which series you want labeled, choose Select. You may decide, however, to select None and let your audience use the scale and grid lines to determine your elements' values. Do this when precise numbers aren't as important or when the scale covers a small range, enabling viewers to see the values for the elements easily.

When you only want to label certain series, do the following:

1. Move the cursor to the Value labels' settings on the second page of the Titles & Options menu.

2. Highlight Select and press Enter.

3. Press PgDn twice to move to the fourth page of the Titles & Options menu.

4. Move the cursor to the Y Label column's row for the series you want displayed. Press the space bar to change the Y Label column option to Yes. You won't see value labels if the column is set to No.

Set Value labels to None when you want to label only a few elements within a series and use the Draw/Annotate Add Text option to add the labels yourself. You can also use Draw/Annotate to place the labels directly in the bars instead of above them.

REFINING COLORS, MARKERS, PATTERNS, AND LINE STYLES

So far you have been using the default colors and patterns for your bar and line charts. You can change the color, marker, pattern, and line style for each series by replacing the existing number on the fourth page of the Titles & Options menu with the one that represents your choice.

In Chapter 4, you learned about combining the patterns and colors and how to call up the available color choices by pressing F6 in the Color column.

You specify numbers in the Marker/Pattern column. *Pattern* refers to the bar shading and *marker* refers to the character that represents a dot when used in point or zigzag, curve, or trend line charts. Table 6.1 shows the 15 different marker styles you can choose from.

In the last column, Line Style, you choose the style you want for your line charts. Figure 6.7 shows the four line styles that are available. When you display more than one series, choose a different style for each. Style 2 is the heaviest line and should be used for your most important series. Styles 1 and 4 should be your next choices, as style 3 is almost invisible when you print in High mode. You might want to use style 3 for a future prediction, illustrating its vagueness.

Set the marker number to zero when you want to display lines without markers.

Use line styles that are darker than your grid lines to avoid confusion. You can also use Draw/Annotate to darken lines that need emphasis.

Table 6.1: Marker styles

OPTION SETTING	MARKER	OPTION SETTING	MARKER
0	none	7	△
1	•	8	✕
2	+	9	○
3	✳	10	▽
4	□	11	✭
5	✕	12	⊠
6	◇	13	✞

Figure 6.7: Line styles

HANDS-ON: CREATING A DROP-GRID GRAPH

Large amounts of data offer unique problems in chart construction. Besides trying to fit them all in a chart, you're faced with trying to identify the values and amounts of those you do place. You need to make your elements readable.

In this section you'll create a life-expectancy chart that shows how many additional years a person at a given age can expect to live. Your chart will show ages from 0 (new born) to 65. Thus, you'll have 66 data elements to display.

This session explores using a technique called a drop grid to show large amounts of data. A *drop grid* is a vertical grid that extends from the X axis to the data value but does not extend through the whole graph. You can't choose a specific drop-grid style, but Harvard will make one when you have many elements and are using the Number X axis type.

To create a drop grid, follow these directions:

1. Select the options to create a bar or line chart. After you select Bar/Line, the X Data Type Menu will appear on your screen.

2. Press **N** to select Number as the X data type and then press Enter. For the Starting with value, type **0** and press Enter. At the Ending with prompt, type **65**. Press Enter twice and you'll see the data-entry screen.

3. Type the following title and subtitle:

   Average Life Expectancy
   by individual age

Because you can only enter one line in the Footnote field on the data-entry screen, you'll have to wait until you're in the Titles & Options menu to enter a two-line footnote.

4. You now have a little typing to do since you're making a large chart. Notice that Harvard entered the 66 X axis labels for you. Move to the Series 1 column and enter the values listed in Table 6.2.

Table 6.2: The life-expectancy data

X AXIS	NAME SERIES 1	X AXIS	NAME SERIES 1
0	74.7	33	43.8
1	74.5	34	42.9
2	73.6	35	42.0
3	72.6	36	41.0
4	71.7	37	40.1
5	70.7	38	39.2
6	69.7	39	38.2
7	68.7	40	37.3
8	67.7	41	36.7
9	66.8	42	35.5
10	65.8	43	34.5
11	64.8	44	33.6
12	63.8	45	32.7
13	62.8	46	31.8

Table 6.2: The life-expectancy data (continued)

X AXIS	NAME SERIES 1	X AXIS	NAME SERIES 1
14	61.8	47	31.0
15	60.9	48	30.1
16	59.9	49	29.2
17	58.9	50	28.3
18	58.0	51	27.5
19	57.0	52	26.6
20	56.1	53	25.8
21	55.1	54	25.0
22	54.2	55	24.2
23	53.3	56	23.4
24	52.3	57	22.6
25	51.4	58	21.8
26	50.4	59	21.1
27	49.5	60	20.3
28	48.5	61	19.6
29	47.6	62	18.8
30	46.7	63	18.1
31	45.7	64	17.4
32	44.8	65	16.7

5. Press F8 to call up the first page of the Titles & Options menu. Type the following footnote:

   Source: U.S. National Center
   for Health Statistics

6. For your X and Y1 axes titles, type

   Person's age
   Life expectancy in years

   Then move to the Type column and set series 1 to Bar.

7. Press PgDn and set Legend location to None.

8. Press PgDn to reach the third page of the Titles & Options menu. Since your chart has many X axis values, set both the X and Y Tick Mark Style options to Out. This will make it easier to see the labels that the drop-grid lines point to.

9. Press F2 to see how your chart looks so far. Notice that it's difficult to identify the values along the X and Y axes. Also notice that the value for 65 is right on the frame. When you have finished checking your chart, press Esc to continue.

10. Press PgDn to move to the fourth page of the Titles & Options menu and type **66** as the Maximum Value in the X Axis column. Then type **5** as the Increment for both the X Axis and the Y1 Axis columns. These changes will help make your chart more readable.

11. Because your Y axis will now show values in increments of five instead of ten, you need to make the Y1 axis labels smaller so they won't be crowded. Press the F7 key to display the Size/Place menu. Use your arrow keys to move to the Y labels field, type **2.5**, and press Enter.

12. Save your chart as DROPGRID using the Get/Save/Remove option and print it. Your finished chart should look like Figure 6.8.

HANDS-ON: CREATING A NO-FRILLS CHART

Some graphic artists adhere to the no-frills chart style, which uses value labels and avoids grids, frames, tick marks, and scales. As an alternative refinement, the clean and simplistic style of the no-frills chart has much to offer.

In this "Hands-on" session, you'll create a chart that shows the U.S. population in 1986. You'll also show the population projections of the U.S. Bureau of the Census for 1990. Follow these steps to begin creating your graph:

1. Choose the options to create a new bar or line chart. When the X Data Type menu appears, simply press the F10 key to

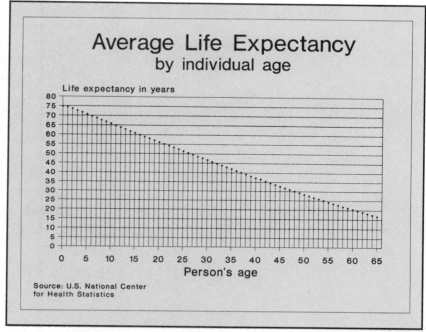

Figure 6.8: Your completed drop-grid chart

accept the X data type default, Name, and continue. The data-entry screen now appears.

2. Type the following title, subtitle, and footnote:

   U.S. Resident Population
   1986 and Projected 1990
   Source: U.S. Bureau of the Census

3. Although you'll label the bars later, you have to give Harvard the series values now so it can create the bars. Therefore, type the following X axis labels and Series 1 and 2 values:

Northeast	50000000	50600000
Midwest	59300000	59800000
South	83000000	87300000
West	48800000	52300000

4. Press F8 to display the first page of the Titles & Options menu. Move the cursor to the Legend Title field, type **Millions of people**, and then press Enter. Type **1986** to replace the Series 1 label for the first series and press Enter again. Then type **1990 Est.** to replace the Series 2 label.

5. Press PgDn to move to second page of the menu. Set the Frame style option to Quarter.

6. To place a simple border around the legend, move the cursor to the Legend frame option and choose Single. Then press PgDn to move to the Titles & Options menu's third page.

7. You'll use Draw/Annotate to directly label your bars so move the cursor to the Y1 Axis Labels settings and choose None.

8. Since you're not labeling the Y axis, disable the display of grid lines and tick marks. To do this, set the X, Y1, and Y2 Grid Lines options and the X and Y Tick Mark Style options to None.

Use light colors to show future projections and estimates.

9. Press PgDn to move to the menu's fourth page. Change the patterns listed in the Marker/Pattern column. For the series labeled 1986, type **4** as the pattern number. For the 1990 Est. series, type **3** as the pattern number. This gives a dark colored pattern to the existing population and a light colored pattern to the estimated population.

10. Press Esc to return to the Main Menu. Select Draw/Annotate and then choose Add and Text.

11. Press the F8 key and change the text size by typing **3.0**. Then press F8 again to begin adding the values for your bars.

12. Type **50.0** and press Enter. Place the rectangle that appears on the first bar for Northeast. (This is the first data element in the 1986 series.) Press Enter to fix the label to that bar.

13. Type **50.6** and press Enter. Place the rectangle on Northeast's second bar and press Enter. Continue to label the other six bars using the values shown in Figure 6.9.

14. Save your chart as NOFRILLS and print it. It should look like the completed chart shown in Figure 6.9.

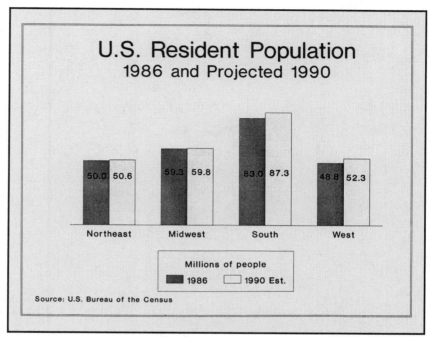

Figure 6.9: A simplistic, no-frills chart

SUMMARY

Your mastery of Harvard has transcended simple graph creation. Since you're familiar with Harvard's subtle features, you can give your charts the type of refinement that only a masterpiece has.

Customizing charts should now be second nature to you. You can control features such as bar characteristics, frame styles, legends, axis labels, grid lines, tick marks, value labels, markers, patterns, and line styles. Through hands-on experience, you learned how to create a drop grid chart and a no-frills chart.

In the next chapter, you'll apply many of the techniques you've learned by creating area charts, high/low/close charts, and multiple charts.

7

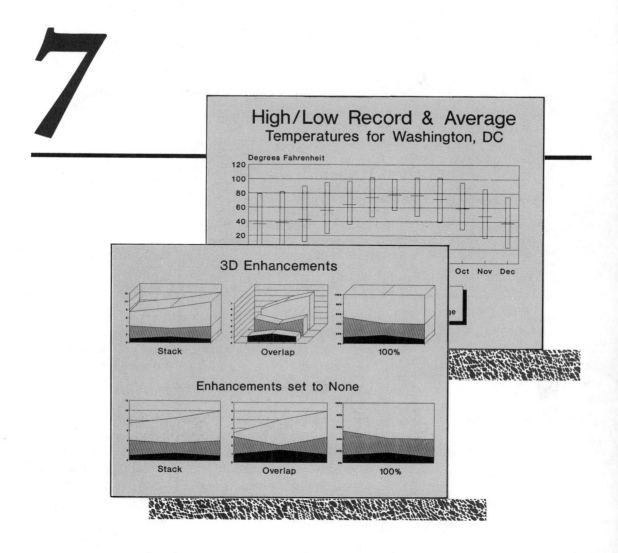

CREATING AREA,
HIGH/LOW/CLOSE,
AND MULTIPLE CHARTS

CHAPTER 7

YOUR FAMILIARITY WITH BAR AND LINE CHARTS should help make this chapter move quickly. Most of the options and menu selections you used for bar and line charts also apply to area and high/low/close charts. You'll also learn a technique that lets you combine several charts into one within a matter of minutes.

WHEN TO USE AN AREA CHART

Area charts combine lines with patterns or colors to indicate volume. In the strictest sense of the term, area charts show several series stacked on top of each other like a stacked bar chart. The top line in the area chart shows the cumulative total of all the series.

Figure 7.1 contains a sample area chart with its layered series, which shows the cumulative totals for your data. You can also identify the total sales of all exported food, the declining rate of exports, and the categories in which exports are declining. Actually, feed and grain is the only series that is declining. Although the fruits and vegetables series seems to fluctuate equally, this is because it is distorted by the changes in the series below it.

Use an area chart for a single series when you want to emphasize changes in its data. You can also use a line chart for a single series, although a line chart doesn't stress the overall pattern as much as an area chart does. However, its data values are easier to pinpoint. See Figure 7.2 to compare an area chart with a line chart.

When you create an area chart, work from dark to light so your darkest patterns will be on the bottom and the lightest on top of the stack. This prevents the layered series from looking top heavy.

> To minimize distortion, place the series with the greatest fluctuation on the top stack.

> Once you have found a perfect color and pattern combination in an area chart, save it as a template for others.

CREATING AREA CHARTS

In effect, you're already familiar with creating area charts because the procedures you follow are almost identical to those for creating bar and line charts.

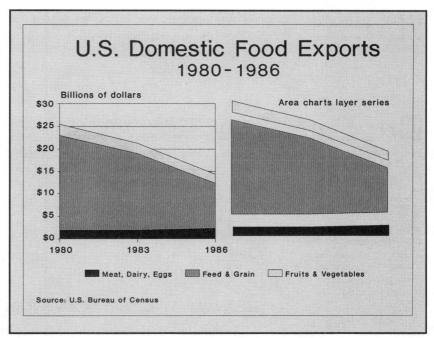

Figure 7.1: Displaying cumulative values with an area chart

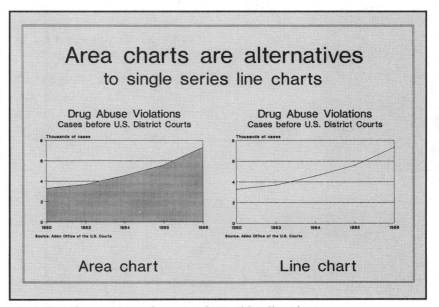

Figure 7.2: Comparison of an area chart with a line chart

Harvard limits you to 100 data elements in an area chart.

If you mix chart types, such as area and bar, you can't use the 3D enhancement effect. Harvard ignores it.

The 3D enhancement holds the same dangers in area charts as it does in bar and line charts—your data are distorted and it's difficult to read the scale.

After pressing **4** at the Create New Chart menu to choose Area, you create an area chart by choosing the X axis type and then entering the data. You can customize your area chart by pressing F8 at the data-entry screen and selecting the options you want. The Area Chart Titles & Options menu, which then appears, comprises four pages.

At the first page of the Titles & Options menu, you can choose from four types of charts: area, line, trend, and bar. Although Type is set to Area by default, you might want to vary the chart type for some of your series to contrast them further.

When you press PgDn to move to the second page of the Area Chart Titles & Options menu, you can select from Stack, Overlap, and 100% for the Chart style option. You also have two enhancement choices: 3D and None. Figure 7.3 shows the results of using these options in your chart.

HANDS-ON: MAKING AN AREA CHART

To familiarize you with how a traditional area chart functions, let's create one. Our sample presents the results of a national study of the concentration of various pesticides in human tissue.

1. From the Main Menu, press **1** to select Create new chart and then **4** to select Area.

2. Once you see the X Data Type Menu, set **Year** as the X axis type, **1971** for the Starting with option, **1983** for the Ending with option, and **3** for the Increment option.

3. You'll now see the Area Chart Data screen where you can type the following title, subtitle, and footnote in the respective fields:

   Pesticide Residue Concentrations
   in sample human tissue
   Source: U.S. Environ. Protection Agency

4. Since Harvard entered the years in the X Axis Year column based on the settings you established in step 2, continue by entering the values for the three series as shown in Figure 7.4.

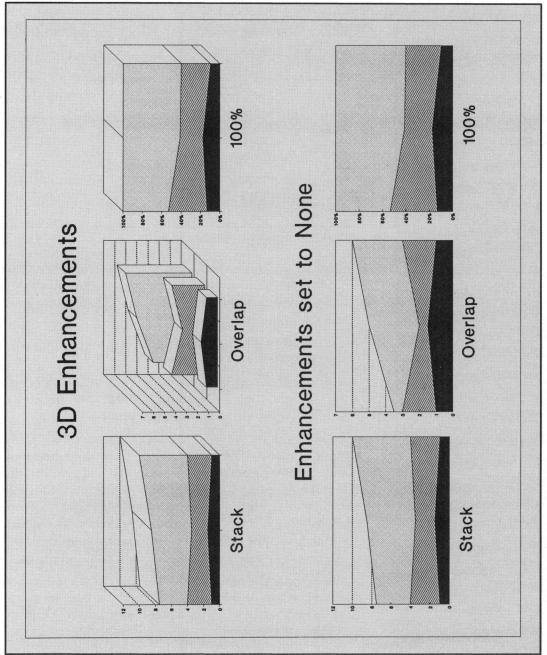

Figure 7.3: Choosing styles and enhancements for your area charts

Area Chart Data

Title: Pesticide Residue Concentrations
Subtitle: in sample human tissue
Footnote: Source: U.S. Environ. Protection Agency

Pt	X Axis Year	Series 1	Series 2	Series 3	Series 4
1	1971	8.06	0.35	0.31	
2	1974	5.15	0.21	0.22	
3	1977	3.14	0.14	0.16	
4	1980	2.82	0.12	0.18	
5	1983	1.67	0.1	0.15	
6					
7					
8					
9					
10					
11					
12					

F1-Help F3-Set X type F9-More series
F2-Draw chart F4-Calculate F8-Options F10-Continue

Figure 7.4: Entering data for your area chart

5. Press F8 to display the first page of the Area Chart Titles & Options menu. Since you can have up to three footnote lines using this screen, type the following as the footnote's second and third line:

    as part of the National Human
    Adipose Tissue Survey

6. Also type **Parts per million** for the Y1 axis title and **Pesticide** for the legend title. Then specify **DDT**, **Beta-Benzene Hexacl.**, and **Other** as the three series' labels.

7. Press PgDn to move to the second page of the Titles & Options menu. The combination of the three-line footnote and the default position of the Legend will give the chart a squashed appearance. Press F2 if you like to see for yourself. Rectify this by setting Legend location to Right, Legend justify to → or ↑, and Legend placement to In. To make your legend box more distinct, set Legend frame to Shadow.

8. Press PgDn to display the third page of the Titles & Options menu. Since the first series (DDT) by default uses pattern 1 (black), which is what you want for the bottom series, set both the X and the Y Tick Mark Style options to Out so you can see the tick marks.

9. Use the Get/Save/Remove menu and save this file using the name MYAREA. Because you didn't change the chart's type, style, or enhancement, it will be a stacked area chart without 3D. You'll use this chart later in this chapter when you learn about multiple charts.

If you want to see what your area chart looks like, print it or press F2. It should resemble Figure 7.5.

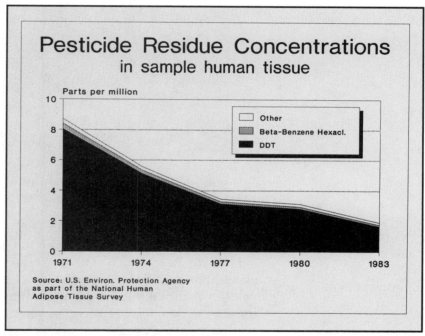

Figure 7.5: Your completed area chart

WHEN TO USE A HIGH/LOW/CLOSE CHART

Close refers to the final or ending prices for a given time period.

Traditionally, you'll find high/low/close charts used for stock market data, such as changes in bond quotes over several months. However, you can use these charts for more than just security transactions. In fact, any data that show ranges and averages are candidates for high/low/close charts. For example, Figure 7.6 provides

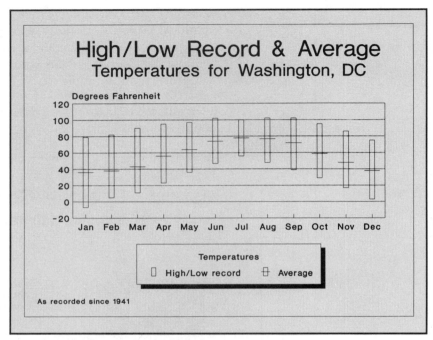

Figure 7.6: A high/low/close chart for temperatures

the record high and low temperatures for Washington, D.C. as well as the average temperature for each month.

Unlike bar and line charts, the nature of the data used in high/low/close charts is such that elements don't usually start at 0. This means you can change the starting value for the X axis without fear of distorting the data. Nevertheless, as you'll notice in Figure 7.6, Harvard automatically makes the grid line at 0 as dark as the X axis line.

You can also create a high/low/close chart for planning work schedules or procedures by using the Horizontal chart option. These charts serve as a graphical to-do list. Figure 7.7 shows an example of such a chart.

Charts that organize and schedule people are often referred to as *Gantt* charts; *PERT* charts are organizing charts that are more task oriented.

CUSTOMIZING A HIGH/LOW/CLOSE CHART

Although you are presented with most of the same options for high/low/close charts as you are with bar and line charts, you actu-

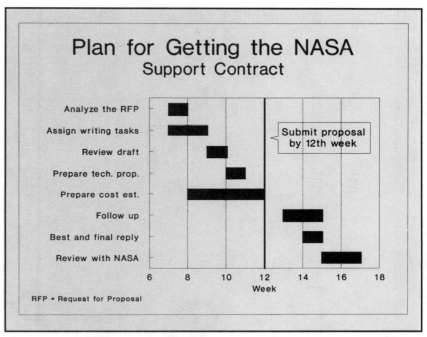

Figure 7.7: A sample PERT chart

Draw patterned boxes over the high/low/close bars using Draw/Annotate when you want to print filled bars.

ally have far fewer choices because many of the options won't work for high/low/close charts. For example, you can't select patterns for your series. However, you can change the chart type to Bar, Area, or Error bar by using the High/Low style option on the second page of the High/Low/Close Chart Titles & Options menu. See Figure 7.8 for a comparison of these selections.

When you are working with a horizontal chart, reset the Bar Width option on the second page of the Titles & Options menu (try 50) so that the bars won't look like thin sticks. Traditionally, financial newspapers show vertical bars as sticks, but there isn't any reason you can't change these as well. Remember, with horizontal charts, the Y axis is the horizontal axis. If you need to show both the month and day for your Y axis values, which can only be numbers, enter the calendar days at the data-entry screen and set the Y1 axis labels option on the third page of the Titles & Options menu to None. Then label the months and days using Draw/Annotate.

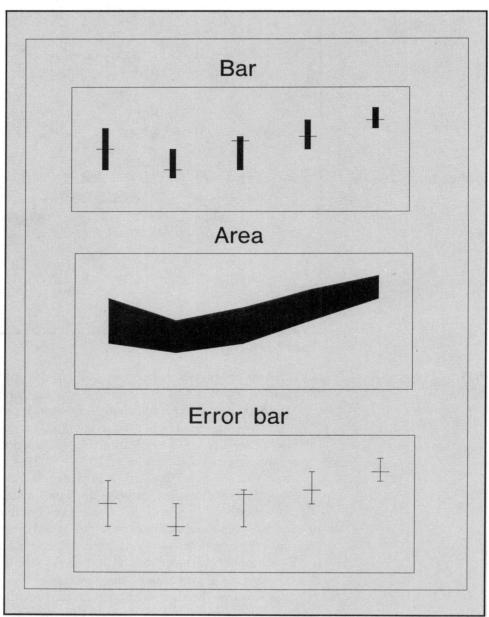

Figure 7.8: Customizing high/low/close charts

HANDS-ON: CREATING A HIGH/LOW/CLOSE CHART

Since providing investment information is probably the most popular use for the high/low/close chart, let's create this type of chart. Things to look out for include setting the legend so it displays properly and setting a currency format for the Y axis. To create the chart, follow these steps:

1. At the Main Menu, press **1** to select Create new chart and then **5** to choose High/Low/Close. You should now see the X Data Type Menu.

2. Select **Month** as the X data type. Next, specify **Jan** for the Starting with option and **Dec** for the Ending with option. Press F10 to continue. The High/Low/Close Chart Data screen will then appear, listing the months in the X Axis Month column.

3. Type the following title and subtitle:

   Custom Computer Corp.
   1988 Monthly Stock Prices

4. Enter the values for the three series in the High, Low, and Close columns as shown in Figure 7.9. If you also wanted to show the opening values for the stock each month, you could enter them in the Open column.

5. Press F2 to see how your chart looks. The High and Low series have the same legend—an outlined rectangle. Press Esc to return to your chart and fix the legend titles. To do this, display the first page of the Titles & Options menu by pressing F8. Then move to the High series label and change it to read High/Low. Delete the Low label by pressing the space bar over it.

6. Press PgDn to display the second page of the Titles & Options menu. Set Legend frame to Single. Press PgDn again to move to the third page of the menu.

7. Set Y1 axis labels to $. This displays the Y axis values as currency. To use two decimal places for cents, type **2** in the Y1 axis format field.

8. Save the completed chart as MYHIGH. Figure 7.10 shows what it should look like. You'll use this chart again in the next section.

```
                     High/Low/Close Chart Data                          ▼

     Title: Custom Computer Corp.
  Subtitle: 1988 Monthly Stock Prices
  Footnote:


            X Axis          High          Low          Close         Open
   Pt       Month

    1      Jan              7             6.5          7
    2      Feb              7.75          6.5          7.25
    3      Mar              7             6.5          6.75
    4      Apr              6.75          6.25         6.75
    5      May              8             5            6.5
    6      Jun              10            7.75         8
    7      Jul              12            9.25         10
    8      Aug              11            10           11
    9      Sep              11.5          9.75         11.25
   10      Oct              11            10           10.5
   11      Nov              11.25         9.75         10.5
   12      Dec              12.5          11           11.75

  F1-Help          F3-Set X type                         F9-More series
  F2-Draw chart    F4-Calculate              F8-Options   F10-Continue
```

Figure 7.9: Entering your high/low/close data

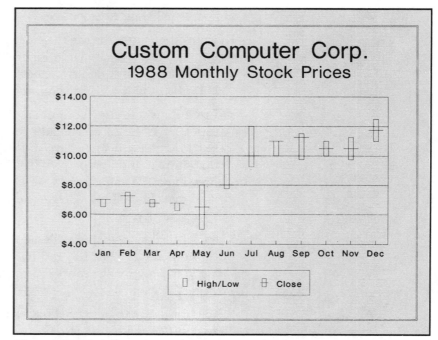

Figure 7.10: Your completed high/low/close chart

You have probably realized by now that one of Harvard's strengths is its consistency. Learning about one chart type's options gives you the skills for working with another type of chart since the same logic applies. Let's continue now by combining many graphs into one chart.

WHEN TO USE THE MULTIPLE CHARTS OPTION

If the charts need any sort of revision, use the Enter/Edit chart option before you put them in a multiple chart.

In Chapter 4, you learned how to combine many charts into one by saving charts as symbols. This is probably the most flexible way to create a multiple chart. However, if you need to create a multiple chart quickly and the charts don't need to be modified, use the Create New Chart menu's Multiple charts option. With the Multiple charts option, you can combine up to six graphs in one chart.

CREATING A MULTIPLE CHART

When you choose the Multiple charts option from the Create New Chart menu, the Multiple Charts Styles menu appears (see Figure 7.11). Select the Custom option when you want to position your charts yourself. The remaining options, Two, Three, and Four, automatically place the respective number of graphs in your chart as

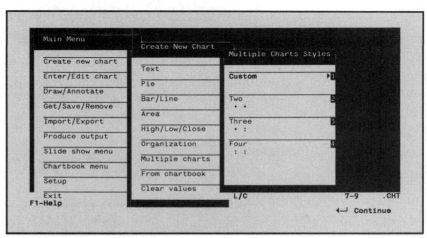

Figure 7.11: The Multiple Charts Styles menu

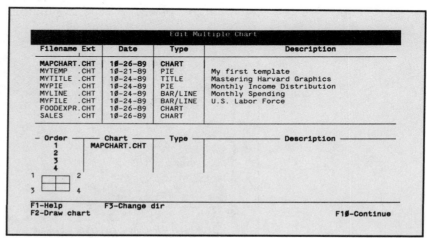

shown by the dots below the option. For example, if you want to place four charts in a rectangular formation, press **4**. After you choose an option, you'll see the Edit Multiple Chart screen (Figure 7.12).

There are two parts to this screen. The top part provides a list of all files, and the bottom part shows those that you've already chosen. (Press PgDn to see your other charts in the top listing if you have more than eight.) You select the files in the order you want them placed. If you selected the Two, Three, or Four option, you'll also see a box diagram in the lower-left corner, representing the charts' placement. The first chart you choose will be displayed in box one. The second chart goes into box two, and so on. Select the files you want for your multiple chart and press F10 when you're done.

To delete a graph from a multiple chart, press Tab to move the cursor to the bottom part of the Edit Multiple Chart screen, highlight the graph, and press Ctrl-Del.

> Use Draw/Annotate if you want to enter a title, subtitle, footnote, or other illustrations.

> You can only move or reposition graphs if you originally chose the Custom option.

HANDS-ON:
MAKING A TWO-GRAPH CHART

This is probably the shortest "Hands-on" session you'll have; that's because creating multiple charts is so easy! To use the two

Figure 7.12: The Edit Multiple Chart screen

charts you created in this chapter's earlier "Hands-on" sessions, follow these instructions:

1. At the Main Menu, press **1** to select Create new chart and then **7** to choose Multiple charts.

2. Press **2** to create a two-graph chart. At the Edit Multiple Chart screen, which then appears, select the MYAREA and MYHIGH charts by highlighting each and pressing Enter.

3. Press F10 to return to the Main Menu and save your chart. Press F2 to see how your chart looks.

That's all there is to creating a multiple chart.

CUSTOM DESIGNING A MULTIPLE CHART

You can choose up to six charts when you use the Multiple Charts Styles menu's Custom option. To arrange their positions, press the F7 key from the Edit Multiple Chart screen. Figure 7.13 shows the Custom Layout menu screen you'll then see.

The Custom Layout menu lists the files you've selected for your customized chart. By default, Harvard lists the files in the order you

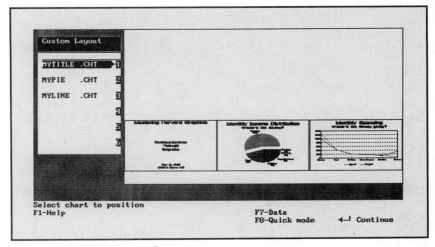

Figure 7.13: The Custom Layout screen

selected them and places them in that order on the screen. If you want to reposition one of the graphs, simply highlight it on the menu or press the number appearing to its right. The cursor will then appear in the chart box. Move the cursor to where you want the graph to start and press Enter to anchor its corner. As you now move the cursor, you'll see the familiar outline showing the graph's position. When you're satisfied with its position, press Enter.

Position the remaining graphs and press F10 when you're done. If you want to see your completed custom-designed multiple chart, press F2. Press Esc when you have finished viewing it and then save your chart.

SUMMARY

Because you learned the details of chart construction in earlier chapters, you were able to create area, high/low/close, and multiple charts quickly and easily in this chapter.

In the next chapter you'll learn how to create organization charts, which will also call on the knowledge you've already acquired. You should find the next chapter just as easy to work with as this one was.

8

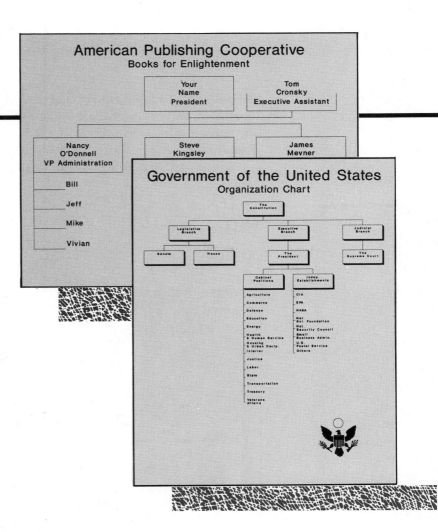

CREATING ORGANIZATION CHARTS

CHAPTER 8

ORGANIZATION CHARTS SHOW THE FORMAL STRUC-
ture of hierarchical groups. By using them, you can transform seem-
ingly complicated organizational schemes into clear visual structures
that are much more effective than words. These charts are ideal for all
types of groups, including clubs, companies, and governments.

UNDERSTANDING ORGANIZATION CHARTS

Figure 8.1 provides an example of an organization chart for the
U.S. Government. Each box represents a branch or department

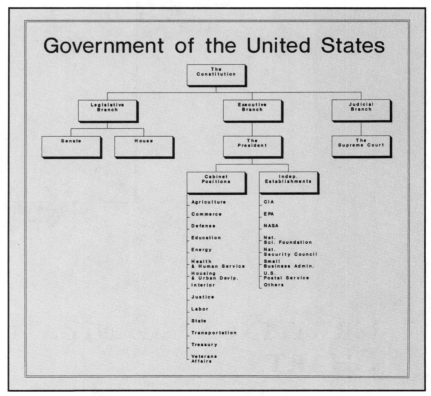

Figure 8.1: Making sense out of the U.S. Government

within the organization. The lines that connect these boxes show the hierarchy of authority. For example, the legislative, executive, and judicial branches have the same level of responsibility as shown by the horizontal line connecting them. The top box shows that each branch is invested with its authority by the Constitution.

You'll also see many departments and independent agencies beneath the executive branch. The chart shows that these branches are all under the control of the president.

Business organization charts aren't much different. Figure 8.2 shows a traditional organization chart for a business. In this case, the chart is organized by the individuals' names and titles.

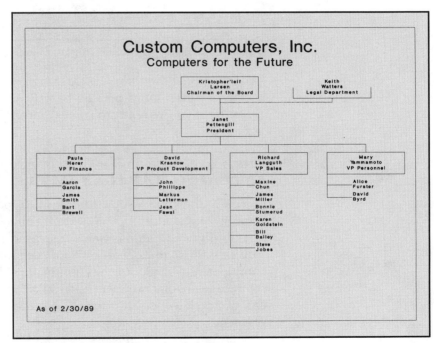

Figure 8.2: A business's organization chart

SETTING UP AN ORGANIZATION'S STRUCTURE

The F5 and F7 keys don't affect the text within your chart's boxes.

You can create an organization chart of up to 8 hierarchical levels and 80 names by first selecting Organization at the Create New Chart menu. Figure 8.3 shows the data screen that will then appear.

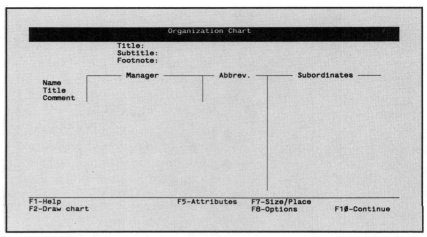

Figure 8.3: The Organization Chart data-entry screen

Start by typing the title, subtitle, and footnote for your chart. Then use the F5-Attributes and F7-Size/Place function keys to format them. Now you're ready to enter the information for your organization chart.

ENTERING MANAGER DATA

You'll enter the people and/or their positions in the Manager column, one at a time. The *current* manager is simply the person (or function) whose name is being displayed in the Manager column. You can use up to 22 characters for each manager's name, title, and comment. You could use the Comment field to specify the manager's room or telephone number. Enter all of your information now. You can decide later which information to exclude if space becomes a problem.

The number of managers you can fit in a chart depends on the organization's structural layout, although it's usually less than 16. Consider making two or more organization charts to show complex structures. For example, if you have more than five managers at the same level, divide them between two charts and present the charts together.

You can also use Draw/Annotate if you need to draw extremely complicated structures.

ENTERING ABBREVIATIONS FOR YOUR DATA

Your chart will display empty boxes if you set the Abbreviations option to Yes without entering data in the Abbrev. column.

When you have many managers, and therefore many boxes, in a chart, you may want to use abbreviations for their names or titles. You can enter up to 11 characters each for the Name, Title, and Comment fields in the Abbrev. column. To display these abbreviations instead of the full names, titles, and comments, press F8 and set the Org Chart Options menu's Abbreviations option to Yes. (We'll explore the rest of this menu's options later.)

ENTERING AND EDITING SUBORDINATES' NAMES

The Subordinates column lets you enter a list of the people who report to the current manager. Simply type their names, pressing Enter after each one.

You can also rearrange the order of the subordinates, and add and delete names. For example, to move a person's name down the list, highlight it and press Ctrl-↓. Conversely, pressing Ctrl-↑ moves it up the list. You can also insert a new name in the list by pressing Ctrl-Ins, and delete a selected name by pressing Ctrl-Del.

ADDING MORE LEVELS

So far you have created one hierarchical level of managers, with their corresponding subordinates. To add an extra level in your chart, highlight one of the subordinates and press Ctrl-PgDn. That subordinate now becomes the current manager. Proceed by adding his or her subordinates. You can add up to eight levels, consisting of seven levels of managers and a final level of subordinates. To return to the previous level, press Ctrl-PgUp.

You can easily move to other managers on the same level as the current manager by pressing PgDn. For example, assume that the current manager is David Krasnow (see Figure 8.2). To make Richard Langguth the current manager, simply press PgDn. If, instead, you want Paula Herer to be the current manager, press PgUp.

HANDS-ON: CREATING AN ORGANIZATION CHART

You'll now create your own organization chart. Use this opportunity to establish your own publishing company's structure by following these instructions:

1. From the Main Menu press **1** to select Create new chart and then **6** to choose Organization. You'll then see the Organization Chart data-entry screen.

2. Type the following title and subtitle:

   American Publishing Cooperative

   Books for Enlightenment

3. Move the cursor to the Manager column and type your name on the first line and **President** on the second line. Press the Tab key twice to move to the Subordinates column.

4. Type the following subordinate names:

   *Tom Cronsky

   Nancy O'Donnell

   Steve Kingsley

   James Mevner

▌ You can only designate one staff position in an organization chart.

The asterisk (*) establishes what Harvard calls a *staff position,* which means the person is on the second level of the hierarchy but does not have anyone below him.

5. Use the arrow keys to highlight Tom Cronsky and press Ctrl-PgDn to make him the current manager. Type **Executive Assistant** for his title. Move to the next horizontal position by pressing PgDn. Nancy O'Donnell now becomes the current manager.

6. Give Nancy the title of **VP Administration** and press Tab twice. Type her subordinates: **Bill, Jeff, Mike,** and **Vivian.** Make Steve Kingsley the next current manager by pressing PgDn.

7. Type **VP Research & Devel.** for Steve's title. Then enter his subordinates: **Alice, Kris, Mary,** and **Ted.** There's only one executive left. Press PgDn to make James Mevner the current manager.

8. Specify **VP Marketing** for James's title and type in his subordinates: **Sam, Shirley, Willis,** and **Sybil.**

9. Oops, we didn't enter James's subordinate list in alphabetical order. Let's correct it by highlighting Sybil's name. Then press Ctrl-↑ and Sybil switches places with Willis. Your list is now in alphabetical order.

10. Save your organization chart using the name MYORG and print it using the Produce output option.

Figure 8.4 shows what your chart should look like. For practice, you'll customize this chart in the next section, where you'll explore the existing options for organization charts.

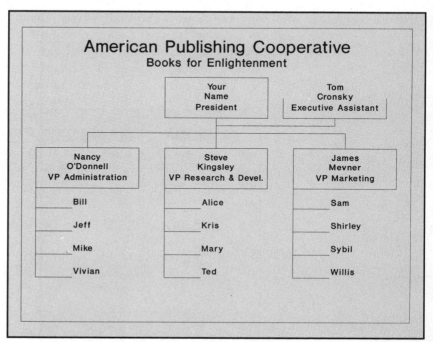

Figure 8.4: Your publishing company's organization

CUSTOMIZING
THE ORGANIZATION CHART

Although your chart is presentable as is, there are several options you can choose from to refine it further. When you press F8 at the data-entry screen, the Org Chart Options menu will appear (see Figure 8.5).

CONTROLLING THE CHART'S DEPTH

The first two choices on the menu let you control how much of your data is displayed. For example, you can use them to show just a small part of your organization's structure. By default, the Start chart at option is set to Top, which means you'll display the chart starting with the first manager. You can also set the Start chart at option to Current manager. Harvard then uses the manager that you had on the data-entry screen when you pressed F8 as the starting point for the chart.

You can control the number of levels that are displayed by selecting a number from 1 to 8 for the Levels to show option. If you leave this option set to All after selecting Current manager for the Start chart at option, Harvard will display all the levels that are below the current manager's level. However, if you set it to 3 instead, then only the first three levels of the organiztion chart are displayed.

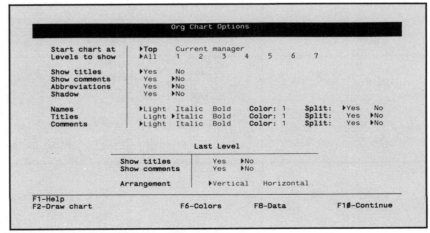

Figure 8.5: The Org Chart Options menu

FORMATTING THE MANAGERS' LEVELS

If your chart's boxes are too crowded, you can hide the titles by setting Show titles to No. Alternatively, you can use abbreviations, as you learned earlier in the chapter. On the other hand, if space isn't a problem and you want to add comments to each box, set Show comments to Yes.

You can also format the boxes themselves by using the Shadow option. For example, the boxes shown in Figure 8.1 have the Shadow option set to Yes, while those in Figure 8.2 don't.

MODIFYING YOUR CHART'S TEXT

You can change the characteristics of your chart's names, titles, and comments by resetting their attributes to the style you want. I recommend you use Bold for the Names, Titles, and Comments option so that all your text will be easy to read. Light is difficult to read unless you give it a color attribute for use in a slide or transparency.

Control how a line splits by placing a vertical bar (|) on the data-entry line between the words you want separated.

You even have some say over how the text is placed in the box. By using the Org Chart Options menu's Split option you can break a long line of text into two lines. By default, names are split into two lines; however, you can also set Split to Yes for the titles and comments.

CUSTOMIZING THE LAST LEVEL

Changes you make to the titles and comments don't affect your chart's last level unless you set the Last Level's Show titles and Show comments options to Yes. Normally, in the interest of space, you have this option set to No so the last level only displays names.

You can also change the Last Level's Arrangement option to Horizontal if you want to list the last level's names horizontally. However, a Horizontal display fits at most a total of six subordinates for the last level.

HANDS-ON: CUSTOMIZING YOUR ORGANIZATION CHART

Let's revise your publishing company's organization chart (Figure 8.4). Use the Get/Save/Remove menu's Get chart option and select MYORG. Then follow these steps:

1. Press **2** from the Main Menu to select Enter/Edit chart. Then press F8 to display the Org Chart Options menu.

2. Set the Shadow option to Yes to emphasize the boxes in your chart.

3. Move to Names and set this option to Bold. Do the same with Titles. This helps make printed charts easier to read.

4. Press F2 to see how your chart looks. Press F8 to return to the data-entry screen.

5. Make Steve Kingsley the current manager by pressing Ctrl-PgDn and then PgUp or PgDn.

6. To change the depth of your chart, showing only Steve's department, return to the Org Chart Options menu by pressing F8. Then set the Start chart at option to Current manager and press F2 to display the chart. It now shows a smaller part of your organization.

You can continue experimenting on your own. Try adding some symbols to your chart or another staff position using Draw/Annotate. Don't forget to save your chart when you're through. Save it as NEWORG so it won't replace MYORG.

SUMMARY

You've now rounded out your graphing experience by creating and customizing organization charts. In the next chapter you'll learn how to use templates and macros to streamline the chart creation process.

9

```
Main Menu                  Get/Save/Remove

   Create new chart
                           Save Template
   Enter/Edit chart
   Draw/Annotate           Directory: C:\HGDATA
   Get/Save/Remove         Template name: MYTEMP
   Import/Export           Description: My first template
                                   W A R N I N G
   Produce output
   Slide show men              This file will be replaced        SCII
   Chartbook menu         Press ←┘ to continue; Esc to Cancel
   Setup
   Exit                                      IE            MYTEMP   .CHT
F1-Help
                                                             ←┘ Continue
```

```
                        Create/Edit Chartbook

Filename Ext    Date      Type            Description

MYTEMP   .TPL  1Ø-21-89  PIE      My first template




Chartbook name: CHARTPAK.CBK
─ Order ─── Template ─── Type ──────────── Description ──────────
    1       MYTEMP  .TPL




Chartbook description: Main chart package for public shows

F1-Help                                              F1Ø-Continue
```

SAVING TIME
WITH HARVARD'S
TEMPLATES AND MACROS

CHAPTER 9

NO DOUBT AS YOU HAVE BEEN PRACTICING MAKING graphs in Harvard, you have been getting more adept at it, churning them out in minutes. You are now ready to streamline the process by using Harvard's templates, which can be kept in chartbooks. After you have mastered these features, you'll explore the use of macros, another time-saving feature.

HOW TEMPLATES AND CHARTBOOKS WORK

Think of a *template* as a predefined empty chart that serves as a pattern for new charts. For example, you could save a no-frills chart (like the one you worked on in Chapter 6) as a template. You could then create another no-frills chart by simply using the template you saved and typing new labels and values. You wouldn't have to reset the options for the chart's frame style, labels, grids, ticks, and values.

In fact, Harvard uses the following templates to create the default settings for your charts:

TITLE	Title text charts
LIST	Simple list text charts
BULLET	Bullet text charts
2_COLUMN	Two-column text charts
3_COLUMN	Three-column text charts
FREEFORM	Free-form text charts
PIE	Pie charts
BARLINE	Bar and line charts
MULTIPLE	Multiple charts

AREA	Area charts
HLC	High/Low/Close charts
ORG	Organizational charts

Although you can change these default templates, I don't recommend it. This way, you'll have them as backups in case you accidentally botch a working template. However, if you do change them, be sure to keep their edited versions in the \HG directory; otherwise, Harvard may not find them.

Chartbooks are simply a feature Harvard provides for organizing your charts. Although you can retrieve a template by using the Get template option on the Get/Save/Remove menu, you may find it easier to group similar templates in one chartbook and work with them there. Furthermore, if you use these templates repeatedly, you can even instruct Harvard to load their chartbook automatically when it starts up. (You'll learn how to do this shortly.)

CREATING TEMPLATES

Place illustrations you use regularly, such as your company's logo, in your template.

You create a template by first making a chart. Once you have formatted the chart exactly as you want it, you save it as a template. Harvard will automatically store the following in your templates:

- Draw/Annotate symbols, drawings, and text
- Attribute settings (F5)
- Text Size/Place settings (F7)
- Titles & Options menu settings (F8)

In addition, you can choose to save X axis labels and series values in your template.

SAVING TEMPLATES

To save your graph as a template, simply choose Save template from the Get/Save/Remove menu. The Save Template dialog box then appears (see Figure 9.1). In the Template name field, specify a name of eight characters or less that matches the type of template

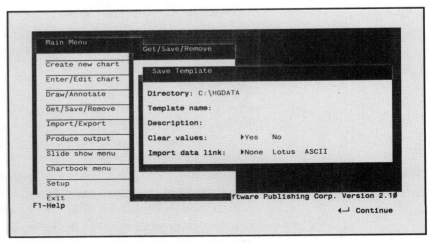

Figure 9.1: Creating a template file

you're creating. For example, use DROPGRID if you're creating a numeric drop grid, or 3DBAR for a 3D bar graph template. You can also provide a 40-character explanation of what the template will be used for (quarterly sales, for instance) in the Description field.

Move between the data screen options by using the Enter, Tab, or arrow keys, and press the F10 key when you're finished. Usually, you'll want to keep Harvard's defaults of Yes for Clear values and None for Import data link. However, when you leave the Save Template screen with the Clear values option set to Yes, the warning shown in Figure 9.2 appears. To continue saving your template, just press Enter.

SAVING VALUES IN TEMPLATES If you want to preserve data values and labels, set Clear values to No. The template will then keep the title, subtitle, footnotes, series values, axis labels, and any other labels you may have created.

SAVING IMPORT DATA LINKS In Chapter 11, you'll work with Harvard's Import/Export feature, which allows you to transfer data from a Lotus spreadsheet file or standard ASCII file to your chart. If you frequently work with outside data, making a template that preserves the data link speeds up your chart creation process

You can make a template for creating Harvard graphs with outside data from programs such as Lotus 1-2-3 by using the Import data link option. You'll learn more about importing data in Chapter 11.

Save values if you regularly compare chronological data, such as monthly or yearly sales. Then you won't have to reenter these values for subsequent charts.

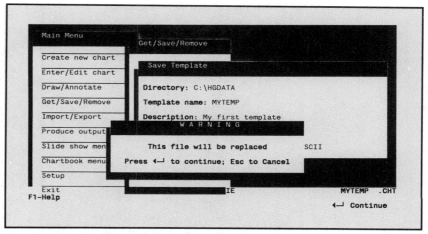

Figure 9.2: Harvard's warning before clearing values

considerably. To do this, set the Import data link option to either Lotus or ASCII.

CHANGING AND DELETING TEMPLATES

You can retrieve and edit a template as if it were a chart. To retrieve a template, select Get template from the Get/Save/Remove menu. Then use Harvard's Enter/Edit chart option to change it. Don't forget to save your template using the procedures described previously when you have finished editing it.

Similarly, you can delete templates just as you would any other file. Choose the Remove file option from the Get/Save/Remove menu. The files you have in your subdirectory will then be listed. As you will see in the listing, Harvard gives template files a .TPL extension. Simply highlight the file you want to delete and press Enter. A warning dialog box then appears, giving you a chance to cancel your deletion instruction. Press Enter again to confirm your instruction and remove the file.

MANAGING CHARTBOOKS

Now that you know how to create templates, select the Chartbook menu option from the Main Menu to help manage them. The Chartbook Menu then appears (see Figure 9.3). You create chartbooks by

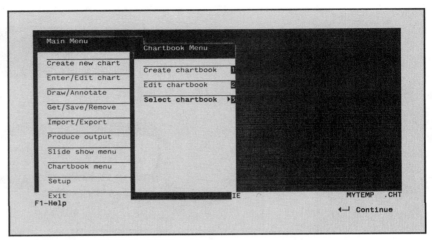

Figure 9.3: The Chartbook Menu

selecting Create chartbook and assign templates to it by selecting Edit chartbook.

CREATING A CHARTBOOK

When you press **1** at the Chartbook Menu, the Create Chartbook dialog box is displayed (see Figure 9.4). As always, the name you specify for the chartbook must have eight characters or less. When you have typed the name, press Enter. Then type a brief description of the chartbook and press Enter again. Harvard then displays the Create/Edit Chartbook screen, so you can add templates to your chartbook.

ADDING TEMPLATES TO YOUR CHARTBOOK

Press **2** at the Chartbook Menu to display the Create/Edit Chartbook screen, which lets you assign templates to the chartbook. Figure 9.5 provides an example of the listings you'll see. Notice that the screen is divided in two, with the top half listing all templates and the bottom half listing the templates already included in the chartbook. (Your lower listing will be blank initially.)

Add templates to your chartbook by highlighting and selecting the files you want from the top listing. After you select a file, it appears on

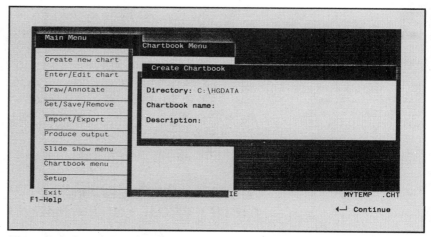

Figure 9.4: Creating a chartbook

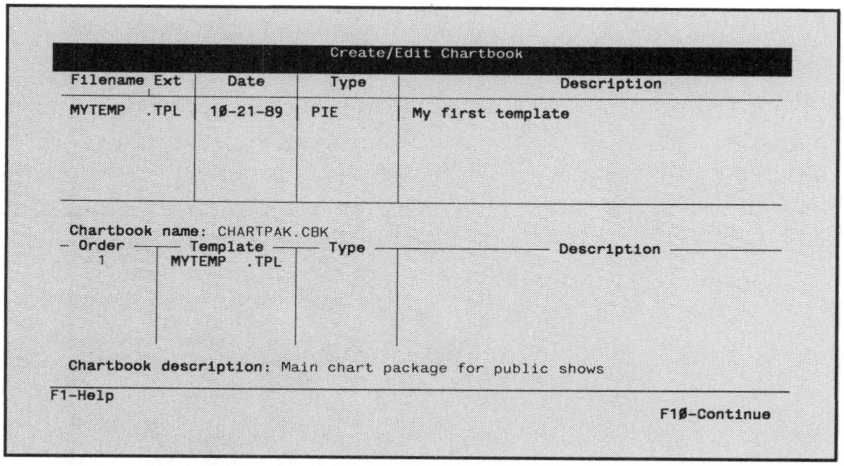

Figure 9.5: The Create/Edit Chartbook screen

the bottom part of the screen as part of the chartbook. When you have finished selecting files, press the F10 key to continue editing the chartbook.

With the Edit chartbook option, you can also delete templates from the chartbook and change their descriptions by using the Tab key.

You must use the Remove file option on the Get/Save/Remove menu to delete a template permanently. Removing it from the chartbook merely deletes it from that chartbook's list; it will still be listed in the top half of the Create/Edit Chartbook screen.

The Tab key acts like a switch. Press it once and Harvard moves the cursor to the templates on the bottom half of the screen; you can remove a file from this listing by highlighting it and pressing Enter. Press Tab again and you'll see the chartbook's description highlighted. You can now change the description if you like. Press Tab a third time to return to the top listing on the screen. From here, you can add templates to the chartbook again. Press F10 to save your changes and return to the Main Menu so that you can practice using your chartbook's templates.

HANDS-ON: CREATING A CHART FROM YOUR CHARTBOOK'S TEMPLATE

To create a chart from a chartbook's template, simply follow these steps:

1. At the Main Menu, press **8** to select the Chartbook menu option.

2. Press **3** to choose the Select chartbook option. The titles of the chartbooks that you created will appear on the screen. Figure 9.6 shows an example of what this list might look like. Highlight the chartbook you want and press Enter. After choosing your book, press Esc until you see the Main Menu.

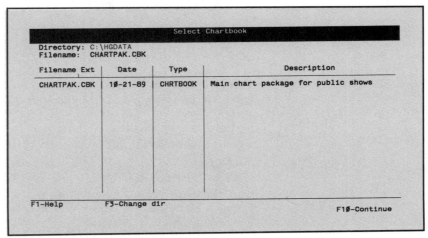

Figure 9.6: The Select Chartbook menu

3. At the Main Menu, press **1** to select the Create new chart option. Then press **8** to choose the From chartbook option. A listing of the chartbook's templates then appears.

4. Highlight the template you want and press Enter. You can now enter the data for your new graph.

5. After entering your data, press F2 to see the completed chart. You shouldn't need to reformat it since the template already customized it. Simply save your new chart with the Save as chart option on the Get/Save/Remove menu, giving it a different name.

When you have finished with this chart, you can continue working with the selected chartbook's templates. To do this, repeat steps 3 through 5 for each new chart.

CONFIGURING HARVARD TO LOAD A CHARTBOOK AUTOMATICALLY

If you find that you use the same chartbook's templates constantly, you might want to have Harvard load it automatically every time you start up Harvard. To do this, choose the Setup option from the Main Menu followed by Default. Then move your cursor to the Chartbook field and type the name of the chartbook you want to use.

CREATING AND USING MACROS

You can't use a mouse when recording macros.

Harvard provides *macros*, which duplicate keystrokes that you type on your computer, as another tool for automating the chart creation process. For example, you can create a macro that will send your current chart to the printer. (In fact, you'll learn how to do this in the "Hands-on" section at the end of this chapter.)

Harvard's MACRO program is a separate utility that you can use with other programs without running Harvard Graphics; for example, you can use it in your favorite word processor. Since running macros takes so few keystrokes, you'll probably find yourself using them regularly. If so, include C:\HG\MACRO in your Harvard startup process.

LOADING AND INVOKING THE MACRO PROGRAM

Use the DOS or OS/2 CHKDSK command to see how much free memory you have in your computer.

If the HG directory is current, you only need to type **MACRO** to load the program into memory.

Harvard Graphics doesn't recommend using other memory-resident programs as they might interfere with Harvard's operation. If you do use other memory-resident programs, load MACRO last.

You should have about 500K free memory available when running the MACRO program with Harvard Graphics. To load the MACRO program from the DOS prompt, type **C:\HG\MACRO** and press Enter. You'll know it is loaded into your computer when you see the message shown in Figure 9.7 followed by the DOS prompt.

Once the MACRO program is ready to use, start Harvard Graphics. Both the macro program and Harvard will then be running together. The MACRO program is a *memory-resident* program, which means it sits in your computer's memory until called.

If you decide to place your macro files in a directory other than C:\HG, use the following DOS SET command before you create any macros:

    SET MACROS = *d:\path*

Substitute the drive letter for *d* and the new subdirectory's name for *path*. Then you won't have trouble running a macro whose name is just one character.

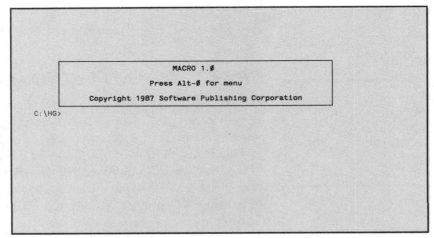

```
                    MACRO 1.0
               Press Alt-0 for menu
      Copyright 1987 Software Publishing Corporation

C:\HG>
```

Figure 9.7: Loading MACRO into memory

⬚ Unload MACRO if you run out of memory in Harvard. This may happen when you have many symbols, illustrations, or elements in your chart.

⬚ Press Esc four times when you first start recording a macro. This should return you to the Main Menu from any place in Harvard. You can then invoke your macro anywhere and it will work.

Since MACRO is in memory, you can invoke it anytime by pressing Alt-0. The MACRO 1.0 menu will then appear (see Figure 9.8). This menu works like the other Harvard menus—simply highlight the option you want and press Enter. Let's examine how to create a macro.

RECORDING A MACRO

When you want to create a macro for some function, think through the steps you need to execute before you choose the Record a macro option. For example, you can't record a macro from the Main Menu and play it back from the Get/Save/Remove menu. You would get different results from those you expected. Because using the Tab and arrow keys in macros can sometimes cause problems, use numbers or letters to select menu and options whenever possible.

To create a macro, select Record a macro. You will then be prompted for the macro's name. Although you can give your macro a name of up to eight characters, use only one letter because you will then be able to use a short-cut method of running the macro; you'll learn about this method soon. Harvard will automatically add the .MAC extension to your file name.

Choose a letter that reminds you what the macro does. For example, if your macro is for printing your charts, name it P. Note

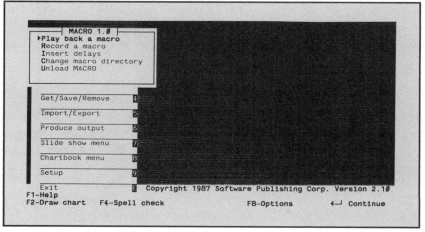

Figure 9.8: The MACRO 1.0 menu

the drive and subdirectory where MACRO plans to save the macro. You can change it by typing over it if you like. For example, you might want to place it in C:\HG so Harvard can find the file without you having to specify its location with DOS's SET command. Press Enter to continue. Every key you now press will be recorded.

Once you have finished recording your macro, press Alt-0. You'll see a revised MACRO menu that includes a Stop recording macro option. Select it to save your macro.

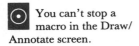
You can't stop a macro in the Draw/Annotate screen.

PLAYING BACK A MACRO

There are two ways you can invoke a macro. You can either use the MACRO menu or press Alt-*n*, where *n* is the single-character file name of the macro.

To use the menu, press Alt-0 and select Play back a macro. You'll then be prompted to enter the macro's name. Simply type the macro's file name and press Enter.

The second method of invoking a macro, pressing an Alt-letter key combination, is the easiest. For example, to run a macro named J, simply press Alt-J. This saves you the bother of having to use the MACRO menu.

STOPPING OR PAUSING A MACRO

To abort a macro that is running, press Alt-End. If you only want it to pause, press Ctrl-Alt instead. You'll then see the Pause dialog box shown in Figure 9.9.

To test each keystroke individually, select the first option, Single-step playback. The keystrokes are then played back slowly enough for you to catch any errors. If you are pretty sure everything will run smoothly, you can double-check your macro by using the second option, Pause playback for # keys. To use this option, replace the # with a number of keys and press Enter. For example, type **3** to pause the macro after every three keystrokes. When you have finished testing your macro, choose the third option, Resume macro playback, to run the macro at normal speed.

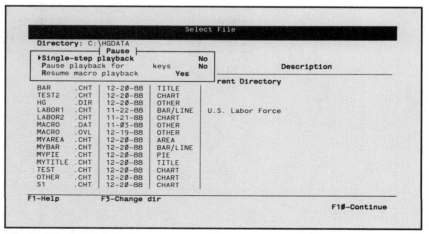

Figure 9.9: Pausing a macro

EDITING A MACRO

If you find that your macro doesn't work properly, you can use a word processor or DOS's EDLIN program to edit it since Harvard saves it as an ASCII file. Table 9.1 shows some of the keystrokes you might need to type or edit.

DELETING AN UNWANTED MACRO

If after testing your macro, you decide it isn't worth the hassle of editing it, simply delete it and then create a new one. It's just as easy to delete a macro as it is to create one; use the Remove file option on the Get/Save/Remove menu. To do this, press **4** at the Main Menu and then press **5** to select Remove file. Next, highlight the file you want in the Select File list and delete it by pressing Enter twice. You can also erase your files from the DOS or OS/2 prompt by using the ERASE or DEL command.

CUSTOMIZING A MACRO

When you press Alt-0 while recording a macro, you can add customized features to it. The revised MACRO menu that appears

Table 9.1: Editing your keystrokes

KEYSTROKES	AS THEY APPEAR IN MACROS
Backspace	< BKS >
Del	< DEL >
End	< END >
Enter	< ENTER >
Esc	< ESC >
F1	< F1 >
Ins	< INS >
←	< LFT >
→	< RGT >
↓	< DN >
↑	< UP >
PgDn	< PGDN >
PgUp	< PGUP >
–	< MIN >
+	< PLS >
Shift-Tab	< ShftTAB >
Alt-1	< Alt1 >
Alt-A	< AltA >
Alt-F1	< AltF1 >
Alt-hyphen	< Alt- >
Ctrl-Del	< CtrlDEL >
Ctrl-Ins	< CtrlINS >
Ctrl-1	< Ctrl1 >
Ctrl-A	< CtrlA >
Ctrl-F1	< CtrlF1 >

contains the additional options, Stop recording a macro (which you have already used) and Type macro commands. However, you can use some of the other options as well. For example, to run a macro within the current one, select Play back a macro (or press Alt-*n*, where *n* is the single-character macro's name). Let's look closer at some of the other ways you can customize your macros.

INSERTING A TIME DELAY If you select the Insert delay option, you'll see the Delays dialog box (Figure 9.10), which presents you with several choices. Let's examine these in order.

Timing delay This delay slows down the execution time of your macros. You can enter a number from 1 (minimum delay) to 999 (very slow). Delays can help you debug your macros when things aren't working right.

Polling delay This delay represents the time that passes before Harvard reads the next keystroke. Set the Polling delay to at least 40, or Harvard might skip some keystrokes. Faster 80286 compters can use a shorter delay, such as 20 or 30.

Real-time delay This delay lets you specify how much time the macro pauses before continuing. The Real-time delay isn't global like the Timing delay. It only affects the macro at the point you set it. To use it, simply type the number of seconds you want the macro to pause. For example, if you type 60, the macro will pause for 60 seconds. You can specify from 1 to 32,767 seconds.

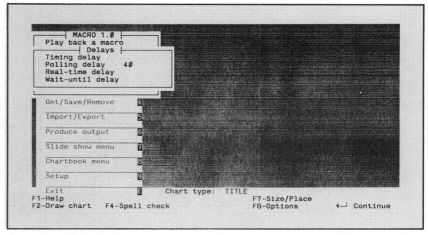

Figure 9.10: Adjusting your macro's timing

You can skip over time delays when playing back a macro by pressing Ctrl-Shift. (Use the Shift key on the right side of your keyboard.)

Use the DOS TIME command to check or set the time on your computer. The Wait-until delay option reads the time from your computer's system clock.

Wait-until delay   Use this delay to have the macro resume processing at a specified time. Use military time to set the clock. For example, type 9:30 to suspend macro processing until 9:30 in the morning and 13:00 to wait until 1 P.M. Use 0:00 to specify midnight. Once the ''alarm clock'' rings, the macro continues processing.

INSERTING MESSAGES IN MACROS   Add messages, instructions, warnings, and comments to your macros by pressing Ctrl-F10. You can enter up to 78 characters. Type the message you want and press Enter. This message will appear during playback, along with instructions telling you to press F10 to continue.

PAUSING THE MACRO FOR MANUAL INSTRUCTIONS   You can momentarily stop the running macro and manually enter your own keystrokes. For example, pressing Ctrl-hyphen simultaneously when you record the macro will pause it at that point in its execution so that you can type a chart name. To continue recording keystrokes, press Alt-0.

HANDS-ON: MAKING AND RUNNING A PRINTING MACRO

Printing charts takes time. In some cases, you have to press eight keys and go through three menus before your chart begins to print. You'll now make a macro that lets you print by simply pressing two keys.

Create your macro by following these instructions:

1. To load the MACRO program, type C:\HG\MACRO at the DOS prompt and press Enter.

2. Start Harvard Graphics.

3. Invoke the MACRO program from memory by pressing Alt-0. The MACRO menu then appears on your screen. Press **R** to select Record a macro. When you are prompted for the macro name, type **C:\HG\P** and press Enter. Harvard will start recording your keystrokes.

4. Press Esc four times to assure that your macro will start from the Main Menu regardless of where you are in Harvard when you invoke it.

5. Press Ctrl-F10. In the dialog box that appears, type

   This program lets you select and print a chart.

   This message will appear when you run the macro. Press Enter to continue recording your macro. The dialog box disappears, and every key you now press will be recorded in the macro.

6. Press **4** and then **1** to retrieve a chart.

7. Press Ctrl-hyphen to pause your macro when it executes.

8. Press Alt-0 to continue recording your keystrokes. Press F10 and Esc twice to return to the Main Menu.

9. Press **6**, **5**, **H**, and then press Enter five times. This sets the options from the Print Chart Options menu in High mode. It also moves the cursor to the last line. It's probably advisable to stop the macro here. This way, you can continue printing by merely pressing Enter, or you can quickly reset any of the printing options.

10. Stop recording your macro by pressing Alt-0 and then **S**. You're now ready to test it.

11. To run your macro, press Alt-P.

12. Within seconds, you'll see the Select File list and a message telling you to press F10 to continue. After you press F10, select the chart you want printed and press Alt-0 when you're finished. The macro will continue for a few seconds and then the Print Chart Options menu will appear.

13. Press Enter to print your graph.

The computer may appear to have ignored your entry but it hasn't; the pause will occur when the macro runs so you can choose a chart to print.

You can see that it is much easier to run a macro than it is to type all the keystrokes every time.

SUMMARY

As you have learned in this chapter, Harvard's chartbooks and templates can help save time in creating and printing your graphs. You have also learned that macros can execute a wide variety of keystrokes, making routine procedures for Harvard, DOS, and other programs quick and effortless.

In the next chapter you'll learn how to draw your own custom graphs in Harvard, and you'll practice making a template for them.

10

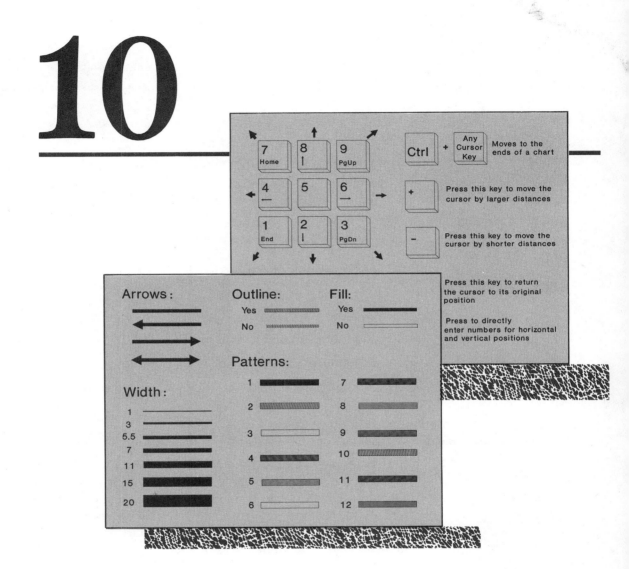

7 Home	8 ↑	9 PgUp
4 ←	5	6 →
1 End	2 ↓	3 PgDn

| Ctrl | + | Any Cursor Key | Moves to the ends of a chart |

| + | | Press this key to move the cursor by larger distances |

| − | | Press this key to move the cursor by shorter distances |

Press this key to return the cursor to its original position

Press to directly enter numbers for horizontal and vertical positions

Arrows:

Width:

1
3
5.5
7
11
15
20

Outline:

Yes

No

Patterns:

1
2
3
4
5
6

7
8
9
10
11
12

Fill:

Yes

No

DESIGNING CUSTOM CHARTS

CHAPTER 10

YOU CAN USE HARVARD'S DRAW/ANNOTATE OPTION to create (*draw*) a custom chart from scratch, or to add illustrations and text to (*annotate*) an existing graph. Using this option, you can create, for example:

- Maps
- Signs and posters
- Personal greeting cards
- Flow charts and diagrams
- Floor plans and layouts
- Letterheads and stationery
- Brochures, announcements, and cover designs

THE DRAW MENU'S FEATURES

If you want to create a custom chart from scratch, choose Create new chart, then Text, and finally Free form. Add your title and subtitle, then leave the Free Form Data screen without entering the body text. Next, choose Draw/Annotate from the Main Menu. You can also start drawing immediately by selecting Draw/Annotate if you're not using a title or subtitle in your chart.

Figure 10.1 shows the screen you'll see. The Draw menu appears on the left. If you want to work on an existing chart, retrieve it using the Get/Save/Remove option and then choose Draw/Annotate. It will then appear in the *chart box* on the right.

As you saw briefly in Chapter 3, the Draw menu lets you choose from a variety of options. Use the Add option to draw a new chart or to add to an existing chart, and the Modify, Copy, and Delete options to edit existing material. The Grid and Symbol options provide further refinements.

Let's take a closer look at some of these options.

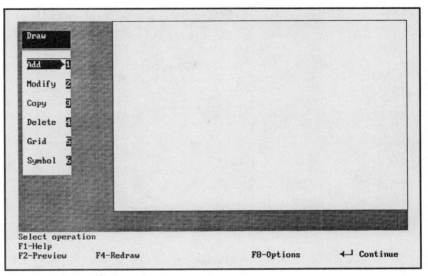

Figure 10.1: The Draw screen

USING THE ADD OPTION

The Add menu provides you with a number of drawing and customization tools: Text, Box, Polyline, Line, Circle, and Polygon. Since you used the Text option in Chapter 3 to create your certificate, we'll explore the other possibilities now.

Moving the cross-hair cursor in the chart box is the same with all the Add menu's options. If you don't have a mouse, your numeric keypad and a few other keys let you move the cursor in all directions. Figure 10.2 shows how each key affects cursor movement. For example, pressing **7** moves the cursor diagonally left. However, if you press Ctrl-7, then the cursor will move to the extreme upper-left corner.

DRAWING BOXES

Use boxes to both emphasize text and create symbols and pictures. Simply follow these steps:

1. Select Box from the Add menu by pressing **2** or **B**.

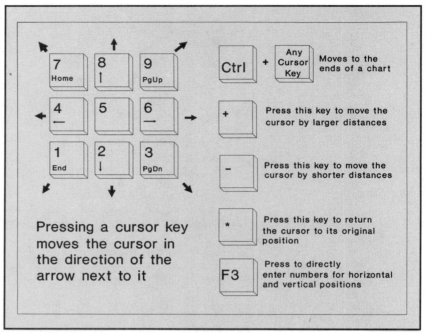

Figure 10.2: The cursor-movement keys in Draw/Annotate

2. Move the cursor to anchor the box's starting corner and press Enter. If you make a mistake, simply press Backspace and repeat this step. (Press Esc if you change your mind and don't want to add a box.)

3. Move your cursor to where you want the box to end. As you move it, Harvard outlines the box to show you its current dimensions. Once you're satisfied with its size and position, press Enter.

To select box options, press the F8 key before you position your box. The cursor leaves the chart box and moves to the Box Options menu. From here, you can select the box's shape, style, and size (see Figure 10.3). If you later decide your box isn't what you want, you can use the Modify option to revise its options or reposition it (see this chapter's "Revising Your Charts" section).

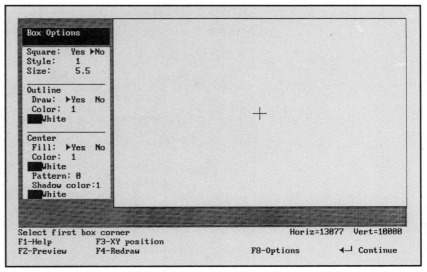

Figure 10.3: The Box Options menu

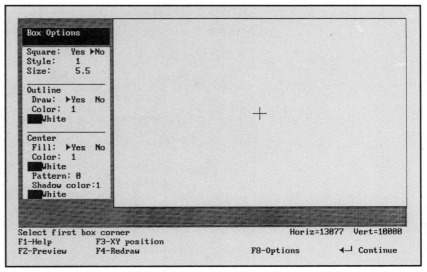
You can also make a box square by simply pressing the Shift key while you move the cursor after anchoring the box's corner. Keep the Shift key depressed until you press Enter.

USING THE SQUARE OPTION The Square option lets you decide whether your box has equal sides. Harvard creates a perfect square when you set this option to Yes; otherwise, you can create a rectangular box.

SELECTING A BOX STYLE Figure 10.4 shows the 21 box styles you can choose from. Select the type of box you want by typing the style's number in the Style field. If you forget the numbers, highlight the Style field and press F6. A Box Styles menu will appear to help jog your memory.

ENHANCING FEATURES WITH SIZE Harvard's terminology is a little confusing in that the Size option doesn't affect your *box's* size, but rather the size of the box's *features*. You enlarge the features as you increase the size. Figure 10.5 shows the effects of changing the features' sizes.

CUSTOMIZING THE OUTLINE The outline customizing techniques not only apply to boxes, but to lines, circles, and polygons as

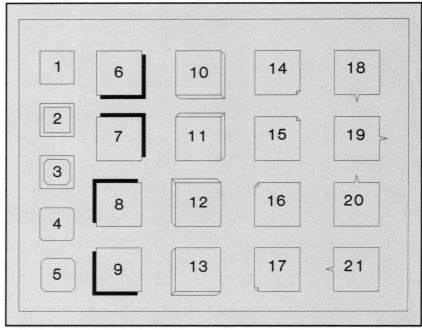

Figure 10.4: Box style options

If you set both Outline Draw and Center Fill to No, nothing is displayed—Harvard won't create the box.

well. You'll normally keep the Outline Draw option set to Yes, unless you want to hide the outline when using fill patterns or colors. You can change the outline's color by typing the color's number in the Outline Color field. Alternatively, you can press the F6 key for a list of colors and select one from there.

CUSTOMIZING THE CENTER You give a pattern or color to your box by typing its number in the Center Pattern or Color field and setting Fill to Yes. Or, highlight the Pattern or Color field and press F6 for a list you can choose from, then set Fill to Yes. As with outlines, customizing the center also applies to lines, circles, and polygons.

Black and white on your screen reverse themselves when printed—the white areas on your screen will be printed black, and black screen images won't print since they represent the white of the paper.

Choosing the right pattern is critical when you're not using a plotter, color printer, or PostScript printer. Other printers can't distinguish color commands and will print any colored box solid black. To prevent this, make sure you specify a pattern other than 0.

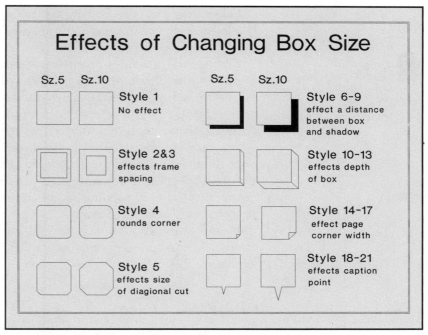

Figure 10.5: Changing the size of a box's features

DRAWING POLYLINES

The Add menu's Polyline option lets you create irregularly shaped lines. They're as easy to create as boxes but give you more flexibility for unusual designs or shapes. To use the Polyline option, follow these steps:

1. Select Polyline from the Add menu. You can change its attributes by pressing the F8 key.

2. Move the cross-hair cursor to the point on your chart where you want the polyline to start and press Enter.

3. Move the cursor to where you want the line to end and press Enter. If you made a mistake, simply press the Backspace key and try again.

4. Repeat steps 2 and 3 until you have added all the lines you want and then press Esc.

To draw a horizontal or vertical line (which is especially difficult to do with a mouse), hold the Shift key down while you draw. Don't release it until you press Enter to finish.

When you press the F8 key, the cursor will move from the chart box to the Polyline Options menu (Figure 10.6). In addition to selecting a color, you can choose one of four styles for your polylines.

Figure 10.7 provides examples of polylines. When you choose Sharp for the Shape option, you draw angular lines that are connected to each point on the chart where you press Enter. Although setting Shape to Curve results in sloping lines, you can make a curved polyline more angular by pressing Enter at short intervals when you want the curve to change directions. If you just press Enter once to change directions, it's a very gradual change, as shown in Figure 10.7. (Each dot indicates where Enter was pressed.) To ensure that a curved polyline touches a particular point in your chart, simply press Enter three times.

If you set the Close option to Yes, Harvard automatically draws another line to connect your first and last drawn polyline, making a geometric shape.

Use polygons instead of polylines when creating shapes that need fill patterns or colors.

DRAWING LINES

To draw straight lines, use the Line option. As with the other drawing options, you have several styles to choose from. For example, you can

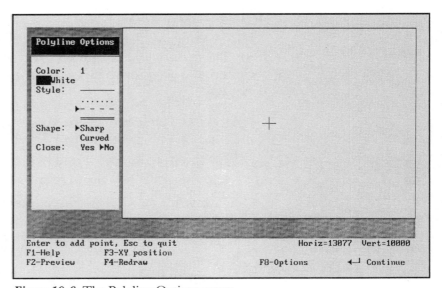

Figure 10.6: The Polyline Options menu

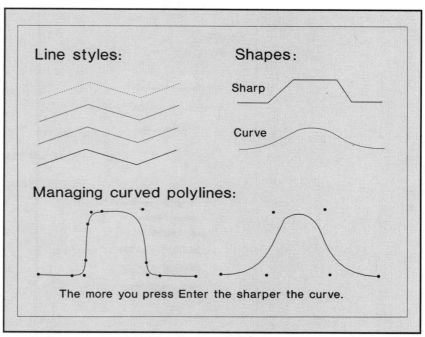

Figure 10.7: Managing polylines

use an arrow instead of a plain line, which is the default. When you want to add a line to your chart, follow these steps:

To draw a horizontal or vertical line, press the Shift key and hold it down until you press Enter again.

1. Choose Line at the Add menu. Press F8 if you want to change any of the line options.

2. Move the cursor to where you'll start the line and anchor it by pressing Enter. If you make a mistake, simply press Backspace and reposition it.

3. Draw your line by using the arrow keys or the mouse.

Set Fill to No when you want text placed inside the arrow. You can then use the Add menu's Text option to label the arrows.

4. Draw the line to the point where you want it to end and press Enter. The new line should now appear on your chart.

When you press F8, the Line Options menu appears. Figure 10.8 shows some of the characteristics you can choose with this menu.

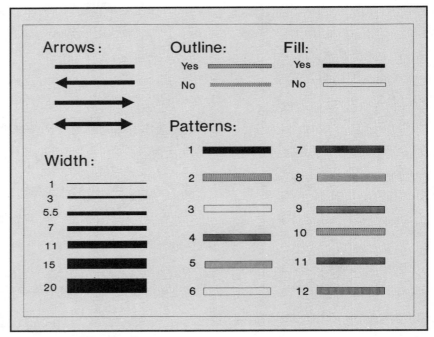

Figure 10.8: Drawing lines

DRAWING CIRCLES

Harvard also lets you draw circles effortlessly. To draw either a circle or an *ellipse* (an oval), follow these steps:

1. Select the Circle option from the Add menu. Press F8 to change any options. For example, set Shape to Ellipse, Outline Color to 5 (blue), and Center Color to 6 (red).

2. Move the cursor to position the center of the ellipse and press Enter.

3. Draw the ellipse by moving the cursor. You'll see a box on the screen that moves in relation to your cursor's movement. Once this box outlines where you want your ellipse placed, press Enter. The box disappears and the circle takes its place.

Figure 10.9 provides examples of the other options you can select from the Circle Options menu.

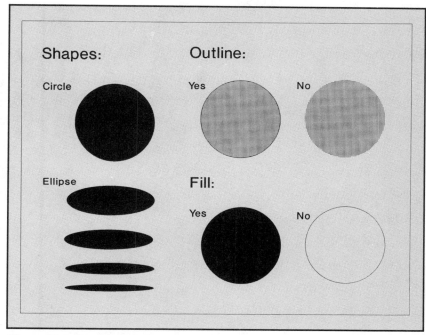

Figure 10.9: Drawing circles

DRAWING POLYGONS

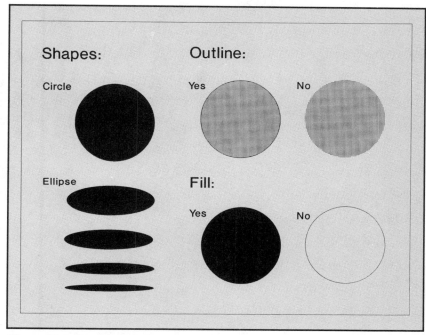

You can draw almost anything by using polygons and polylines. Most of Harvard's symbols use these two features.

A polygon is so similar to a polyline that after choosing Polygon from the Add menu, you create it by following the same steps. However, when you are drawing a polygon, its beginning and end will always meet, which enables you to place colors and patterns inside it, unlike curved polylines. Figure 10.10 shows examples of polygons that you can draw.

The Polygon Options menu differs slightly from the Polyline Options menu. In addition to the standard Outline Draw and Color options, there is an Outline Style option that lets you choose one of four styles for your polygon's outline (see Figure 10.10).

If you set the Polygon Options menu's Fill option to No, you might as well use a polyline. Polylines let you use curved lines and require less memory. Memory becomes an issue in charts with many drawings and illustrations.

CHANGING DRAWING DEFAULTS

After using these drawing tools a couple times, you may find that you are consistently changing Harvard's defaults to the same set-

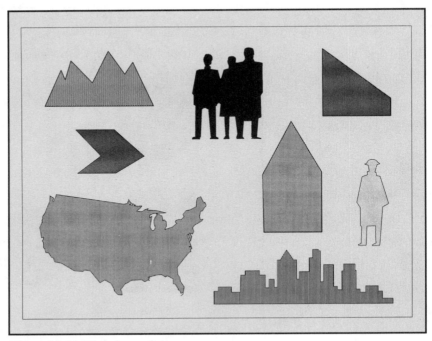

Figure 10.10: Drawing polygons

tings. If this is the case, there is an easier way to change the options
than calling up the Line Options or Box Options menu every time.
You can simply reset Harvard's defaults. To do this, press F8 at the
Draw menu.

When you first press F8, you'll see the Default Options menu,
which is similar to the Add menu. It lists each drawing tool (polyline,
box, line, circle, and polygon) and a Global option. Simply highlight
the tool whose default you want changed and press Enter. The
Options menu for that tool then appears, enabling you to change the
defaults. For example, you can stop the default shading (or coloring)
of a box by setting its default Fill value to 0.

Besides changing the individual defaults, you can also change
defaults for all the drawing tools by selecting Global. The Global
Options menu then appears (see Figure 10.11).

The options in this menu affect the entire chart. For example, if
you reset Display to Quick, your chart will be displayed without any
of its text attributes. This means you'll see changes to your chart

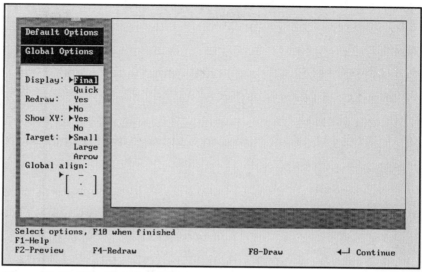

Figure 10.11: The Global Options menu

Save time by setting Redraw to No and Display to Quick. You can then press F4 when you want the screen redrawn to remove holes created by editing. You will still be able to see chart details by pressing F2.

more quickly when you redraw the chart by pressing F4. If you reset the Redraw option to Yes, you'll see the revised chart every time you make a change; this can be time-consuming.

When you set Show XY to No, you hide the cursor's X and Y positions, which would otherwise be displayed on the bottom of your chart, as in

Horiz = 3847   Vert = 9388

These numbers give you the exact location of the cursor, which helps when you must place symbols or drawings, such as your logo, on two or more charts in the same place. The X, Y position of 1, 1 refers to the bottom-left corner of your chart.

The remaining options, Target and Global align, influence the positioning of the objects in your chart. Target specifies the cursor type; by default, it is a small cross-hair cursor. If you reset it to Large, you may have trouble positioning small objects. On the other hand, setting Target to Arrow may make it easier to position objects. Global align lets you set a common point in every chart for positioning objects. This is especially useful for aligning text into columns that are centered or justified.

REVISING YOUR CHARTS

Now that you can draw shapes and lines in your charts, let's examine changing the chart's layout and design. Remember that you select Modify from the Draw menu when you need to edit your chart. Use Copy to duplicate objects and Delete to remove them. Be careful when deleting a group of objects because you can't use the Undo option to bring them back.

When you choose Modify, the Modify menu appears, containing five options (see Figure 10.12). Figure 10.13 shows the effects of using them.

CHOOSING THE OBJECTS TO MODIFY

You need to identify the objects you want revised, copied, or deleted. After choosing the editing option you want, the cursor will appear in the chart box. You're now ready to select the object (or objects) you want modified.

SELECTING AN INDIVIDUAL OBJECT   Move the cursor to the object you want modified and press Enter to select it. You should

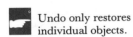 Undo only restores individual objects.

Save your chart before modifying it. This way you can retrieve the original version if you make a serious mistake during the editing process.

You can't modify objects that weren't created with Draw/Annotate. Instead, save them as symbols and then modify them after you import them back into your chart.

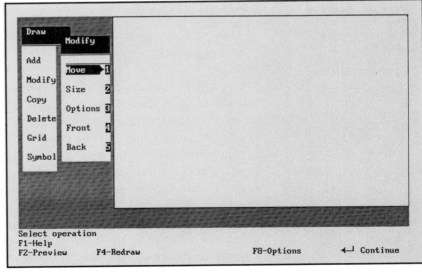

Figure 10.12: The Modify menu

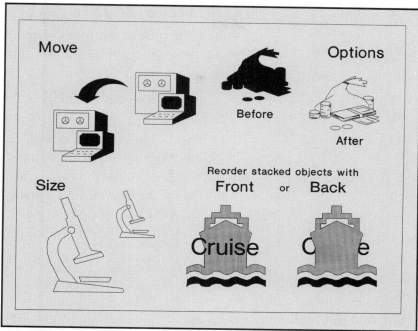

Figure 10.13: Modifying your chart's objects

see four hollow dots surrounding the object. You'll also see a pop-up menu on the left side of the screen, listing the Choose this, Select next, and Retry options.

Press Enter again to select the default, Choose this. If the dots don't surround the object you want, press the space bar to highlight Select next and press Enter. Keep pressing Enter until the dots surround the correct object and then press the space bar twice to highlight Choose this and press Enter. If you want to start over again instead, press the space bar twice and select Retry. Press Esc if you want to cancel your selections.

SELECTING A GROUP OF OBJECTS

To select a group of objects, enclose them in a box. First, move the cursor to an empty corner, press Enter to anchor the box, then move the cursor until all the objects are inside the box, and press Enter again.

Each object in the group will then be surrounded by four dots. As with individual objects, pick Choose this and press Enter to start modifying the objects.

Choose the Select next option to see all the parts of a symbol. Sometimes, several objects appear as one, especially stacked polylines and polygons.

RESIZING OBJECTS

You can increase or decrease the size of your chart's objects by following these steps:

1. Press **2** at the Modify menu and select the object(s) you want resized. Harvard then outlines the object(s) you selected with a box.

2. If you want to move as well as resize an object, press the Backspace key. Then move the cursor and press Enter to reanchor the object.

3. Change the box's size by moving the arrow keys. If you want to maintain the object's original proportions, press the Shift key as you move the cursor. If you made a mistake and want to start over, press Esc.

4. When you're satisfied with the new size, press Enter. The box outline will then be replaced with the resized object(s).

RECALLING THE OPTIONS MENUS

You can recall a drawing tool's Options menu for an object by pressing **3** at the Modify menu. Then select the object you want modified and the corresponding drawing tool menu will appear. You'll see a different menu, however, if you choose a group of objects. The Group Options menu only lets you change the group's outline, fill, and shadow colors.

Use this menu to change any symbols that your printer turns into black blotches. To do this, set Outline Color to 1 (white), Fill Color to 0 (no fill), and Shadow Color to 1 (white). Figure 10.13 shows how this helps print the money symbol on non-PostScript or black and white printers.

MOVING OBJECTS TO THE FRONT AND BACK

Move text and illustrations to the front or back of a group by using the Modify menu's Front or Back option. To bring a selected object forward, type **4** or **F**. Type **5** or **B** if you want to push an object to the back. Then select the object you want reordered and press Enter. Figure 10.13 shows this effect using the word Cruise as the selected object.

COPYING OBJECTS

It's easy to copy objects. First, select the object(s) you want copied. Harvard then places an outline in the chart box, which you move to where you want the copied objects placed. Press Enter and the objects will appear. The outline also reappears, allowing you to create additional copies. When you have positioned all the copies you want, press Esc.

HANDS-ON: CREATING A SIGN

Now let's practice using the drawing tools. You'll create text, polylines, boxes, circles, polygons, and lines, resulting in a sign similar to that shown in Figure 10.14.

Don't worry if you make a mistake since it's easy to correct it. For example, if a polyline or arrow doesn't look right, simply press the Backspace key and reposition it. You can also delete it and try again, or use a Modify option, such as Move or Size.

If you have a color monitor, follow the instructions for creating this sign in color and also use patterns so you can print it on any printer.

1. At the Main Menu, press F8. Choose the Portrait orientation and press F10 to return to the Main Menu.

2. Press **3** to display the Draw menu. Notice that the shape of the chart box changes to reflect the portrait orientation.

3. Press **1** to display the Add menu and then press **6** to select Polygon. You'll use this tool to create the large clock case.

4. Press F8 and set Fill to Yes, Color to 14 (crimson), and Pattern to 2 for the polygon. Press F8 again to return to the chart box.

5. Using Figure 10.14 as a guide, move the cursor to the lower-left corner and start drawing the clock case. Press Enter and move the cursor to the right while holding the Shift key. At the right corner, press Enter again. Continue drawing the case; when you're done, press Esc several times to return to the Add menu.

6. Press **5** to add a circle, which you'll use for the clock face. Change the circle's Center Color option to 0 (no fill). Then

Figure 10.14: A sample sign

position the circle in the clock case polygon using the procedures described earlier in this chapter. When you're done, press Esc until you see the Add menu.

7. Select Box and use this tool to create a solid black base for the clock case.

8. Next, choose the option to add Text. Press F8 and set the text size to 5.5. Press F8 again to return to the chart box and place the numbers 3, 6, 9, and 12 on the clock face. Use a text size of 8 and add the sign's messages, **Clocks for Sale** and **$5 to $20**. Place them below the clock. Return to the Add menu when you're finished.

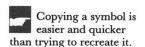

Copying a symbol is easier and quicker than trying to recreate it.

9. Choose the Add menu's Circle option to draw a small circle that you'll use on the clock face to represent the missing numbers. Set both the Outline and Center Color options to 1, and the Pattern option to 0. Place the circle at the one o'clock position and then press Esc twice to return to the Draw menu. Use the Copy option to duplicate it. Place a copied circle at the remaining hours where you are missing a number.

10. Place the two clock hands in your chart using the Add menu's Line option.

11. Add a circle on the top of the clock for decoration. Make it look like a sun by setting both the Outline and Center Color options to 7 (yellow), and the Pattern option to 3. Now use the Add menu's Polygon option to create the mountains in front of the sun and its Polyline option to simulate the wood carvings.

Save and print your completed sign. In making this sign, you used all of Harvard's drawing tools. You're now ready for advanced drawings, where a grid can come in handy.

USING A GRID

A grid helps you draw and align the different objects in your chart for an accurate, uniform composition. When you select Grid from the

Draw menu, Harvard presents the Grid menu (see Figure 10.15).

Harvard's grids are composed of dotted lines. To adjust the density of the dots—that is, how closely the dots are spaced—enter a number from 1 to 25 for the Size option. Size 1 gives the greatest dot density. (You may need to experiment with the grid's size when you start drawing.) To display the grid in your chart box, set the Show option to Yes.

When you set Snap to Yes, all lines, boxes, and circles you draw will then be forced to start and end on a grid dot. Use Snap as a tool to align boxes, lines, and other objects in your chart. You'll find this function invaluable when creating flow charts and diagrams. It gives your lines and boxes a neat, symmetrical appearance. Snap won't affect the objects you created before turning it on unless you modify them.

Figure 10.16 shows how drawing over an image on paper and using Harvard's Grid option can help in reproducing the image in Harvard. It's easier to draw if you only concentrate on one grid box at a time and not the entire picture. After you complete each box, your illustration will piece itself together for a near-perfect reproduction.

Because Snap restricts the placement of your lines, set the Grid menu's Size option to 1 for greater flexibility.

The changes you make using the Grid menu don't always show on your screen. If this happens, just press the F4 key to redraw the chart and you'll see them.

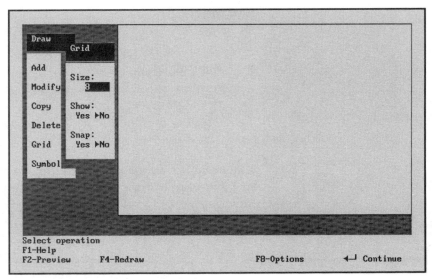

Figure 10.15: The Grid menu

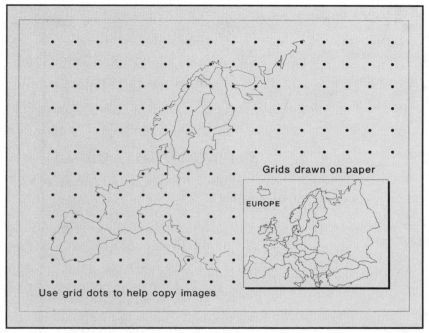

Figure 10.16: Reproducing an illustration by using Harvard's grid

TRANSFORMING
YOUR DRAWINGS INTO SYMBOLS

After you create a complex drawing using Harvard's Grid option, you should turn it into a symbol and save it for future use. To do this, you use the Symbol menu's Group option. Press **6** to select Symbol from the Draw menu. Now follow these steps to turn your drawing into a symbol:

1. From the Symbol menu, select Group. Move the cursor to the edge of your drawing and press Enter to anchor a corner. Drag the cursor across the other objects you want included and press Enter.

2. Each of the objects within the group should have four circles around it. If those are the objects you want grouped, press

If you select Group for objects in a stack, Harvard places them at the top of the stack. If you don't want this, use the Modify menu's Back option to reposition the objects.

Enter to select the Choose this option; otherwise, press the space bar and choose Select next to continue choosing other objects.

3. Once you've selected all the objects you want included in the symbol, press Esc.

You now need to save the symbol.

SAVING YOUR SYMBOLS

Here are the steps for saving a symbol:

1. Press **2** to select Save from the Symbol menu. Select your symbol as if you were modifying it. After selecting Choose this, you'll see a list of symbol files.

2. Highlight and select the file where you want to save the symbol, or type the name of a new file. Harvard adds a .SYM extension to all symbol files.

Keep your symbols for color and Post-Script printers in files together, separate from those for black and white printers.

You can place up to 20 symbols in a file. Symbol files store a symbol's shape, screen location, and the options used for its objects.

REMOVING SYMBOLS

You'll probably find yourself removing symbols often as you improve the ones you have. Do this by following these steps:

1. Select Remove from the Symbol menu. A list of symbol files will then appear on your screen.

2. Highlight the file that contains the symbol you want removed and press Enter. All the symbols in the file are then displayed.

3. Move the cursor to the symbol you want removed and press Enter. Press Enter again to confirm its removal or press Esc if you made a mistake.

To transfer a symbol into a different file, get the symbol, place it in your chart, and resave it to a new chart by following the steps in "Saving Your Symbols."

HANDS-ON: CREATING A MAP TEMPLATE CHART WITH A MAP SYMBOL

All versions of U.S. Mapmaker work perfectly when you have a color printer, plotter, or PostScript printer.

Although Harvard sells an accessory program called U.S. Map-Maker that helps you make maps, Version 1.0 doesn't work with a dot matrix or a HPLC printer such as the HP LaserJet II; its charts are printed as solid blotches. If you have one of these printers, you can simply use the colorful U.S. map symbol that you'll find in Harvard's COUNTRY.SYM file.

Map charts show at a glance the geographical composition of your statistics. They're excellent for showing population compositions since you can shade each state based on the number of people within it. You can also use map charts to show acres in agriculture or forests, sales revenue, average income levels, and a host of other statistics.

You'll create a simple U.S. map chart template containing labeled states. You'll then use the template to create a chart whose purpose is to identify the North, South, Midwest, and West regions of the United States. To create your template and chart, follow these steps:

1. Create a new free-form text chart. Type the following title, subtitle, and footnote:

   Title
   Subtitle
   Footnote

   These values are simply placeholders so you don't place symbols in their space. They will be cleared when you save the chart as a template. Now press F10 to return to the Main Menu.

2. Press **3** and then **6** to select the Symbol option from the Draw menu.

3. At the Symbol menu, press **1** to select Get. Highlight the file named COUNTRY.SYM and press Enter. Figure 10.17 shows what your screen should like. Move your cursor to the U.S. map chart in the third column's top row and select it by pressing Enter. You'll then see an outline representing the map symbol in the chart box.

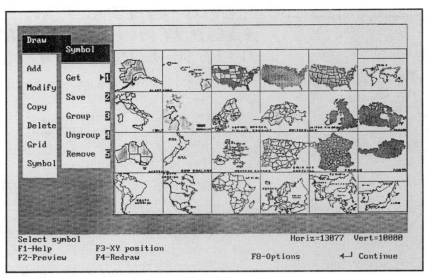

Figure 10.17: The maps in the COUNTRY.SYM file

4. Press Backspace, move the cursor to the map's starting corner, and press Enter to anchor it. Keep the map's proportions by pressing the Shift key while moving the cursor to the opposite corner. Press Enter. Your map now fills most of the chart.

5. Repeat steps 3 and 4 to place the symbols for Alaska and Hawaii in the lower-left corner of your chart.

6. Press Esc until you see the Draw menu. Press **2** and then **3** to display the Options menu. Move the cursor to the map chart and select it by pressing Enter twice. The Group Options menu then appears. Set Outline Color to 1 (white), and Fill Color and Shadow Color to 0 (no fill). Repeat this step for Alaska and Hawaii.

7. Press Esc twice to return to the Draw menu. Press **6** and then **4** to choose Ungroup from the Symbol menu. Move the cursor to the map and press Enter to ungroup it. Then do the same with Alaska and Hawaii.

8. Use the Draw menu's Delete option to remove text and polylines individually from Alaska and Hawaii. If you accidentally remove the wrong object, use Delete's Undo option.

You won't see any messages when you ungroup a symbol. To double-check the ungrouping process, press Enter until you see the "Not a group" message.

9. Select Text from the Add menu. Press F8 to move to the Text Options menu and set Size to 2.5. Place the two-letter abbreviation on each state using Figure 10.18 as a guide. If the state is too small to label, place its label next to it. You can then add a line to connect the label to the state, if necessary.

You've now created a chart that will make a great template for hundreds of other map charts. To turn it into a template, follow these steps:

10. Press Esc until you see the Main Menu. Then press **4** twice to choose Save template from the Get/Save/Remove menu and type **USMAP** for the template's name. Press F10 to accept the other default values, including Clear values. To return to the Main Menu, press Esc.

11. To create a chartbook of map templates, press **8** and then **1**. Type **MAPCHART** for the chartbook's name and press

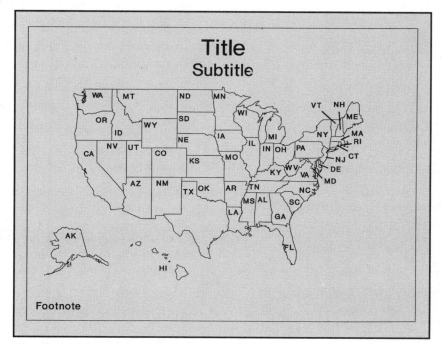

Figure 10.18: Your template map

Enter. Type **A collection of map templates** for the description and press Enter again. Highlight USMAP.TPL and press Enter to place it in your new chartbook. Press Esc until you see the Main Menu.

To use this template at any point, you would return to the Main Menu and select the Chartbook menu option. From the Chartbook Menu choose Select chartbook and then pick MAPCHART. However, since you just created this chartbook, it is still in memory, ready to be used.

12. Press **1** and **8** to select the Create New Chart menu's From chartbook option. Highlight USMAP and press Enter to select it.

13. Type the following title, subtitle, and footnote:

    U.S. Map Chart
    showing census regions
    Source: U.S. Bureau of the Census

14. Press F10 to return to the Main Menu and then press **3**, **1**, and **2** to choose the Add menu's Box option. Using Figure 10.19 as a guide, create a legend box for each of the four regions. Use the Options menu to give each box one of these patterns:

    6 (white)
    3 (light grey)
    5 (medium grey)
    4 (dark grey)

15. Add a legend label to each of the four boxes using West, Midwest, North, and South.

16. Press Esc until you see the Draw Menu. Press **2** and then **3** to select Options from the Modify menu.

17. Select a state and give it a pattern number representing the legend it uses. For example, choose **3** for the Midwest, **4** for the North, **5** for the South, and **6** for the West.

For uniform legend box sizes, just draw one. Use Copy to create the others.

Pattern 1 (black) shows a good contrast in map charts. However, text and symbols won't print (except on color printers) if placed in states using this pattern.

18. Repeat step 17 for all 50 states. When you're finished, save your chart under a different name (not as a template) and print it. It should resemble Figure 10.19.

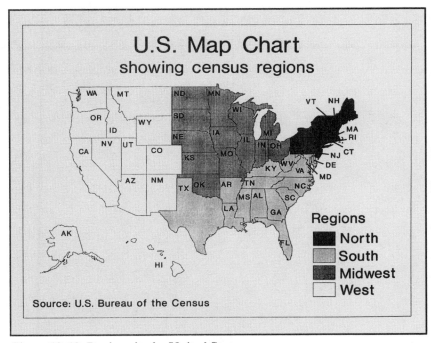

Use an arrow cursor instead of a cross-hair for tracing symbols. The cross-hair cursor sometimes covers areas you need to trace. Select Global from the Default Options menu to change it.

The U.S. map you just created came from a symbol where each state was a polygon. This allowed you to change each state's pattern to match the statistics you wanted to display. Unfortunately, polylines in symbols can't be modified, and Harvard uses polylines for many parts of its other map symbols. The best you can do with these symbols is to trace them using polygons and save your drawing as a map template.

When you trace a symbol, add a separate feature, such as a small circle or box, and group it with the original symbol. Then select the small circle or box to delete it and the associated symbol. (Once you have completed your drawing, the original symbol is unnecessary and will take up too much memory.) If your drawing disappears, press F4 to redraw it. By saving your drawing as a template, you can then use it to create map charts.

Figure 10.19: Regions in the United States

TURNING YOUR CHART INTO A SYMBOL

If you want to use an entire chart as a symbol in another chart to illustrate an example, you shrink your chart and reposition it, as follows:

1. Use the Get/Save/Remove option to retrieve the chart you want. Press Esc until you see the Main Menu.

2. Press F7 at the Main Menu and the cross-hair cursor will appear on the screen. Move it to where you want the new chart to begin and press Enter. This anchors the bottom corner for relocating your chart. A box will now appear on your screen as you move the cursor.

3. Move the cursor until the box outlines the area where you want the chart placed and press Enter. You'll see that Harvard redraws the chart within the outlined area. Press Esc until you see the Main Menu. You can now add text to describe your chart symbol and complete the chart.

SUMMARY

You have now used polylines, circles, boxes, lines, and polygons to create your own illustrations. You can even turn your illustrations into symbols and modify them so they'll print on any type of printer. You've also modified symbols to create a professional map chart.

This chapter rounds out your graphing experience. You're now ready to use Harvard with your data from other programs.

11

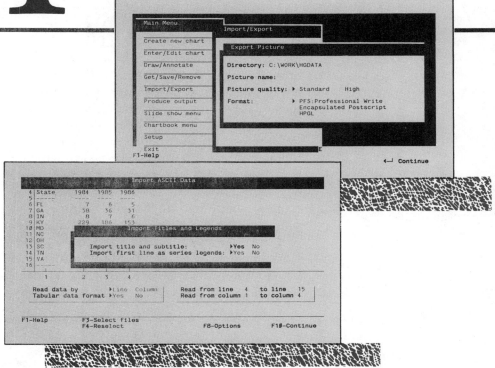

TRANSFERRING INFORMATION BETWEEN HARVARD AND OTHER PROGRAMS

CHAPTER **11**

WHEN YOU WORK WITH SEVERAL PROGRAMS, importing and exporting data can save you a considerable amount of time. By using Harvard's Import/Export feature, you won't have to retype data from other programs. For example, you can import a Lotus spreadsheet to Harvard and use its data in a chart. You can also export a Harvard graph for use in other programs. To do these data and file transfers, you use the Main Menu's Import/Export option. When you choose this option, the Import/Export menu appears, presenting you with seven options (see Figure 11.1).

Harvard provides you with five importing options so that you can import data from virtually any program. If you work with the Lotus 1-2-3 or PFS:GRAPH program, you have options geared specifically to it. If you work with another program, you can probably save your work in either the standard ASCII or delimited ASCII format and use the appropriate ASCII importing option. Dozens of programs, including database managers, word processors, and graphics and

The Lotus options will also import charts and data files created with Symphony.

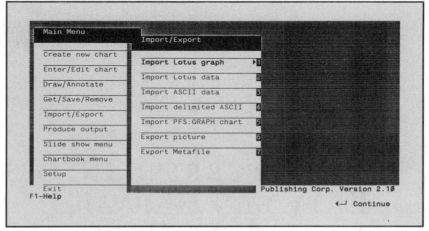

Figure 11.1: The Import/Export menu

communications programs, use the ASCII format for data portability. You may find that your programs refer to ASCII formats as DOS, text, or nondocument files.

IMPORTING GRAPHS

You can't import Lotus .PIC files as graphs.

Press F3 at the Import Lotus Graph screen to select a different Lotus graph than the one currently displayed.

Because Harvard produces better looking graphs than Lotus does, you might want to import Lotus graphs into Harvard and modify them. To choose the Import Lotus graph option, press 1 at the Import/Export menu. You'll then see a listing of files that you can select. Simply highlight the file you want and press Enter.

Since each Lotus file contains more than one graph, you'll first see a list of graphs within that file. Highlight the graph you want and press Enter. Set Import data only to No, press F10, and the Import Lotus Graph will then appear, containing the selected graph. You can edit and save the graph as you would any Harvard chart.

Importing graphs from the PFS:GRAPH program is even quicker. You just press 5 to select the Import PFS:GRAPH chart option, choose the file you want, set Import data only to No, and press F10. Because each file only contains one graph, the graph is then imported to your screen and you can modify it as you wish.

IMPORTING LOTUS DATA

If you don't have a Lotus chart you can import, try importing a Lotus data file. It may take a few extra steps, but it is still faster than retyping lots of data. If you regularly create charts from a Lotus file, you should create a template. (We'll do this in this chapter's "Hands-on" session.)

Before you start importing data, use Lotus to print a copy of your spreadsheet. Assume that you have a Lotus file named FRUIT and that it looks something like Figure 11.2. Notice the columns are headed A to D. Each row is numbered 1 to 7. Each element sits within a cell. For example, the element 1278 is in the B5 cell and the word Peaches is in the A7 cell. The A1 cell contains the spreadsheet's title and overlaps into cells B1 and C1.

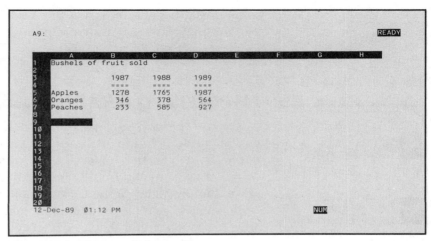

Figure 11.2: The sample Lotus data

After printing your spreadsheet, start Harvard and choose the type of chart you want to create. For example, you might create a bar chart using Year as the X data type. Once you see the data-entry screen, press the F10 key to return to the Main Menu. Your newly created chart is still active and is ready to receive the Lotus data.

At the Main Menu, select Import/Export and then choose Import Lotus data. A list of Lotus data files you can import will be displayed. Simply highlight the file you want and press Enter. If you don't see the file, press F3 to search other subdirectories. When you press F3, Harvard first checks the import directory that was specified with the Setup menu's Default option. If you didn't specify one, it uses the current data directory.

Figure 11.3 shows the screen you'll now see. This Import Lotus Data screen will appear in place of the file listing the next time you select the Import Lotus data option. (Harvard always assumes you want to make changes to the previous Lotus file you imported.) If this assumption is incorrect, simply press F3 and select a different file.

Always choose a chart or template before importing Lotus data. Otherwise, Harvard will give you the error message, "Cannot import data to the current chart type."

DESIGNATING DATA RANGES

Look at your printout of the Lotus spreadsheet and identify the rows or columns that you'll use in your Harvard chart. Specify these rows and columns in the Import Lotus Data screen. For

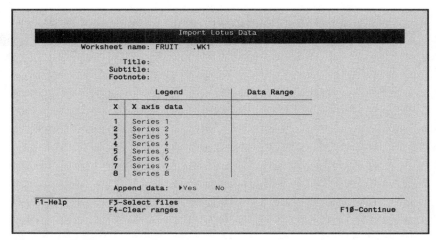

Figure 11.3: The Import Lotus Data screen

example, type **\A1** in the Title field. The slash tells Harvard to take values from the cell as opposed to literally entering A1 for the chart's title.

Continue by designating data ranges. Look at the spreadsheet and find the X axis data range. Type **B3..D3** in the Data Range field to use 1987, 1988, and 1989 for the X axis. (The two dots are a Lotus code meaning B3 to D3.) Next identify each series on your spreadsheet and specify their labels and data ranges in the data-entry screen. For example, type **\A5** for the first series' legend. The legend will then be Apples. Next, enter the Apples range by typing **B5..D5**. Figure 11.4 shows what your screen should look like when you've finished specifying the Lotus data Harvard should use.

COMPLETING YOUR LOTUS IMPORT

With your ranges established, decide whether you're replacing or appending data into a Harvard chart. Notice the Append data option at the bottom of the data-entry screen. In this case, set it to No since you are replacing the ranges with the Lotus data and your chart doesn't contain other data. If you are modifying a chart in which you entered data in Harvard, leave Append data set to Yes. The Lotus data are then added to those your chart is already using. After you choose a setting for this option, press F10 to return to the Main Menu and then save your chart.

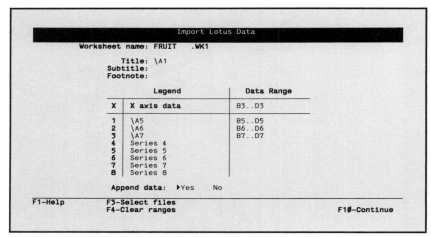

Figure 11.4: Your completed data references

HANDS-ON: USING A
TEMPLATE TO IMPORT YOUR LOTUS DATA

If you use Lotus 2.0 or later, load UNITS.WKS and resave it so Lotus can change the file's extension to .WK1. You need to do this if you want to change the spreadsheet file later. Simply substitute .WK1 for .WKS in this session.

If you work with Lotus frequently, you'll find a template convenient for importing data. To see how this works, copy the UNITS.WKS file to the \HGDATA directory. Harvard includes this Lotus file on its Utilities disk (Disk 3) for you to practice with. Thus, you can try this "Hands-on" session even though you don't have Lotus. However, if you do, load the file and print it for reference as you work through this section. Follow these steps to import the spreadsheet:

1. At the Main Menu, press **1** to select Create new chart.

2. Press **2** to choose Bar/Line and then press F10 twice to return to the Main Menu.

3. Press **4** to select Import/Export.

4. Press **2** to choose Import Lotus data, highlight UNITS.WKS, and press Enter. You'll then see the Import Lotus Data screen.

5. Type **\A3** in the Title field to use the contents of cell A3 as the chart's title. Press Enter three times.

6. Type **B1..I1** as the values for the X axis data range.

7. Move your cursor to the Series 1 label by pressing Enter and then Shift-Tab. You'll replace this and the next two labels.

8. Type **\A4**, press the Delete key 5 times, and press Enter. Type **\A5**, press the Delete key 5 times, and press Enter. Type **\A6**, press the Delete key 5 times, and press Enter.

9. Type **B4..I4** for the **\A4** data range and press Enter. Type **B5..I5** for the **\A5** data range and press Enter. Type **B6..I6** for the **\A6** data range and press Enter.

10. Move your cursor to the Append data option and set it to No.

11. Press Enter. The Bar/Line Chart data screen will then appear, allowing you to reformat the imported data. When you've finished designing your chart, press Esc until you see the Main Menu.

To keep your completed graph, save it as a chart before you save it as a template.

Now that you have created a chart of imported data, you need to save it. So that you don't have to go through all these steps every time you want to use imported data in your Harvard charts, save it as a template by following these steps:

12. At the Main Menu, press **4** to select Get/Save/Remove.

13. Press **4** to choose the Save as template option. You'll then see the Template menu.

14. Type **UNITS** as the template's name and press Enter.

15. Type **Units shipped (lotus import)** as the description. Notice that Clear values is set to Yes and Import data link is set to Lotus. Since this is just what you want, press F10 to continue.

Clearing the values saves the importing procedure without the actual data. This way, when you modify the Lotus file (for monthly reports, say), the revised data will then be imported to Harvard automatically.

16. When the "Chart values to be cleared" message appears, press Enter.

17. Press Esc until you see the Main Menu. You've now created a template that can automatically find your Lotus file and import its data.

CREATING A CHARTBOOK Before you use the template, create a chartbook for storing templates that import Lotus data and put your template in it. Then, when you create templates for the other Lotus files you use frequently, you'll have a place to store them. To do this, follow these steps:

1. At the Main Menu, press **8** to select Chartbook menu.

2. Press **1** to select Create chartbook.

3. Type **LOTUS** for the chartbook's name and press Enter.

4. Type **Lotus templates** for its description and press Enter.

5. Highlight UNITS.TPL, press Enter, press F10, and then press Esc until you see the Main Menu.

USING A TEMPLATE   Now make changes to the UNITS.WKS spreadsheet using Lotus. For example, you can update the spreadsheet by simply changing the quantities shipped. Let's see what happens when you use the template for this file:

1. At the Main Menu, press **8** to select the Chartbook menu option and then **3** to choose the Select chartbook option. Highlight LOTUS, press Enter, and then press Esc to return to the Main Menu.

2. Press **1** to choose the Main Menu's Create new chart option and then press **8** to select From chartbook. Highlight and select UNITS.TPL.

As you can see, your bar chart now contains the revised data, and the chart is already complete—your template formatted the data as you specified when you created it.

IMPORTING ASCII DATA

You can easily import ASCII data into Harvard as text or graphic charts. Suppose, for example, that you want to import an ASCII file containing the information shown in Table 11.1.

You start by creating a bar chart, keeping Name as the data type for the X axis. Then return to the Main Menu, where you choose Import/Export. Next, select Import ASCII data from the Import/

You can use a template to create your bar chart.

At the DOS prompt, enter **TYPE** *d:\path\filename* when you want to see if a file uses the ASCII format. If you can read the text on the screen, you're probably working with an ASCII file.

Table 11.1: Tobacco acreage by state (numbers in thousands of acres)

STATE	1984	1985	1986
FL	7	6	5
GA	38	36	31
IN	8	7	6
KY	229	186	153
MD	23	20	18
NC	272	251	215
OH	12	8	7
SC	47	43	37
TN	75	62	49
VA	54	43	38
Total	792	688	584

Export menu and press Enter. A list of all the files in your current directory will appear on the screen. Just choose the ASCII file you want to import and press Enter. Figure 11.5 contains the Import ASCII Data screen that you'll now use.

As with the Import Lotus data option and its screen, you'll see this screen instead of the file listing when you've previously imported an ASCII file. If you want to select a different file, simply press F3 to display the listing and choose another file.

UNDERSTANDING ASCII LINES AND COLUMNS

Let's look closer at the options on this screen. The numbers along the left margin are the line numbers. For example, you'll see the figures for Maryland (MD) on line 10. To see additional lines in the file, press Ctrl-↑. On the bottom of the screen, you'll see the Read from line 4 to line 243 setting. (If you created a text chart [the default is a free-form chart], you'll see Read from line 1 to line 49.) This means that Harvard plans to take data from lines 4 to 243 and use

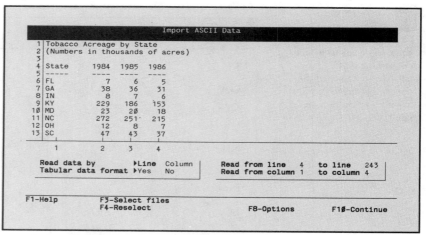

```
┌─────────────────────────────────────────────────────────────────────┐
│                          Import ASCII Data                            │
│   1│Tobacco Acreage by State                                          │
│   2│(Numbers in thousands of acres)                                   │
│   3│                                                                   │
│   4│State    1984  1985  1986                                         │
│   5│-----    ----  ----  ----                                         │
│   6│FL          7     6     5                                         │
│   7│GA         38    36    31                                         │
│   8│IN          8     7     6                                         │
│   9│KY        229   186   153                                         │
│  10│MD         23    20    18                                         │
│  11│NC        272   251   215                                         │
│  12│OH         12     8     7                                         │
│  13│SC         47    43    37                                         │
│           1        2     3     4                                      │
│                                                                       │
│   Read data by        ▶Line  Column    Read from line    4  to line   243 │
│   Tabular data format ▶Yes   No        Read from column 1  to column 4 │
│                                                                       │
│ F1-Help          F3-Select files                                      │
│                  F4-Reselect                 F8-Options    F10-Continue │
└─────────────────────────────────────────────────────────────────────┘
```

Figure 11.5: The Import ASCII Data screen

them in the graph. We'll have to change the last line from 243 to 15, which has the last X axis value. To do this, move to the setting by pressing Tab twice and type **15**.

You can only import ASCII files that are 256 characters or less in width.

Immediately below the imported data, you'll see column numbers 1, 2, 3, and 4. That is because Harvard detected four columns in this ASCII file. If Harvard can't detect columns, it gives each character's position a column number. For example, a text chart would show a scale of character positions from 1 to 77. Notice the Read from column 1 to column 4 setting below the line numbers setting. Since we want all the columns in our chart, we won't change them. However, if you wanted to limit which columns are imported, you would tab to these numbers and change them. For large files, press Ctrl-→ until you see all the columns.

REFINING IMPORT SPECIFICATIONS

After you have chosen which ASCII data to display, use the remaining two options, Read data by and Tabular data format, to specify how Harvard should present the data. For example, set Read data by to Line if the series labels are in the lines. Set it to Column when they are at the top of the columns. Set Tabular data format to Yes when the data are arranged in columns as shown in Figure 11.5. If there aren't tabs between the columns—that is, you have rows of nonaligned data, where each character is treated as a column—set Tabular data format to No.

You can refine the columns that you import by pressing the F8 key. You'll see one of your columns marked by a highlighting block. You move the highlighting between the data columns by using the Tab key. Delete a highlighted column from the import list by pressing Ctrl-Del. (Notice that its column number disappears.) To add a column, press Ctrl-Ins, use the arrow keys to move to the new column's position, and press Enter. To change the width of a highlighted column, use the left and right arrow keys. Press Esc when you have finished arranging your data.

FINISHING THE ASCII IMPORT

Once you're satisfied with the columns you're importing, press F10. You'll then see the Import Titles and Legends dialog box as shown in Figure 11.6. Set the Import title and subtitle option to Yes since you are using the first two lines in the ASCII file as the title and subtitle. Also set the Import first line as series legends option to Yes so that Harvard will use the line after the subtitle (line 4) as the series legend.

After you set Import first line as series legends to Yes, press Enter. Figure 11.7 shows the data screen that will then appear. You can

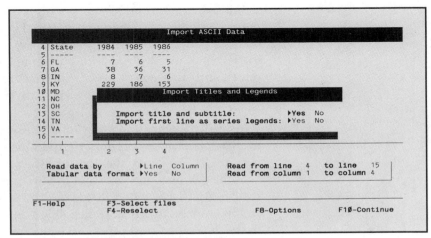

Figure 11.6: The Import Titles and Legends dialog box

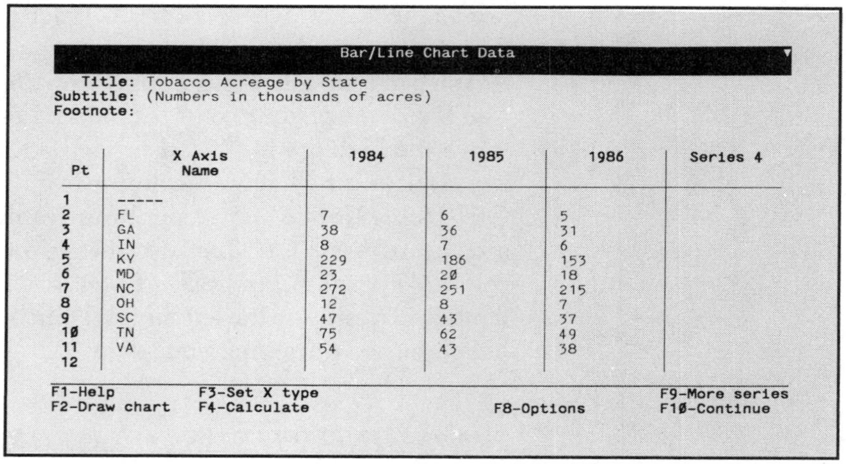

Bar/Line Chart Data

Title: Tobacco Acreage by State
Subtitle: (Numbers in thousands of acres)
Footnote:

Pt	X Axis Name	1984	1985	1986	Series 4
1	-----				
2	FL	7	6	5	
3	GA	38	36	31	
4	IN	8	7	6	
5	KY	229	186	153	
6	MD	23	20	18	
7	NC	272	251	215	
8	OH	12	8	7	
9	SC	47	43	37	
10	TN	75	62	49	
11	VA	54	43	38	
12					

F1-Help F2-Draw chart F3-Set X type F4-Calculate F8-Options F9-More series F10-Continue

Figure 11.7: Working with your bar chart's imported ASCII data

delete the dashes in the first row by moving the cursor to that line and pressing Ctrl-Del. Continue to modify your bar chart as you wish and then save it.

IMPORTING DELIMITED ASCII DATA

Before you import delimited data, let's examine its data arrangement. It is called *delimited* because each individual segment of data is set off by certain marks from the rest of the data. Traditionally, but not necessarily, you'll find text enclosed in double quotes (") and elements separated by commas (,) which are known as *end-of-field delimiters*. Records usually end with a delimiter that comprises a carriage return and line feed (#13 #10). Each record then starts on a new line. For example, Figure 11.8 shows how the lines of the tobacco file look when they are delimited.

As with the other importing options, select the type of chart you want to create, then go to the Import/Export menu, and select Import delimited ASCII. You'll see the familiar listing of files to select from. Highlight the delimited file you want to import and press Enter. You'll now see the ASCII Delimiters dialog box shown in Figure 11.9.

If your delimited ASCII file follows the conventional formats listed in the dialog box, just press F10 to continue. If not, reset the delimiters and then press F10. Harvard then displays another dialog box

```
"Tobacco Acreage by State"
"(Numbers in thousands of acres)"
""
"        ","____","____","____"
"FL",7,6,5
"GA",38,36,31
"IN",8,7,6
"KY",229,186,153
"MD",23,20,18
"NC",272,251,215
"OH",12,8,7
"SC",47,43,37
"TN",75,62,49
"VA",54,43,38
"        ","____","____","____"
"Total","792","688","584"

_
```

Figure 11.8: A sample delimited file

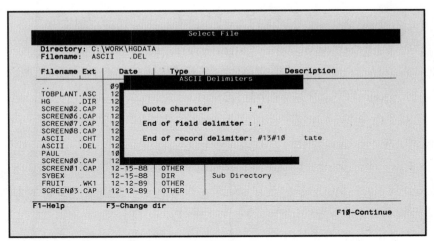

Figure 11.9: The ASCII Delimiters dialog box

asking if you want to import the record as a series legend. Select Yes if your data file uses one and press Enter. You'll now see the chart's data-entry screen containing the imported data.

EXPORTING PICTURES

Suppose you want to use a Harvard graph in a word processing or desktop publishing program to illustrate a report you're creating with that program. With Harvard's Import/Export option, this is easy to do. First, use the Get/Save/Remove option to retrieve the chart you want to export. Next, use the Import/Export option and select Export picture. You'll then see the Export Picture menu (Figure 11.10).

Specify the directory you want to send the picture to if it is not the directory Harvard has already entered. For example, you might want to send the picture to the subdirectory where you keep desktop publishing files. If you have already saved the file (which would normally be the case), its name will already be listed; otherwise, type the picture's name using eight characters or less and press Enter. Then select the resolution for your picture. Choose either Standard (150 dots per inch) or High quality (300 dpi) and press Enter.

Now select the format you want. Harvard provides you with three choices. PFS:Professional Write lets you send your picture to that program. If you choose Encapsulated Postscript, you can export your graph to programs such as Ventura Publisher and PageMaker. Select HPGL to export to programs that read HPGL formats. HPGL, Hewlett-Packard Graphic Language, is a special set of instructions for plotters.

Before selecting Encapsulated Postscript, make sure the HGPRO-LOG.PSC file is in your \HG subdirectory. Harvard includes this file on the Utility disk.

Harvard doesn't automatically add an extension to the name you specify here; however, you can add one if you like.

Only Ventura Publisher Versions 1.1 and later can read Encapsulated PostScript, HPGL, or CGM files.

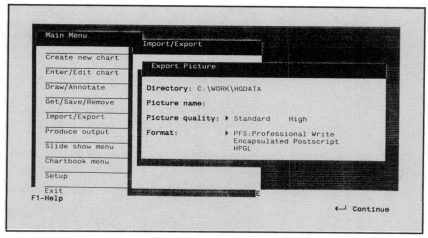

Figure 11.10: The Export Picture menu

EXPORTING METAFILES

The final option on the Import/Export menu is Export Metafile. The CGM (Computer Graphic Metafile) format is fast becoming the standard for vector graphic pictures. When you choose this option, you'll see the Export Metafile dialog box. Specify the directory you want to export the file to, type the file name, and tell Harvard if you want to use its graphic fonts. Using this option requires that you've configured your computer system to use VDI drivers. The Harvard manual contains explicit instructions on doing this. It also describes how to convert CGM files into Harvard symbols, which lets you import images from Ventura and PageMaker. You can add new symbols and pictures into Harvard using this technique.

SUMMARY

You're now familiar with Harvard's import and export techniques. You can make a polished graph out of any program's data. In today's world, where computer users tend to work with several programs and always need to present their data well, this is an essential tool.

In the next chapter you'll explore Harvard's options for presenting your charts, the culmination of all the chart construction techniques you have acquired.

12

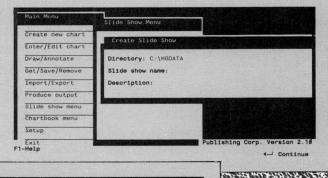

CREATING SLIDE SHOWS

CHAPTER *12*

You can use templates to create consistently styled graphs for your slide show. When you include a template in your slide show, Harvard uses its attributes for the files that follow it in the show. To stop using the template, you need to add another template. When Harvard encounters the second template, it switches to that template's formatting. If a template has a footnote, the text will be repeated on each of the subsequent slides. Similarly, any Draw/Annotate features will be reproduced on the slides.

YOU'RE NOW FAMILIAR WITH ALL OF HARVARD'S capabilities and you can create professional looking charts quickly and effectively. In this chapter, you'll learn how to tie all the loose ends together for a powerful presentation.

You can organize and plan your presentation by using Harvard's slide show feature. As with any slide show, you specify the order in which the slides are presented. In this case, though, the slides are charts, either Harvard Graphics chart files or bit-mapped files from other programs. By using this slide show feature, you can produce output for your presentation with just one command—all the files included in the slide show will be printed, plotted, or recorded on film together. Alternatively, you can present the slide show as a *screen show,* an interactive presentation on your computer's screen, complete with special effects.

Once you've selected your charts, you're ready to create a slide show. For now, let's look closer at the production aspects of your show.

CREATING AND EDITING A SLIDE SHOW

Creating a slide show is simple. Press **7** from the Main Menu to get the Slide Show Menu (Figure 12.1). Then press **1** and you'll see the dialog box as shown in Figure 12.2.

Harvard displays the directory where it plans to store your slide show. You can change it by typing a different directory in its place. To create a slide show, type its name, using eight characters or less, and a description. Harvard then takes you automatically to the Create/Edit Slide Show screen (Figure 12.3). This is the same screen you'll see when you press **2** at the Slide Show Menu.

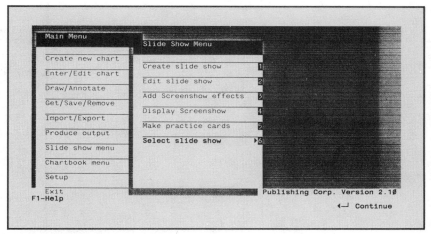

Figure 12.1: The Slide Show Menu

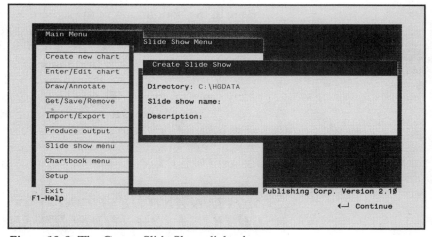

Figure 12.2: The Create Slide Show dialog box

The top half of the screen shows a listing of charts you can select from. Those listed on the bottom part of the screen are those that you've already selected.

ADDING CHARTS TO THE SLIDE SHOW

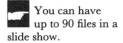 You can have up to 90 files in a slide show.

To add a chart to a slide show, highlight the file you want on the top part of the screen and press Enter. You'll then see the chart's

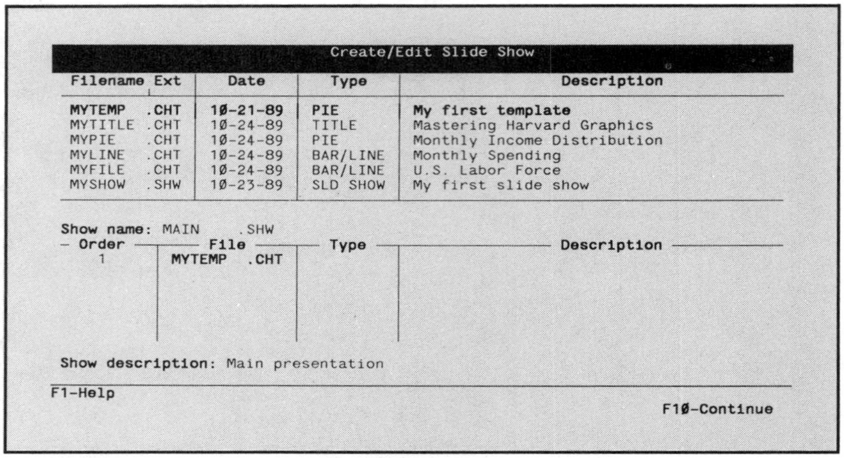

Figure 12.3: The Create/Edit Slide Show screen

name in the bottom part of the screen, which shows that you selected it. When you're finished selecting charts, press F10.

You can also include screens and files from other programs. For example, you can include bit-mapped files that you created with PC Paintbrush, Publisher's Paintbrush, PC Paint, Dr. HALO, and many other programs. These files must have a .PIC or .PCX extension so Harvard knows they are bit mapped. You can also use an add-on program from Harvard called ScreenShow Utilities, which lets you capture screen images and saves them as .PCX files.

You can only print .PIC and .PCX files in Harvard when they are part of the slide show. Harvard will simply ignore your command if you try to print a .PIC or .PCX file individually (unless you import it into Harvard; for more on importing, see Chapter 11).

MOVING AND DELETING CHARTS FROM THE SLIDE SHOW

To delete a chart from a slide show, press Tab until the highlighting moves to the bottom half of the screen. Then highlight the chart you want removed and press Ctrl-Del.

If you want to reorganize your charts, you just change the order of the slides in the list. Simply highlight the file you want moved and press Ctrl-↓ or Ctrl-↑, depending on the direction you want the file moved.

CHANGING THE SLIDE SHOW DESCRIPTION

You can edit and change the description you gave the slide show when you created it. Press Tab until you see the Show description line highlighted. Then simply type the show's new description and press F10 when you're done.

DISPLAYING THE SLIDE SHOW

When you have finished adding files to your slide show and editing it, you can view it by choosing Display Screenshow. You can use your mouse or keyboard to move through your screen show. Pressing the right mouse button or Enter displays the next slide. To view the previous slide, press the left button or Backspace. If you want to start the show over again from the first slide, press Home. Conversely, pressing End displays the last slide.

A useful shortcut, Ctrl-E, presents the chart's data on the screen. By pressing this key combination, you can edit the graph you are viewing. To return to your slide show, press Esc until you see the Main Menu and start the show over. Unfortunately, you can't simply pick up where you left off in the slide show. While viewing your show, press both mouse buttons or Esc to return to the Slide Show Menu.

MAKING PRACTICE CARDS

When you're satisfied with the general structure of your slide show, you might want to make *practice cards* for your speech. These cards are Harvard's version of old-fashioned index cards. You can fill in any information to guide you through your speech.

To make or edit a practice card, select Make practice cards from the Slide Show Menu. As you can see in Figure 12.4, the Practice Cards screen contains the number, name, and description for each chart in your presentation. The large area in the center is for you to type your notes, key words, outline, or other information that you'll need for your presentation.

When you have finished entering the information, you can have the chart's data printed when you print the practice card by setting

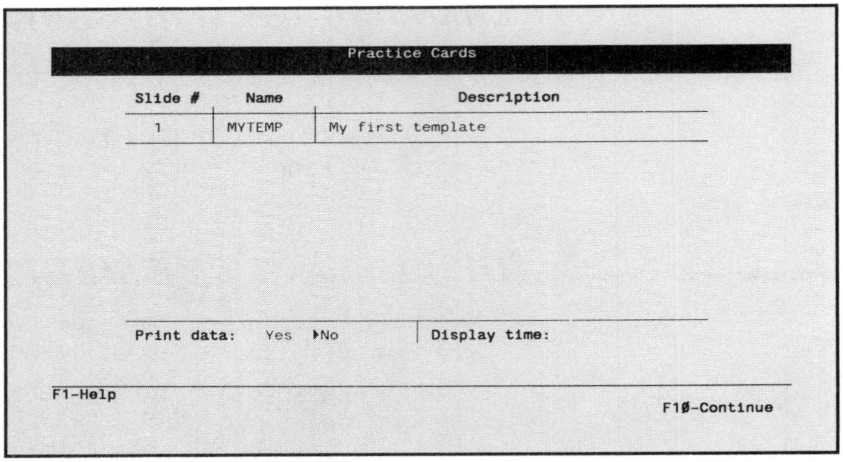

Figure 12.4: The Practice Cards data-entry screen

To move to a partic-
ular practice card,
highlight the Slide #
column's number and
replace it with the num-
ber of the card you want.

Print data to Yes. The remaining option, Display time, which shows
how many seconds Harvard waits before presenting the next chart, is
part of Harvard's feature that lets you display your show automatically. You'll learn about this feature later in this chapter.

To create the next practice card, press PgDn or F10. Continue
doing this until you have cards for all your slides. Press Home to
return to the first practice card. When you want to see the last card in
your slide show, press End. Press Esc when you're done to return to
the Slide Show Menu.

To print your practice cards, select Print practice cards from the
Produce Output menu. If you previously set Print data to Yes on the
Practice Cards data-entry screen, the chart's data will also be printed
separately. Figure 12.5 shows an example of a printed practice card.
Notice that Harvard also prints your chart. (You might want to think
of practice cards as practice sheets since they print on an entire
8½-by-11-inch sheet of paper).

SELECTING SLIDE SHOWS

If you have other slide shows, you can work with another show by
choosing Select slide show from the Slide Show Menu. You will then
see a list of the shows that you've created. Simply highlight the one
you want and press Enter.

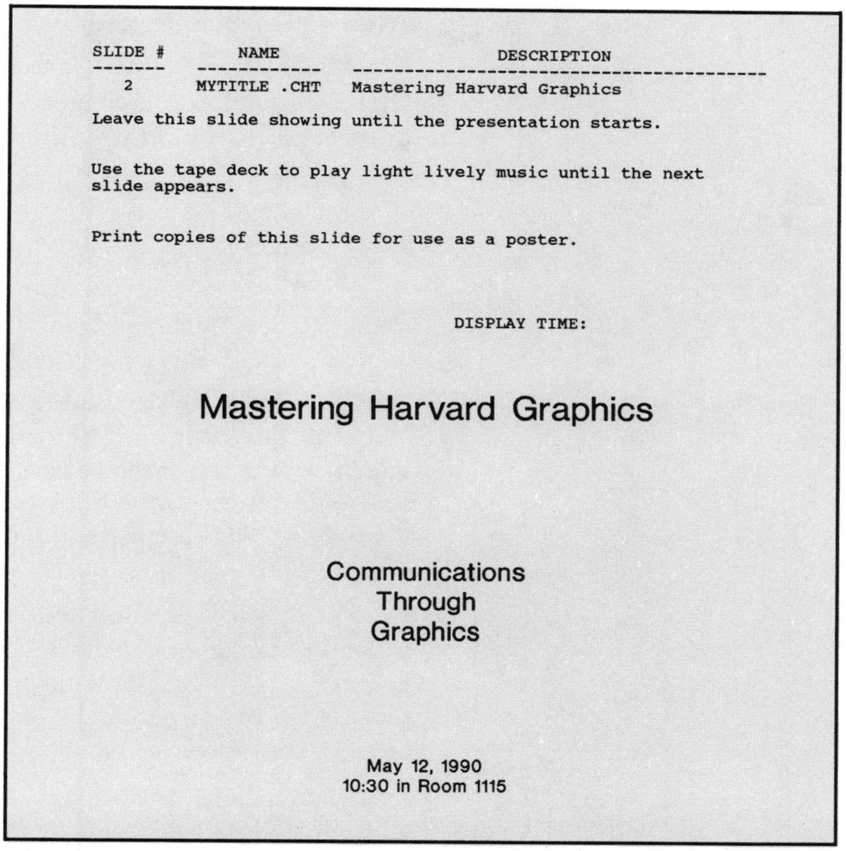

```
SLIDE #      NAME                    DESCRIPTION
-------   ------------   ------------------------------------------
   2      MYTITLE .CHT   Mastering Harvard Graphics
Leave this slide showing until the presentation starts.

Use the tape deck to play light lively music until the next
slide appears.

Print copies of this slide for use as a poster.



                         DISPLAY TIME:


                 Mastering Harvard Graphics




                      Communications
                         Through
                        Graphics




                       May 12, 1990
                     10:30 in Room 1115
```

Figure 12.5: A printed practice card

HANDS-ON: CREATING A SLIDE SHOW

You'll now create your own slide show and practice cards. Here are the steps to follow:

1. From the Main Menu, press **7** and **1** to display the Create Slide Show screen.

2. Type the following name and description for your slide show:

   MYSHOW
   My first slide show

When you press Enter after typing the description, Harvard will take you to the Create/Edit Slide Show screen.

3. Highlight the files you created in earlier chapters and press Enter to place them in your slide show list. Include

MYPIE
MYTITLE
MYHIGH
MYAREA

If you don't have these files, simply choose other files.

Press F10 to continue and you'll see the Slide Show Menu.

4. Press **4** to select Display Screenshow to preview your slides. You'll then see the first chart (slide) appear on the screen. Move through the slide show by pressing Enter at each screen. When you reach the last chart, press Esc to end the show and return to the Slide Show Menu. By previewing your show, you discovered that you need to fix the order of your slides.

5. Press **2** to select the Edit slide show option. Press Tab to move the highlighting to the bottom half of the screen. Highlight the MYTITLE chart and press Ctrl-↑ to make it the first slide. Press Esc to return the Slide Show Menu again. The order of your slides is fine now.

6. Press **5** to make a practice card. Type the following note to yourself about the first slide in your presentation:

Show until the presentation starts.
Introduce yourself and the topic.

Press PgDn when you are done. Now use your imagination to make practice cards for the other slides. For example, you could type a few comments about each type of graph and how they're used. When you're done, press Esc several times to return to the Main Menu.

7. To print the practice cards, press **6** at the Main Menu and then **8** at the Produce Output menu. Accept all the default values by pressing Enter until your practice cards start printing.

8. When your cards finish printing, you'll see the Produce Output menu again. Press **9** to choose the Print slide show list

option. This sends a list of the charts you've selected for your slide show to the printer.

Use the printed practice cards and list to double-check your presentation's organization. Once you're satisfied with it, determine the media you'll use for your presentation and produce the charts you'll need.

PRODUCING THE SHOW

Now that your slide show is organized, you are ready to produce it for others to see. First, you need to decide how you're going to present it—what media to use.

CHOOSING THE MEDIA

Chapter 2 discussed the advantages of using paper copies, plotters, transparencies, and 35mm slides to show charts.

If you want to produce your show on 35mm slides, use the Produce Output menu's Record slide show option. You can also print or plot your entire slide show using the Print slide show or Plot slide show option. Harvard's printing options for slide shows save you time since you don't have to print, record, or plot each chart individually. To print the slide show you just created, follow these steps:

1. At the Main Menu, press **6** to select Produce output.

2. At the Produce Output menu, press **5** to select Print slide show. A dialog box similar to that used for printing individual charts will appear.

3. Select the printing options you want for your presentation. For example, set Quality to High.

4. When you have chosen the options you want, press F10. Harvard will start printing your slide show.

Depending on the number of people viewing your presentation, you have three additional media choices for your slide shows. If your audience will be 10 to 20 people, you can present your screen shows on 19-inch monitors or LCD overhead panels. If you are working with a larger group, you can give your screen shows on video projectors and 33-inch to 37-inch monitors.

Panels don't show color well. They project images using a blue or gray color scale. CGA resolutions are blurry and difficult to read.

WORKING WITH LCD PANELS   LCD panels function much like transparencies but offer the additional advantage of screen shows. The LCD panel sits on the overhead projector and is connected to your computer. When you use the panel with the Display Screenshow option, the panel displays the images instead of the monitor. The overhead projector then transfers the images to a screen using either CGA, EGA, or VGA resolutions.

WORKING WITH LARGE MONITORS   Large 33- to 37-inch monitors are suitable for presentations to larger audiences, but are costly. Many of these monitors have input and output jacks that let you put your presentations on a VCR tape. However, don't bother hooking up your computer to a television set because TVs don't provide the resolution a quality presentation needs.

PC Emcee is a device that lets you hook up sound from a tape deck to your show and also works as a remote control device. Alternatively, you can use a mouse with a long cord to control the slide show.

WORKING WITH VIDEO PROJECTORS   There are several commercial companies that make video projection units. Although the projected images aren't as crisp as a 4,000-line resolution slide, they are adequate for most screen shows.

ADDING SPECIAL EFFECTS TO YOUR SCREEN SHOW

You can also create a presentation on a LCD panel, monitor, or video projector that shows special effects. For example, you can show a slide that fades in while the old one fades out, or you can present a slide that opens from the center of the screen, enlargening to replace the previous one. There are dozens of effects you can use.

Start by selecting the slide show you want to present. Then select Add Screenshow effects to begin customizing your show. Figure 12.6 shows the data-entry screen that will then appear.

You can't change data in the first three columns as they only provide information about your slide. The first column gives you the slide number, the second gives the chart's file name, and the third tells you the type of chart. The remaining columns categorize the functions you can specify for each slide, as follows:

Draw   Sets the screen effect for drawing the chart

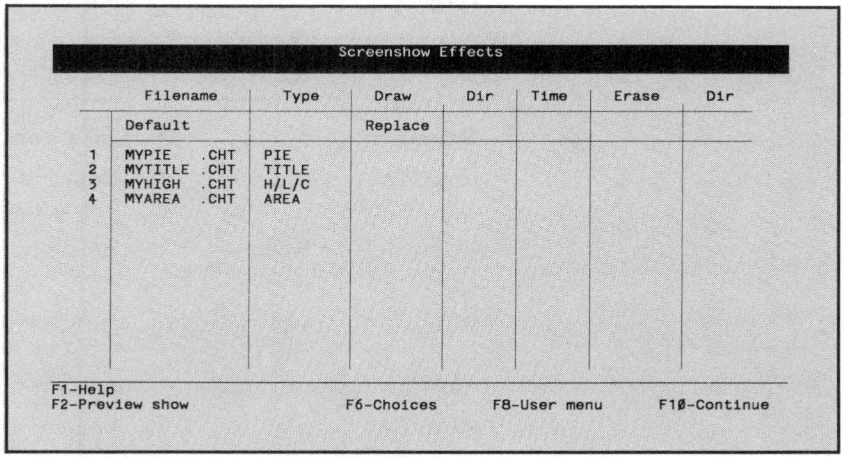

```
                        Screenshow Effects

            Filename      Type    Draw    Dir    Time    Erase    Dir

          Default                Replace

      1   MYPIE    .CHT  PIE
      2   MYTITLE  .CHT  TITLE
      3   MYHIGH   .CHT  H/L/C
      4   MYAREA   .CHT  AREA




   F1-Help
   F2-Preview show            F6-Choices      F8-User menu      F10-Continue
```

Figure 12.6: The Screenshow Effects data-entry screen

Dir	Determines the direction the drawing goes in
Time	Sets the length of time that the chart is displayed
Erase	Sets the screen effect for erasing the chart
Dir	Determines the direction erasing takes

Move the cursor to the column you want to use and press the F6 key for a list of the effects you can choose from. Table 12.1 also lists the special effects you can choose and their default directions. As you can see, some effects don't use directions. Although the Fade option doesn't have a default direction, you can specify Up or Down for special effects.

Use the Tab and arrow keys to move among the columns and rows and add effects to each slide. To remove an effect, press Ctrl-Del.

When you add a Draw effect to a chart, you can also specify the direction it moves in. For example, say you choose Scroll. You can then specify Left in the Dir column so that the chart scrolls on the screen from right to left. (If you don't specify the direction, Harvard uses the default direction for the chosen effect.)

Similarly, you can also decide how you want your chart erased. Before the next chart is displayed, Harvard removes the current chart using the effect you specified in the Erase column. For example, say you specify Wipe in the Erase Column and Down in the

Whenever you select a Draw effect for a chart, you can also specify how long the chart is displayed and how it is erased. If you don't specify a time period, the slide will stay on the screen until you press Enter. If you don't specify how it's erased, Harvard will quickly clear the screen and show the next slide.

Table 12.1: Harvard's special effects for screen shows

EFFECT	DEFAULT	FUNCTION
Replace	n/a	Clears and replaces the screen
Overlay	n/a	Replaces but doesn't erase the previous screen
Wipe	Right	Erases a screen from one side to the other
Scroll	Up	Scrolls slides on from one side to the other
Fade	n/a	Fades a slide on or off the screen
Weave	n/a	Weaves slides in several directions at once
Open	Up/Down	Draws slides from the center to the border
Close	Up/Down	Draws slides from the border to the center
Blinds	Up/Down	Displays slides using vertical strips
Iris	Out	Draws slides diagonally (similar to Open/Close)
Rain	n/a	Fades a slide on or off the screen using strips instead of dots

Dir column. Your chart will then be wiped off the screen horizontally, starting at the top.

Some draw effects blend together better than others. For example, if you erase a chart using Scroll from one direction, display the next by scrolling from the opposite direction. Similarly, if you erase a chart using Iris Out, show the next one using Wipe Right. Experiment and see which combinations work best for you. You can set default Draw and Dir values by typing the effects and directions you want in the row labeled Default. You can then vary some of the charts by setting just their rows to other effects; leave the remaining chart's rows blank in the Draw and Dir columns to accept the defaults.

Don't use the timing feature for live presentations since your timing might not always match your trial run. Use the keyboard or mouse and change charts manually.

Vary display times in an active screen show to maintain your viewers' interest. You might try reading your spiel about the chart out loud to help judge the time needed.

One file stores all the information for a particular slide show, including its practice cards and special effects. Thus, when you make changes at the Screenshow Effects screen, you change the other lists as well.

ADDING TIME DELAYS   You can add time delays to automate your screen show. For example, you might want to do this for a trade booth or convention presentation. You can also use these delays for precision timing when you're using a tape recorder or other audio device in your presentations.

To set a display time for a chart, move the cursor to the chart's row in the Time column and enter the time in minutes or seconds. For example, you can type 30 for 30 seconds or 1:30 for one minute and 30 seconds.

To create an ongoing screen show, one that continually repeats itself (for example, for a trade booth), move the cursor to the last file and press F8. You'll then see the Key/GoTo dialog box. Move the cursor to the Go To column, press **1**, and then press Esc without typing anything in the Key column. Now you won't have to restart the show every time it ends.

CHANGING YOUR SLIDES' ORDER   You can easily change the order of the slides in your show. Simply highlight the slide you want moved and press Ctrl-↑ or Ctrl-↓ to move it.

CREATING AN INTERACTIVE SLIDE SHOW   You can create a menu for your slide show so audiences can choose the part of the show they are interested in. In effect, you can divide your slide show into independent sections, where the audience decides the order they are presented. Even if your slide show needs to be seen from beginning to end, this feature is useful for viewers who have already seen your presentation and want to review a particular section.

For example, suppose you want to use the menu shown in Figure 12.7. To set up this menu system for your show, create a text chart containing the menu and make it your show's first chart. Then select Add Screenshow effects from the Slide Show Menu and highlight the first file (the menu chart). Press F8 and you'll see the Key/GoTo box (Figure 12.8).

This box lets you jump about the slide show, selecting the slides you want viewers to see for each part. For example, if you enter **2** in the Key column and **10** in the Go To column, Harvard will display the tenth chart when the user presses **2**. Continue typing Key and Go To instructions until you've covered all your menu choices.

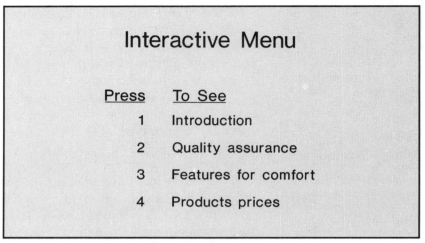

Figure 12.7: Introducing your interactive show

Figure 12.8: Creating a branching screen show

If you leave the Key column's row blank and enter a number in the Go To column, Harvard jumps to that chart if the user doesn't press any of the other keys listed in the Key column. This way, your slide show will always run; you have created a default order. This technique also lets you enter unconditional jumping instructions. For instance, you can jump to the first chart at the end of every section by typing **1** in the Go To Column and leaving the Key column blank for each section's last chart.

The Key/Go To box can handle up to ten sets of instructions per chart. The Key column can contain numbers or letters, but the Go To column can only use digits that refer to slide (chart) numbers. When you add branching instructions for a chart, a diamond character appears to the left of the file name on the Screenshow Effects listing. Use this screen as a reference when you are checking or adding Key/Go To commands.

USING HARVARD'S SCREENSHOW UTILITIES

Harvard sells an optional add-on program called ScreenShow Utilities, which lets you transfer a screen show to a computer that isn't running Harvard Graphics. This means you are less restricted as to when or where you present your slide show; you can even use a portable laptop.

One of ScreenShow's utilities is a memory-resident program called Screen Capture, which lets you save an image that appears on the screen and turn it into a .PCX file as part of your show. For example, you could capture a spreadsheet program's display and place it in your slide show.

HANDS-ON:
PRODUCING A SCREEN SHOW

Try out some of the special screen show effects for yourself by adding a few embellishments to the simple slide show you created in the last "Hands-on" session.

1. At the Main Menu, choose Slide show menu by pressing **7** and then press **6** to choose the Select slide show option. Highlight the show you want and press Enter.

2. Press **3** to select the Add screenshow effects option.

3. Move the cursor to the Default row under the Time column. Press **3** and Enter to set the default time to three seconds. This sets up your show as a self-running demo.

4. Move to the Draw column for your first slide (MYTITLE) and type **S** for Scroll. Press Tab and type **L** for Left in the Dir column. Now move to the Erase column and type **S** for Scroll again. Press Tab to move the cursor to Erase's Dir column and type **R** for right. When the screen show runs, Harvard will erase your chart by scrolling it to the right.

5. Enter effects and directions for the other slides in your show until your Screenshow Effects screen looks similar to Figure 12.9.

	Filename	Type	Draw	Dir	Time	Erase	Dir
	Default		Replace				
1	MYTITLE .CHT	TITLE	Scroll	Left		Scroll	Right
2	MYHIGH .CHT	H/L/C	Iris	In		Iris	Out
3	MYAREA .CHT	AREA	Wipe	Left		Wipe	Right
4	MYPIE .CHT	PIE	Fade	Down		Fade	

Screenshow Effects

F1-Help
F2-Preview show   F6-Choices   F8-User menu   F10-Continue

Figure 12.9: Choosing your special effects

6. Press F10 to return to the Slide Show Menu. Then Press **4** to select Display Screenshow and watch your show run by itself.

SUMMARY

This chapter pulled together all the techniques and enhancements that you learned throughout this book. By combining charts you create in Harvard, charts you import from other programs, and templates to ensure consistency, and adding special effects, you can create slide show presentations worthy of a Harvard Graphics master.

A

TO INSTALL HARVARD GRAPHI
PC-compatible computer equipped with tl

- A hard disk or two 720K floppy-di
  that Harvard is better suited to h
  only will a hard disk store all your
  with, but Harvard also runs faster

- A minimum of 512K (kilobytes) of
  computer, or 640K of memory if
  puter network or plan on using l
  gram. You'll need 2Mb (megabyt
  OS/2's DOS mode.

- DOS Version 2.0 or later, or OS/2

- Harvard Graphics Version 2.1 c
  manual and either six 5¹/₄-inch r
  3¹/₂-inch micro floppy disks. You
  blank disks for backup copies, or
  Harvard disk.

INSTALLING HARVARD

APPENDIX *A*

TO INSTALL HARVARD GRAPHICS, YOU'LL NEED A PC-compatible computer equipped with the following:

- A hard disk or two 720K floppy-disk drives. Note, however, that Harvard is better suited to hard-disk installation. Not only will a hard disk store all your files and be easier to work with, but Harvard also runs faster on a hard disk.

Don't use memory-resident programs such as SideKick when running Harvard; the makers of Harvard claim that funny things can happen, such as disappearing files or frozen computers.

- A minimum of 512K (kilobytes) of memory installed on your computer, or 640K of memory if you're attached to a computer network or plan on using Harvard's MACRO program. You'll need 2Mb (megabytes) of memory if you use OS/2's DOS mode.

- DOS Version 2.0 or later, or OS/2 in DOS mode.

- Harvard Graphics Version 2.1 or later, consisting of the manual and either six 5¼-inch mini floppy disks or three 3½-inch micro floppy disks. You will also need three to six blank disks for backup copies, or one blank disk for each Harvard disk.

INITIAL PREPARATIONS

Once the previous list is assembled, you're ready to install Harvard. Start by following these instructions:

1. Boot your computer by turning it on. Within a minute or so you'll see the system prompt, telling you that DOS is ready for a command. It usually looks like A >, C >, or some other variation that shows the name of the drive you're using.

2. Once you see the system prompt, type **CHKDSK** and press the Enter key. If the CHKDSK command didn't work, one

of the following situations occurred:

- You didn't have a complete DOS disk when booting. Find your original DOS disk and reboot your computer.

- You didn't have a path established on your hard disk for your operating system to find your DOS files. Try typing **PATH C:\DOS** and press Enter. (Many systems use a subdirectory called \DOS to store DOS programs.) Then reenter the CHKDSK command. If it still doesn't work, find your original DOS floppy disk and boot from it.

3. Read the line showing the number of bytes free on your disk. To install Harvard, you should have at least 2,000,000 bytes of disk space available. If you don't, you'll have to delete or move files from your disk to provide enough space for Harvard to function.

4. Now read the last line telling you how much memory your computer has. If you have at least 426,000 bytes of memory free, you can run Harvard Graphics. If not, you'll have to take your computer into the shop and have more memory installed.

> If you don't have enough memory available, check whether your computer has any loaded memory-resident programs. Unloading them will free up memory. (These programs interfere with Harvard's performance anyway.)

5. Proceed by making backup copies of all your Harvard disks. Type **DISKCOPY A: B:** and press Enter. Take a Harvard Graphics disk and gently insert it into drive A. Place a blank disk in drive B. Then press Enter to continue. The drives will whirl, and the disk lights will flicker on and off while copying.

    If you have only one disk drive on your computer, follow the copying instructions that appear on your screen. When the computer tells you to place a *source* disk in the drive, it is referring to the Harvard disks. The *target* disk means the blank disks you're using to copy Harvard.

6. After copying the disk, place an identifying label on it. Include the following:

    Disk number
    Disk name
    Version number

The version number appears in the gold box on the bottom right of the Harvard disk label.

7. When you're asked if you want to copy another disk, press **Y** and repeat steps 5 through 8 until you copy all your disks. Press **N** when finished.

8. Put your original Harvard disks away in a safe place. You'll now use your new backup disks to complete the installation.

INSTRUCTIONS FOR INSTALLING HARVARD ON YOUR HARD DISK

Using your backup disks, follow these steps to install the program on your hard disk:

1. Create a new subdirectory to store your Harvard program files by typing **MD C:\HG** and pressing Enter. This DOS command creates the \HG subdirectory on drive C. On large computer systems, replace the C with the drive on which you want Harvard installed.

2. Type **MD C:\HGDATA** and press Enter. This creates a data directory to store your graphs.

3. Place the Harvard Utilities disk in drive A.

4. Type **A:INSTALL** and press Enter. Harvard's INSTALL program will then lead you through the installation process, prompting you for instructions.

5. Press **A** and then Enter to tell Harvard to get files from drive A.

6. Type **C:\HG** and press Enter, telling Harvard to copy the files from drive A to the \HG subdirectory on drive C.

7. You're then prompted to insert the first program disk in drive A. Place Disk 1 in drive A and press Enter. You'll see the files copied from drive A to your hard disk.

8. Read the instructions on the screen and insert the next disk, Disk 2, into drive A. Press Enter. Repeat this step to copy all the backup disks. If you insert the wrong disk, don't worry.

Harvard can tell it is the wrong disk and will ask if you want to retry. Insert the correct disk and then press **Y** to continue.

You are now ready to start using Harvard Graphics. Follow the steps in Chapter 1 for running Harvard Graphics and configuring it to your system.

B

Table B.1: Supported printers

COMPANY	PRINTER NAME
Apple	LaserWriter
AST	TurboLaser
CalComp	ColorMaster
Epson	EX
	FX
	GQ-3500
	JX
	LQ-800 *
	LQ-1000
	LQ-1500
	LQ-2500
	LX
	MX

SUPPORTED DEVICES

APPENDIX **B**

You can also create special VDI drivers that are supported by Harvard and used for high-resolution film recorders. The Harvard Graphics manual discusses VDI drivers in detail.

TABLES B.1 THROUGH B.4 LIST THE PRINTERS, PLOT-ters, film recorders, and video screen controllers that are supported by Harvard Graphics Version 2.1. Like a racing car's system, Harvard fine-tunes itself to these specific models. To avoid problems, stick with them; unsupported devices may not work the way you expect them to.

Table B.1: Supported printers

COMPANY	PRINTER NAME
Apple	LaserWriter
AST	TurboLaser
CalComp	ColorMaster
Epson	EX
	FX
	GQ-3500
	JX
	LQ-800 *
	LQ-1000
	LQ-1500
	LQ-2500
	LX
	MX
	RX
HP	DeskJet
	LaserJet 500 Plus

Table B.1: Supported printers (continued)

COMPANY	PRINTER NAME
IBM	LaserJet Plus
	LaserJet Series II
	PaintJet
	QuietJet
	QuietJet Plus
	Color Jetprinter
	Color Printer
	Graphics Printer
	Personal PagePrinter
	Proprinter II
	Proprinter XL
	Proprinter XL24
	Proprinter X24
	Quietwriter II
	Quietwriter III
Matrix	TT200
NEC	CP6
	CP7
	LC-860 (LaserJet)
	LC-890 (PostScript)
	P5
	P6
	P7
	P5XL
	P9XL
Okidata	LaserLine 6
	MicroLine 84

Table B.1: Supported printers (continued)

COMPANY	PRINTER NAME
	MicroLine 92
	MicroLine 93
	MicroLine 182
	MicroLine 183
	MicroLine 192
	MicroLine 193
	MicroLine 292
	MicroLine 293
	MicroLine 294
Qume	LaserTen
	LaserTen Plus
Tektronix	4696
Toshiba	PageLaser 12
	P321
	P341
	P351
	P351C
	P1340
	P1350
	P1351
Xerox	4020
	4045

*The Epson 800 printer has limited support. You can't print a chart in High mode because its form feed forces printing onto another page when only half the chart has been printed.

Table B.2: Supported plotters

COMPANY	PLOTTER NAME
Enter Computer	SP600
Houston Instrument	DMP 29
	DMP 40
	DMP 40-2
	PC Plotter
HP*	ColorPro
	7470A
	7475A
	7475A B-size
	7550A
	7550A B-size
IBM	6180
	6182
	6182 B-size
	7371
	7372
	7372 B-size

* Harvard also supports many of the HPGL-compatible plotters that are available.

Table B.3: Supported film recorders

COMPANY	FILM RECORDER NAME
Bell & Howell	CDI IV
	Quintar 1080
General Parametrics	ColorMetric
	GPC file

Table B.3: Supported film recorders (continued)

COMPANY	FILM RECORDER NAME
	VideoShow
Lasergraphics	RASCOL II/PFR
Magi	Slide Service
Matrix Instruments	PCR
	QCR
Polaroid	Palette (CGA)
	Palette Plus (EGA)
PTI	ImageMaker

Table B.4: Supported video screen controllers

COMPANY	CONTROLLER NAME
DGIS	Direct Graphics Interface Standard adapter
Hercules	Graphic Card (monochrome)
IBM*	Color Card (CGA)
	Enhanced Graphics (EGA)
	PS/2 Display Adapter (VGA)
Toshiba	T3100 monochrome

* Note: Many companies make IBM-compatible screen controllers that will work with Harvard Graphics. However, only VGA cards that are register compatible with IBM can be used with Harvard.

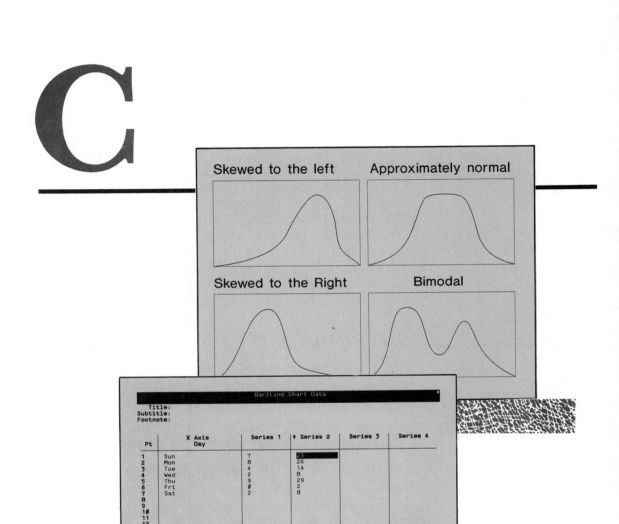

STATISTICS AND CALCULATIONS

APPENDIX C

BY WORKING WITH GRAPHS, YOU HAVE USED STATIS-
tics throughout this book. You're also familiar with some calculations
that Harvard does for you. For example, you know that Harvard will
mathematically compute and plot a trend line. This appendix
reviews other statistical functions that are built into Harvard.

INTRODUCING BASIC STATISTICS

When you need to show minimum and maximum statistical values, use a high/low/close chart as described in Chapter 7.

This appendix doesn't purport to teach statistics. But this simple
introduction does highlight some important basics that you should
know when creating charts.

UNDERSTANDING POPULATIONS AND SAMPLES

When creating frequency distributions, let your audiences know
whether you're using a population or a sample. This distinction is
important in statistics. For example, if you are trying to find the percentage of smokers in a town, a population study requires that you
talk to each resident within that town. However, a sample study only
requires that you communicate with a random number of people to
see if they smoke. A sample study assumes that the percentage of
smokers in your randomly selected group approximates the population of the town, which is not necessarily true.

USING THE THREE M'S

The three M's in statistics are the mean, median, and mode. They
help analyze data and are often included in charts. Harvard does not
directly support these functions, but you can easily compute them
yourself.

Suppose you want to graph test scores. You can show the mean, median, and mode in your chart by using Draw/Annotate or by entering them in a footnote. Let's determine the mean, median, and mode of these test scores: 40, 50, 60, 70, 80, 90, 90, 100, 100, 100, 100.

The *mean* is simply an average, obtained by adding all your individual measurements and dividing it by the number of values you have added. For example, our 11 test scores added together total 880. Divide this by 11, and the mean is 80.

To find the *median*, order the values numerically and find the middle number. Since you have 11 test scores, the middle number is the sixth score, or 90.

Figuring the *mode* of a group of numbers is also easy. It's the peak of a distribution—the most common occurrence. As with the median, sort your values and then see which one occurs most often. In our text score example, there are four scores of 100, more than any other score. Thus the mode in our collection of test scores is 100.

The Harvard @AVG function averages a row on the data-entry screen, which contains data from a group of series. It does not average a series column.

UNDERSTANDING SKEWS

Frequently distributions follow certain patterns since there are always a mean and median. For example, a population study showing human intelligence has a symmetrical distribution. However, an income population study is skewed to the right because the median figure is less than the mean.

Figure C.1 shows the four terms that are used in describing frequency-distribution charts. Notice that the first graph is skewed to the left; this is called a *negative* skew. When a graph is skewed to the right, it has a *positive* skew. Graphs that are approximately normal have a *symmetrical distribution*. On the other hand, bimodal graphs are less common; they occur when your data include two distinct modes.

USING THE CALCULATE FEATURE

In Chapter 5, you learned that the Calculate feature (F4) lets you move, swap, and clear columns of series. You can also enter calculations to help analyze data and do statistical calculations. By entering a formula in the Calculation field, you can

- Execute arithmetic functions

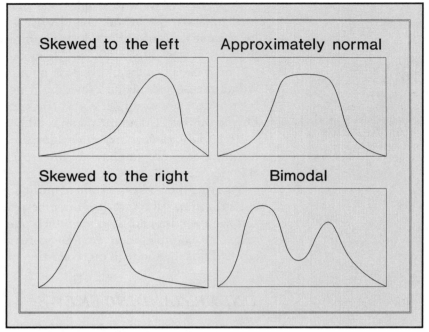

Figure C.1: Types of skews

- Use row calculation functions
- Use series calculation functions

Remember that you move the cursor to the row or column the data will be entered in before you press F4.

USING ARITHMETIC FUNCTIONS

Use arithmetic functions to compute a single data element. You can also use arithmetic functions on all of a series' rows on the data-entry screen. Either way, you can add (+), subtract (–), multiply (*), or divide (/) numbers.

Follow these steps to enter a calculation:

1. At the data-entry screen, move the cursor to the element you want calculated. To calculate an entire series, just move the cursor to the column.

2. Press the F4-Calculate key. When the Calculate menu appears, move your cursor to the Calculation field.

3. Type the calculation you want and press Enter. Use the pound sign (#) when you want to use a column calculation, or Harvard will only change a single data element.

For example, if you enter **3*2 + 1**, Harvard will only change the value at the current cursor location. It interprets this line as 3 times 2 plus 1 and will place the value of 7 in that data element. Harvard always calculates in the order you enter your equation, working from left to right.

However, if you type **#1*3 + 2** for the calculation, Harvard will interpret the #1 as meaning column one. In other words, the calculation reads column one times 2 plus 1. If you entered this calculation in the Series 2 column, your data-entry screen might look like Figure C.2.

USING ROW CALCULATION FUNCTIONS

Harvard has four built-in functions that affect rows of data for the columns you designate. For example, the rows in columns 1, 2, and 5 are added together when you type **@SUM(#1,#2,#5)**. Replace the *n*

Pt	X Axis Day	Series 1	◆ Series 2	Series 3	Series 4
1	Sun	7	23		
2	Mon	8	26		
3	Tue	4	14		
4	Wed	2	8		
5	Thu	9	29		
6	Fri	0	2		
7	Sat	2	8		
8					
9					
10					
11					
12					

Figure C.2: Computing a column's data

in the following row calculation functions with the column number you're computing:

@AVG(*#n,#n*)	Computes the average value of the row
@MAX(*#n,#n*)	Finds the largest number in each row
@MIN(*#n,#n*)	Finds the smallest number in each row
@SUM(*#n,#n*)	Adds the designated values in each row

You can specify up to 7 different column numbers within the brackets. For example, if you want to find the averages of columns 1 to 4, type **@AVG(#1,#2,#3,#4)** in the Calculation field and press Enter.

You must have at least one empty column for the results of the series calculation functions.

USING SERIES CALCULATION FUNCTIONS

Unlike row calculations, series calculations only use values from one column. Replace the *n* in the following series functions with the number of the column you want affected. You'll also notice that some functions don't need a column number.

Use the @DUP function to save your series' values before you start working with them. This way, you'll still have the original column in case you make a mistake in your calculations.

@CLR	Erases elements from the current column (where you pressed the F4 key).
@COPY(*#n*)	Copies a series from the designated column.
@CUM(*#n*)	Shows cumulative totals.
@DIFF(*#n*)	Shows the difference between the current element and the preceding element.
@DUP(*#n*)	Duplicates the specified series.
@EXCH(*#n*)	Exchanges data between columns.
@MAVG(*#n*)	Calculates moving averages.
@MOVE(*#n*)	Moves the specified column to the current cursor location.
@PCT(*#n*)	Shows the percentage value of each element when compared to the series total.
@REDUC	Sorts and combines duplicate X axis labels. This option affects all columns in your chart.

@RECALC	Updates calculations to account for any change made in column values. It affects all columns.
@REXP(*#n*)	Calculates exponential regression curves.
@RLIN(*#n*)	Calculates linear regression curves.
@RLOG(*#n*)	Calculates logarithmic regression curves.
@RPWR(*#n*)	Calculates power regression curves.

To work with one of these functions, follow these steps:

1. Move your cursor to an empty column. This column will store the new calculations.

2. Press the F4-Calculate key. You'll then see the Calculate menu.

3. Move the cursor to the Calculation field and type the calculation you want to use.

4. Press Enter.

HANDS-ON: USING THE CALCULATE FEATURE

You can use Harvard's Calculate feature to generate statistics in bar, line, and area charts. Practice using this feature by following these steps:

1. Select the necessary menu options to create a new bar chart.

2. When the X Axis Data Type appears, simply press the F10 key to accept Name as the X axis type and continue.

3. Type **1986 Home Video Sales** for the chart's title.

4. Type the data as shown in Figure C.3, remembering to use the F4-Calculate key to add the Units Shipped and Retail Sales series labels.

5. With your cursor in column 3, press the F4 key. Type **Average** for the series name. You're going to use this column

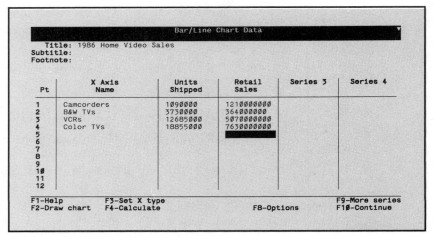

Figure C.3: Entering your data

When you enter a calculation function, think of each series as a sequential column number starting with one. For example, think of Units Shipped as column 1, Retail Sales as column 2, and Series 3 as column 3.

Notice in Figure C.4 that Harvard automatically converted the numbers in the Retail Sales column to scientific notation when it used them in its calculations.

Calculated columns have a diamond character (◆) next to their series label.

to calculate the average sales price. Press Enter and your cursor will move to the Calculation field.

6. Type **#2/#1** and press Enter. You've just told Harvard to take column 2 and divide it by column 1. You get the average sales price of a unit by dividing retail sales by the units shipped. For example, you'll see that $1110.092 is the average retail price of a camcorder.

7. Move your cursor to column 4 and press F4. This time, type **$ Market Share %** for the series name and press Enter. At the Calculation field, type **@PCT(#2)** and press Enter. This function shows the percentage of each element in column 2 compared to the column's total amount. Your data-entry screen should look similar to the screen shown in Figure C.4.

8. Create another column that will display the figures in column 4 as whole numbers with a decimal point. This new column will show 0.085 as 8.5 and 0.534 as 53.4 simply by multiplying column 4 by 100. Press the F9 -More series key and move your cursor to column 5.

9. Press F4. Type **#4*100**, and you'll see the new percentage values that you can add to your graphs.

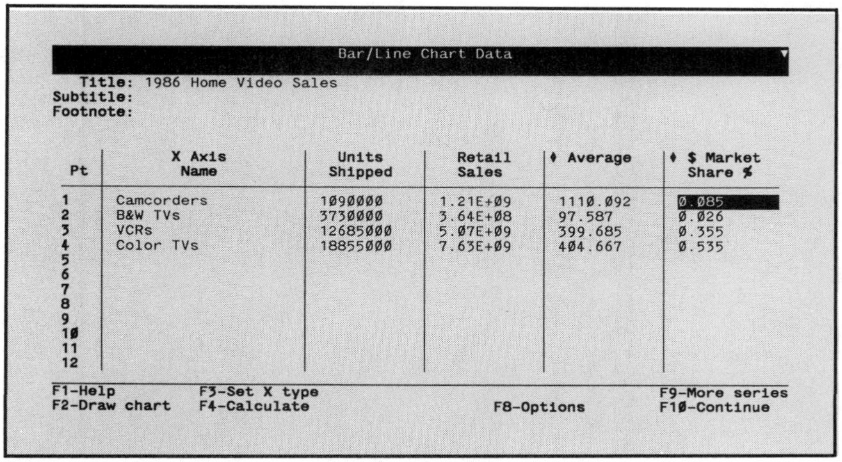

Figure C.4: Harvard computes your calculations.

You have now doubled the amount of material you can graph by creating the average price and percentage columns. This short hands-on exercise demonstrates how you can use Harvard to help generate statistics for a varied presentation.

D

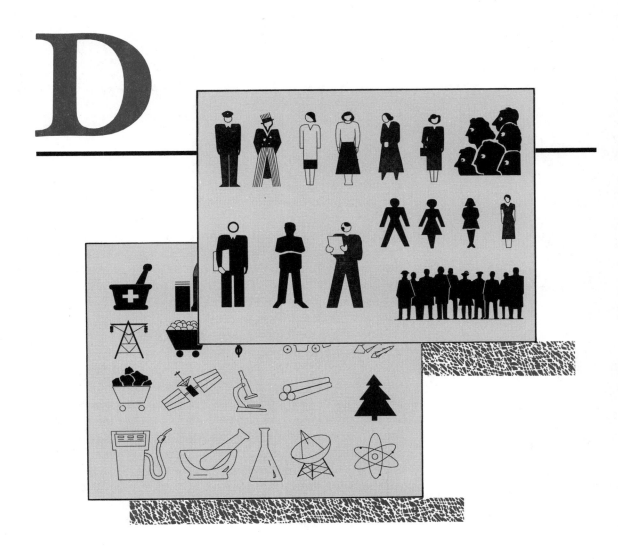

Symbols, Symbols, and More Symbols

APPENDIX D

FIGURES D.1 TO D.16 PRESENT ALL THE SYMBOLS included in Harvard Graphics Version 2.1. Use the Draw menu's Symbol option to add these symbols to your charts (for more information, see Chapter 10).

Once you have added the symbol to your chart, you can move it, copy it, change its attributes—all the things you can do to your own drawings. If the symbol is made up of a group of objects, you can also use the Symbol menu's Group option to select some of its parts.

Say you want to move a couple of objects from a symbol to another part of your chart. First, select the Group option, position the cursor on one of the symbol's objects, press Enter to select it, position the cursor on the next object you want, and press Enter again. When you have finished selecting the objects, press Esc and choose Modify from the Draw menu. Then select Move from the Modify menu. A positioning box appears on the screen; move it to where you want the selected objects to go and press Enter to anchor the box. Next, move the cursor to adjust the length and width of the box and press Enter again when it outlines the proportions you want. Harvard then places the objects in their new location. Delete the original symbol if you no longer need it.

Remember, you can print the following symbols or record them on film. However, you can't use these symbols with plotters.

Selecting the same object twice *deselects* it.

Figure D.1: The ARROWS.SYM file

Figure D.2: The BUILDING.SYM file

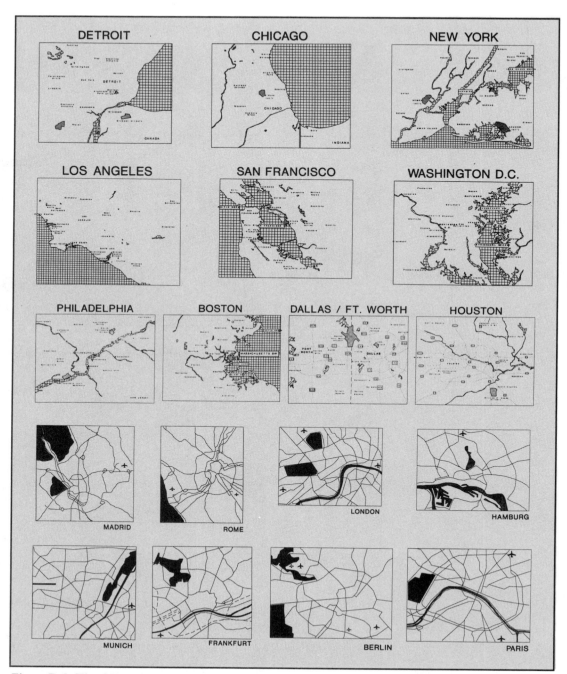

Figure D.3: The CITIES.SYM file

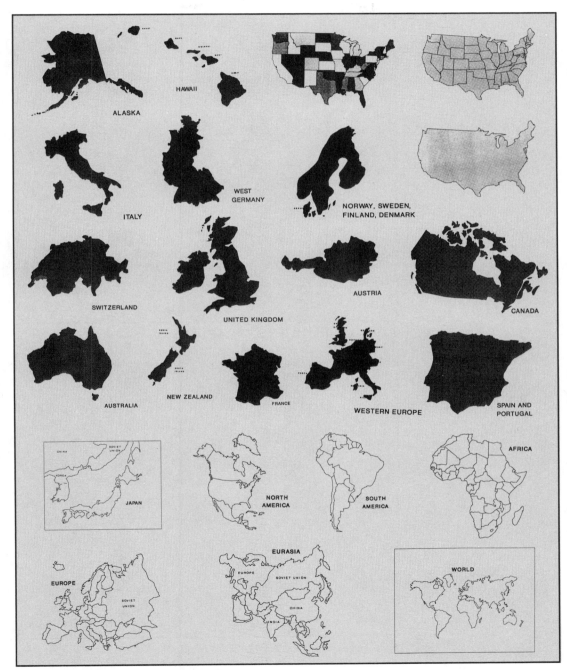

Figure D.4: The COUNTRY.SYM file

Figure D.5: The CURRENCY.SYM file

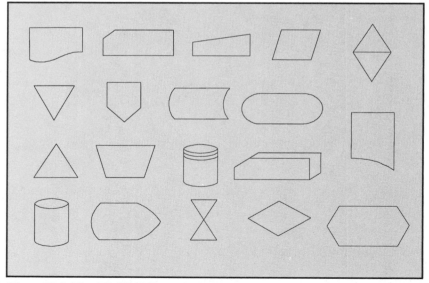

Figure D.6: The FLOWCHAR.SYM file

Figure D.7: The FOODSPRT.SYM file

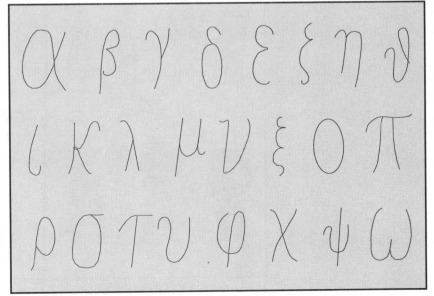

Figure D.8: The GREEKLC.SYM file

Figure D.9: The GREEKUC.SYM file

Figure D.10: The HUMAN.SYM file

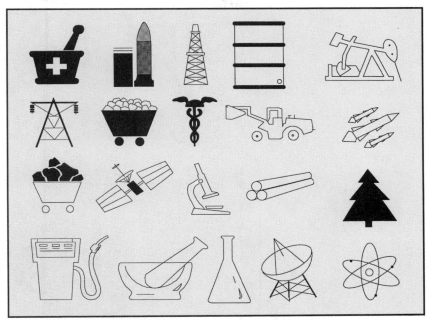

Figure D.11: The INDUSTRY.SYM file

Figure D.12: The MISC.SYM file

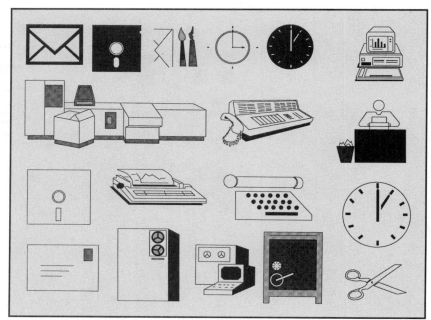

Figure D.13: The OFFICE.SYM file

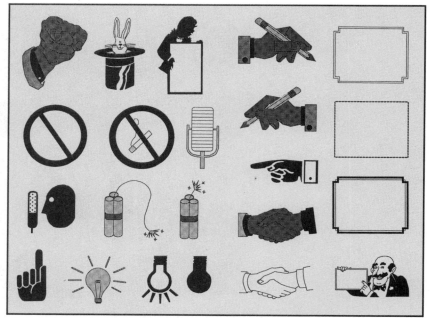

Figure D.14: The PRESENT.SYM file

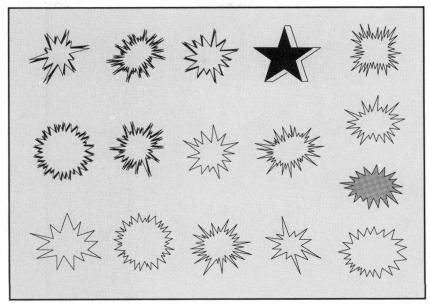

Figure D.15: The STARS.SYM file

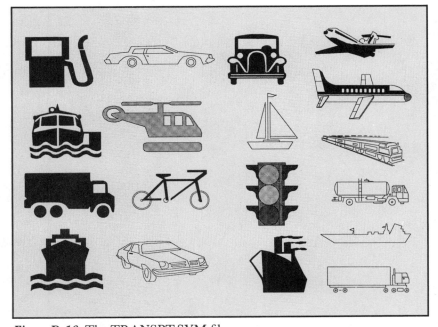

Figure D.16: The TRANSPT.SYM file

INDEX

TO JOIN THE SYBEX MAILING LIST OR ORDER BOOKS
PLEASE COMPLETE THIS FORM

NAME _____ COMPANY _____

STREET _____ CITY _____

STATE _____ ZIP _____

☐ PLEASE MAIL ME MORE INFORMATION ABOUT **SYBEX** TITLES

ORDER FORM (There is no obligation to order)

PLEASE SEND ME THE FOLLOWING:

TITLE	QTY	PRICE
_____	____	____
_____	____	____
_____	____	____
_____	____	____

TOTAL BOOK ORDER _____ $_____

CUSTOMER SIGNATURE _____

SHIPPING AND HANDLING PLEASE ADD $2.00 PER BOOK VIA UPS _____

FOR OVERSEAS SURFACE ADD $5.25 PER BOOK PLUS $4.40 REGISTRATION FEE _____

FOR OVERSEAS AIRMAIL ADD $18.25 PER BOOK PLUS $4.40 REGISTRATION FEE _____

CALIFORNIA RESIDENTS PLEASE ADD APPLICABLE SALES TAX _____

TOTAL AMOUNT PAYABLE _____

☐ CHECK ENCLOSED   ☐ VISA
☐ MASTERCARD   ☐ AMERICAN EXPRESS

ACCOUNT NUMBER _____

EXPIR. DATE _____ DAYTIME PHONE _____

CHECK AREA OF COMPUTER INTEREST:

☐ BUSINESS SOFTWARE

☐ TECHNICAL PROGRAMMING

☐ OTHER: _____

THE FACTOR THAT WAS MOST IMPORTANT IN YOUR SELECTION:

☐ THE SYBEX NAME

☐ QUALITY

☐ PRICE

☐ EXTRA FEATURES

☐ COMPREHENSIVENESS

☐ CLEAR WRITING

☐ OTHER _____

OTHER COMPUTER TITLES YOU WOULD LIKE TO SEE IN PRINT:

_____

_____

OCCUPATION

☐ PROGRAMMER   ☐ TEACHER

☐ SENIOR EXECUTIVE   ☐ HOMEMAKER

☐ COMPUTER CONSULTANT   ☐ RETIRED

☐ SUPERVISOR   ☐ STUDENT

☐ MIDDLE MANAGEMENT   ☐ OTHER:

☐ ENGINEER/TECHNICAL   _____

☐ CLERICAL/SERVICE

☐ BUSINESS OWNER/SELF EMPLOYED

CHECK YOUR LEVEL OF COMPUTER USE

☐ NEW TO COMPUTERS

☐ INFREQUENT COMPUTER USER

☐ FREQUENT USER OF ONE SOFTWARE

   PACKAGE:

   NAME _____

☐ FREQUENT USER OF MANY SOFTWARE

   PACKAGES

☐ PROFESSIONAL PROGRAMMER

OTHER COMMENTS:

_____

_____

_____

_____

_____

_____

PLEASE FOLD, SEAL, AND MAIL TO SYBEX

SYBEX, INC.
2021 CHALLENGER DR. #100
ALAMEDA, CALIFORNIA USA
              94501

SEAL

A QUICK REFERENCE TO HARVARD'S MENUS

Main Menu	
Help	F1
Draw chart	F2
Spell check	F4
Options	F8
Create new chart	1
Enter/Edit chart	2
Draw/Annotate	3
Get/Save/Remove	4
Import/Export	5
Produce output	6
Slide show menu	7
Chartbook menu	8
Setup	9
Exit	E

Create new chart	1
Help	F1
Text	1
Title chart	1
Simple list	2
Bullet list	3
Two columns	4
Three columns	5
Free form	6
Pie	2
Bar/Line	3
Area	4
High/Low/Close	5
Organization	6
Multiple charts	7
Custom	1
Two	2
Three	3
Four	4
From chartbook	8
Clear values	9

Enter/Edit chart	2
Help	F1
Draw chart	F2
Attributes	F5
Size/Place	F7

Continue	F10

Draw/Annotate	3
Help	F1
Preview	F2
Redraw	F4
Options	F8
Add	1
Text	1
Box	2
Polyline	3
Line	4
Circle	5
Polygon	6
Modify	2
Move	1
Size	2
Options	3
Front	4
Back	5
Copy	3
Delete	4
Grid	5
Symbol	6
Get	1
Save	2
Group	3